Education Essays from My Perspective:

50 Years as a Professional Educator Offering You

Pearls of Wisdom for Your Journey

BOOK 2

Education Essays from My Perspective:

50 Years as a Professional Educator

Offering You Pearls of Wisdom for Your Journey

BOOK 2

DR. MARSHA DIANE AKAU WELLEIN

Author

DR. CAROLE FREEHAN

Senior Editor

NICHOLAS PATRICK WELLEIN

Technical Editor

Education Essays From My Perspective: 50 Years as a Professional Educator Offering Pearls of Wisdom For Your Journey, Book 2

Edition: First Edition

Copyright © December, 2021 by Marsha Diane Akau Wellein.

All Rights Reserved

Senior Editor: Dr. Carole Freehan

Technical Editor: Nicholas Patrick Wellein

Graphics Designer: Samuel Naah

Cover design: Nicholas Patrick Wellein

Cover photo: John Waipa

Library of Congress Control Number: 2022900064

ISBN: 978-1-7364147-2-9   eBook ISBN: 978-1-7364147-3-6

Categories: Multicultural Education in Elementary, Secondary, Post-Secondary Education; Gender & Racism; Bias in Children's Literature; Bilingual Education; Adult & Higher Education; Army & Army Reserve Education; Military Tuition Assistance; Job Corps; Change; Planning; Veterans Affairs Education Benefits; Distance/Online Education; Schools; Diploma Mills; Fake Degrees; Graduate School Preparation.

OTHER BOOKS & PUBLICATIONS BY MARSHA DIANE AKAU WELLEIN

Education Essays from My Perspective: 50 Years as a Professional Educator Offering Pearls of Wisdom for Your Journey, Book 1, January 2021, author, by MD Wellein, Inc., available from Amazon.com in softcover and eBook Kindle format.

Factors Associated with Army Reservists Using Educational Programs and Services at 9th Mission Support Command, a doctoral dissertation published in 2010, Hawaii (Available free from ProQuest Dissertations and Theses database; UMI No. 3429228).

Duellberg, D. J., & Wellein, M. D., March 18, 2011, **Innovation in Learning Communities, a Collaboration of U.S. Coast Guard and U. S. Army Reserve Education Programs and Services,** *De Quarterly, DEHub Journal*, No. 7, autumn 11, ODLAA Education Summit: Global Challenges and Perspectives of Blended and Distance Education, Sydney, Australia.

Biographical Entry in **Remembering Those Who Have Made a Difference in United States Military Voluntary Education, 2006,** by Dr. Clinton L. Andy Anderson, Department of Defense & Servicemembers Opportunities Colleges, Washington D.C.

Contracts Writer, U.S. Army Fort Shafter for 9th Mission Support Command, Honolulu, HI, as part of the duties as Army Reserve Regional Director of Education, Pacific & Asia, for Non-Personal Services Contracts (2004-2008) at the Education Services Office; serving also as Installation Technical Representative, Quality Control, and Contract Officer Representative.

The Military Educator, a professional Newsletter of the AAACE Armed Services Continuing Education Unit & later, Commission on Military Education and Training. (Clinton L. Andy Anderson, Editor.) Author, **Be All You Can Be**, **The True Meaning of Adult Education**: Vol. 4, No. 3: Sept 1996, **The James Eddie Thompson Story**. Vol 5, No. 1: Dec 1996 **The PV2 Anthony Gilbert Story**. Vol. 12, No. 2: Aug 2004, **The Steven Hebrank Story**. Vol 13, No. 2: July 2005, **The Scott Martin Story**.

Kalihi Kids Can Communicate, Editor, a Language Arts Resource Book for educators, published in 1976, Honolulu, Hawaii; Trude M. Akau is author.

The Endless Summer – An Adventure Story of Guam, author, a hardback children's chapter book, published in 1976, New York.

Day Care Centers on Guam, author, an extensive 1973 study, available at University of Guam Library System, Richard Flores Taitano Micronesian Area Research Center (MARC), Guam.

Author Marsha Diane Akau Wellein, September, 2020   Photographer: John Waipa, Hawaii

SO, WHAT ARE YOU WAITING FOR?

Your Journey Continues! READ BOOK 1

Education Essays From My Perspective: 50 Years as a Professional Educator Offering Pearls of Wisdom For Your Journey, Book 1

The capacity to learn is a gift; The ability to learn is a skill; The willingness to learn is a choice.

Brian Herbert

Dr. Wellein is truly a most remarkable lifelong learner, an inspiration to her peers, and a passionate speaker . . . [who] immensely enjoyed helping military members and their families pursue their educational dreams. Dr. Wellein has reflected upon her extensive career to assemble some precious **"Pearls of Wisdom"** with the hope that her experience will inspire fellow educators and others.

Dr. Donna J. Duellberg, Program Manager, Voluntary Education Liaison Officer, Coast Guard Navy Community College Program, Wash. DC; Army Warrant Officer, Ret., Former Professor at 8 Universities, Undergrad & Graduate

When I read [Wellein's] latest **Book [1]** I was not surprised at all by its organization, ease to read and insight into public education. The book should be required reading of anyone interested in becoming a teacher regardless of the field. Her experience in Public Education and the Army Civilian Education program gives her great insight! I look forward to her next book.

Charles Dennis Fritts, Army Continuing Education System, 31 Years, Ret. & 17 Years in Elementary Education & Professor of Postsecondary Education

Marsha's **Book [1]** would have helped me a lot when I first started teaching as it is written in a clear and precise way. Each chapter enlightens the reader about new ways of how to interact with the students, introduce new ideas and make learning fun rather that a chore. I would have her book in my classroom as the Number 1 reference book and would share it with all my colleagues. **[Book 1]** holds so many "**Pearls**" just ready to be used during the teaching day and should be recommended for required reading and enjoyment in Teacher Training classes. I am very much looking forward to the next book.

Irene Anneliese Mann, M.Ed.
Defense Language Institute, Lackland AFB, TX, Ret. Instructor,
General & Specialized English in Orlando, Slovenia, Slovakia, Cairo, Kabul, & Abu Dhabi.

Dr. Wellein uses the subject of education to address many social-political matters. I am awed by this creativity. It is one thing to write, but another to write with authority. She does not only write with authority here**; she is an authority**. There is absolutely no guesswork. She is experienced in what she wants to pass [on]. I recommend **[Book 1]** to anyone …in education.

Online Book Club

I worked with Dr. Wellein for five years on the island of Guam in the late 1970s. She was always an inspiring teacher and coworker and provided lots of educational workshops. She had a huge amount of experience and could always come up with new and helpful ideas. Read her Book 1.

Michele Drayton, M.Ed.
Title I Reading, (Washington State & Guam) Ret.,
International Longshore & Warehouse Union, Seattle, WA

Dr. Marsha Wellein was an outstanding Educator for the U.S. Army Continuing Education (ACES) program. Marsha was never afraid of tough assignments and serving in very remote locations as you can see from her biography. There is hardly anyone more qualified to discuss adult education than Marsha. What I liked most about **[Book 1]** was the interesting way it was presented and obviously with a lot of thought.

Dr. Wellein has experience and great skills in working with military personnel and their family members, from the very basic skills programs (reading, writing and arithmetic), technical programs, distance learning, managing learning centers to coordinating college programs from the associate degree level all the way through doctoral programs. She can speak with authority in **Education Essays from My Perspective: 50 Years as a Professional Educator Offering Pearls of Wisdom for Your Journey, Book 1** as she has been a practitioner for her entire working career.

J. Willard (Will) Williams, M. Ed
Director of Ed., U.S. Army, Wash DC; Army Ed. Svcs. Ret., 33 years
Ed. Officer, MO, Korea, HI, GA, Germany; 1995 Military Educator of the Year Award.
Intl. Hall of Fame, Adult & Continuing Ed. & Distance Learning, 2010.
Reginal Manager, Franklin Covey Company for Leadership & Management Training

Book 1 is encyclopedic! You always had the energy, talent, intelligence to communicate in all methods from verbal to this most extensive production **[Education Essays from My Perspective: 50 Years as a Professional Educator Offering Pearls of Wisdom for Your Journey, Book 1.]**

It is gratifying to know that we've made a positive impact on so many! And we have! I maintain that you were by far one of the most independent, resourceful, caring, successful special staff I had the honor knowing at Army Reserve, HI.

Colonel Marcia Andrews
U.S. Army (Retired, 30 years of active duty & reserve)
Many Bases, Units, Locations

FOREWORD
BY NICHOLAS PATRICK WELLEIN

If you know **what Dr. Wellein has actually accomplished** - not talked about - but **initiated and completed,** you might understand the reason for her writing this **Book 2** for you.

She has seen it. She has done it, with all the difficult, snarly, unspeakable obstacles facing her, and now, she wants **to share** with you what she has learned. You will be delighted when you read about Dr. Wellein's experiences as she explains different theories on **three major areas** in real-life terms: <u>Multiculturalism, Prejudice, Racism, and Lies,</u> then <u>Change is the Only Constant</u>, and finally <u>Adult and Higher Education: Life's Challenges</u>. When she made mistakes, she tells you why, so YOU can avoid the pitfalls.

Her philosophy: if you do not make any mistakes, it means you are not doing anything! Just try not to make the same mistakes, the next time!

Do You Know that Dr. Wellein was the FIRST

- Female teacher at Hawaii Job Corps to work there for over 2 years.
- Master's Degree in Reading Education Candidate at the Univ. of Guam who brought in her own IBM Wheel Writer typewriter, typed 36 pages, single spaced, in one day for the Written Exam, doing so brilliantly that Dr. Donald Kenneth Maas, her professor waived the Oral Exams.
- mother with her youngest son of 5, to ride their own horses in Guam's Liberation Day Parade, bedecked with hundreds of flowers, wreathes, and flowing silks, representing the village of Sinajana, U.S. Territory, Guam. She taught for the Dept. of Education and University of Guam for over eight years.

Dr. Wellein was the FIRST Education Services Officer, U.S. Army

- in Sinai, Egypt, under the U.S. State Department, Multinational Forces &

Observers, (an international military force that monitors the decades-old Israeli-Egyptian peace accord) who renovated a kindergarten building to that of a fully functioning education center. She brought in trailers, outfitted them with computers & printers, offered Head-Start language courses in Spanish, French, Arabic to several thousand active-duty military on base from 11 countries. She developed a college program bringing in professors from Germany on Military Air Command (MAC) flights to teach University of Maryland & Big Bend Community College courses, open to all, at North Camp, El Gorah, Sinai, Egypt.

- in Soto Cano Air Base, Honduras, Central America, (flying in every 6 weeks from Panama), to establish a series of permanent Spanish Survival language courses, hire a permanent test examiner, and make that center fully operational, with Central Texas College courses (with an on-site permanent instructor).

- in Panama, Central America, following *Operation Just Cause*, at Fort Kobbe Education Center who instituted **day time college courses**, based on company commanders' requests. Military members especially loved the lunch-time and late afternoon specials!

- in Camp Doha, Kuwait, Middle East, (following *Desert Storm/Desert Shield*) to establish a series of computer courses by flying in professors from Germany on C-5 cargo planes loaded with computer equipment. She orchestrated a fully wired room for these University of Maryland classes, inviting personnel from all services to enroll. And they did!

- in Camp Zama, Japan, to create a unique telephone – facsimile tuition assistance request procedure, reducing hours that soldiers spent waiting in line to register for courses, to just minutes.

- in Puerto Rico, for U.S. Army Southern Command, after that major command transitioned from Panama to Puerto Rico, taking charge of Army military personnel testing in 24 nations: South and Central America, U.S. Virgin Islands,

Puerto Rico, the Caribbean, and part of Florida. She was the first to bring in bachelors and master's degree programs to Fort Buchanan, and expand the associate degree programs as well.

Returning to America in 2001, Dr. Wellein transitioned from Active-Duty Army education to the Army Reserve education, where she was the:

FIRST Education Services Officer, U.S. Army Reserve

- to authorize 200K of tuition assistance (TA) to reservists in Pacific and Asia in the first year (2001), and over 1 million dollars a decade later. She attended numerous college graduations (invited by soldiers) who told her, **"If it wasn't for YOU, I never would have gotten my degree!"**

- to provide information by facsimile, telephone, e-mail, and in person about college programs, testing, scholarships/grants to reservists and family members throughout Pacific and Asian: Alaska, Hawaii, Northern Mariana Islands, American Samoa, Guam, Japan, Korea.

- to purchase over 70 computers, 12 printers and 25 webcams with microphones and cameras for reserve centers in a **special, unique outreach initiative allowing** family members and military **to communicate when military personnel trained for or served in war zones**. She paid the annual Internet charges from her budget!

- to organize joint services (Coast Guard and Army Reserve) education fairs in Hawaii, Guam, and Saipan with counselors, military personnel, and colleges' representatives from the U.S. mainland, Veterans Affairs, ROTC, and additional local schools and agencies.

- to establish a Veterans Affairs Work Study Program at Ft Shafter, Honolulu, with VA paying participants while attending school.

- to establish a Basic Skills program in partnership with Hawaii State Dept. of Education paying for certified instructors and the Army Reserve providing classroom and supplies.

- to win the '*Federal Program Manager of the Year – U.S. Pacific*' in HI, representing 9th Mission Support Command, HI, and U.S. Army Pacific levels; the *Unsung Hero Award*, Headquarters, Department of the Army, Wash., DC; *the Education Services Officer of the Year* (worldwide) by Army Reserve Headquarters, MO.

- to present (with Coast Guard Education Officer, Dr. Donna Duellberg) in worldwide competition in Sydney, **Australia** at the DEHub (Innovations in Distance Learning), a prestigious international symposium: **The Education Summit 2011-2021, Global Challenges and Perspectives on Blended and Distance Learning**. Dr. Wellein and Dr. Duellberg also wrote '**Innovation in Learning Communities, a Collaboration of U.S. Coast Guard and U.S. Army Reserve Education Programs and Services,**' a professional journal article in the *DEQuarterly DEHub Journal*, funded by the Australian Government Dept. of Education, Employment and Workplace Relations.

- to initiate **hosting 18 college counselors weekly (Army Reserve and Coast Guard education offices on their respective bases)** to meet with interested, perspective students.

Dr. Wellein recently received the **2021 Albert Nelson Marquis Lifetime Achievement Award**, featured in the Lifetime Achievement section of **Who's Who in America** for more than 20 years of excellence in education. She was also recognized as a member of the prestigious **International Society of Female Professionals**, including those from 75 countries. Other accomplishments are too long to list here.
She is supremely qualified to talk about educational issues in the military and civilian arena, as someone who has been there, done that, and asked the hard questions!

In **EDUCATION ESSAYS FROM MY PERSPECTIVE: 50 YEARS AS A**

PROFESSIONAL EDUCATOR OFFERING PEARLS OF WISDOM FOR YOUR JOURNEY, <u>BOOK 2,</u> Dr. Wellein continues the conversation from her Book 1, and discusses a myriad of topics: **Multiculturalism, Prejudice, Racism, and Lies**, then **Change is the Only Constant**, and finally **Adult & Higher Education: Life's Challenges** – from her viewpoint. She uses real-life experiences as a teacher (most grade levels, subjects, undergraduate and graduate college instructor on Guam and Hawaii), summer school principal, grants writer, military counselor, education officer, and education director to explain many theories and practical application of these theories, to offer Pearls of Wisdom to you in the process.

How do I know Dr. Wellein and what has she done for me?

I have had the privilege of knowing her for over half a century – okay, 53 years, to be exact. She has been a major force in my life, modeling behavior I needed to see, guiding me in my own educational journey; I finally earned my masters at age 32 – but who is counting! She once told me that there is no such thing as being too old to return to school or becoming skilled in something. After all, in one year, I would be a year older anyway, with or without the added education or skills! I took that sage advice and am better because I did.

So, dear readers, I strongly recommend, indeed greatly urge, you to read this Book 2 (and of course, Book 1) and benefit from the Pearls of Wisdom for your own academic journey.

I am Nicholas Patrick Wellein, BA, MA, devoted youngest son, and can only sign this as "U.S. Federal Agent, Government Employee," but you can figure out the rest!

EDUCATION ESSAYS FROM MY PERSPECTIVE

BOOK 2

TABLE OF CONTENTS

DISCLAIMER

I have taken liberties with some names, agencies, and locations, to protect the privacy of individuals.

Therefore, any resemblance to actual persons, living or dead, or actual events might at times be purely coincidental. Any commentary, analysis, opinions, advice, and/or recommendations contained in this book are based on my personal experiences.

I have strived toward accuracy about specific topics, writers, named resources, references, and whenever the source of the information is known. But this is my own educational journey.

As publisher and author, I do not assume any liability to any party for any loss, damage, or disruption caused by errors or omissions, whether such errors or omissions result from negligence, accident, or any other cause.

I recognize that my memories of the events described in this book may be different than others who were there.

The views and opinions expressed here are mine and do not necessarily reflect the official policy or position of any agency of the U.S. government and are not intended to malign any religion, ethnic group, organization, company, or individual.

DEDICATION

Book 2 is dedicated to **educators – military and civilian everywhere**, especially to those in Guam, Hawaii, Asia & Pacific areas, Europe, South and Central America, and the Middle East to share information and promote life-long learning.

To all **military warriors of all American service branches including the U.S. Coast Guard**, it has been my great honor to serve you in my quest for educational excellence for yourselves and your family members.

My military work at Fort Shafter and Schofield Barracks, Hawaii, followed by my Germany tour (Wurzburg), then by three years with the Multinational Peacekeeping Force in the Sinai Peninsula as our American troops helped enforce the Camp David Accords in Egypt, were eye-opening experiences. Then, two years in Central America after Operation Just Cause in Panama and Honduras, and bringing educational programs to the Middle East (Kuwait, Saudi Arabia) following Desert Storm/Desert Shield made me realize how powerful the American forces are, and how underappreciated they are in America.

I spent two years as Deputy Director, U.S. Army Japan (Camp Zama) and later, over a year as Director, Camp Howze, South Korea (Paju) near the Demilitarized Military Zone near the 38th Parallel, serving troops who protect the demarcation line between South and North Korea.

Education Director for U.S. Army Southern Command in Puerto Rico included responsibilities for U.S. Army military testing for South and Central America; I finally returned to Fort Shafter, Hawaii, in mid-2001. As Army Reserve Director of Education for Pacific & Asia, responsible for education of our troops on Oahu, Kauai, Maui, the Big Island of Hawaii, Fairbanks & Anchorage, Alaska, and U.S. Territories of Guam & American Samoa, Commonwealth of the Mariana Islands (Saipan, Rota, Tinian), Japan, & Korea, the journey was awe inspiring. To military family members, I acknowledge the tremendous adversities you face, and **to our American Military Warriors – I thank you for your service.**

Finally, I dedicate this book **to my family**, for without their continuous support, my 50 years as a professional educator would not have been possible. My sweet, beloved, recently deceased spouse, **Daniel Navarro Atoigue** held Book 1 in his hands, and chucked when he read parts of it, before he was hospitalized and subsequently, passed. These 50 years with Danny have given me many indelible, indeed incredible memories!

Daniel Navarro Atoigue, born in Sinajana, U.S. Territory of Guam

Spouse, Family Nurturer, July 17, 1948 – February 23, 2021, Mililani, Hawaii. ALOHA

ACKNOWLEDGMENTS

Thank you, children – Geoffrey Michael Wellein, Nicholas Patrick Wellein, and Daniet Hokule'a Naomi Atoigue for your continual support and patience, and dear late-husband Daniel Navarro Atoigue who held our family together as the nurturer. Geoffrey – your energy and spirit provided me with great strength. Nicholas – your devotion was so remarkable, as were your computer skills so unbelievably keen. Thank you for your insightful Foreword!

Grandchildren Max Andrew and Stephen Daniel Wellein, Daniel Kekaimalu and Naomi Kauhiwai Legaspi served as an inspiration to me. To my sweet older sisters Nadya 'Tuka' Akau Glatzer and Ilsa Michelson Akau Greenwald, both of Edmonds, WA (but nee Hawaii), I thank you both for your daily conversations which bolster me tremendously. I love you all.

To my late departed educator-mother, Trude Michaelson Akau, I still miss you dearly!

I also want to acknowledge and thank some very special people. Judith F. Champaco of the HI Army Reserve; Jonell Y. Calloway, presently Chaplain & Bereavement Coordinator, MO, but formerly Army Reserve Director of Education (worldwide), and Abdul R. Ali, former Deputy Director (worldwide) Army Reserve Education, GA – warmest ALOHA for helping me personally and professionally.

I want to especially thank Charles Dennis Fritts, formerly Education Director, U.S. Army South, Panama & Honduras, Central America, (1992-1999) retired, and residing peacefully in Roanoke, Virginia and Dr. Donald Kenneth Maas, Professor of Education retired from California Polytechnic Institute at San Luis Obispo by way of New York and Guam, and author of several important education textbooks. I want to thank you both for instilling in me the desire to excel.

To Dr. Clinton L. "Andy" Anderson, and Dr. Steve F. Kime, both inducted into the U.S. Military Education Hall of Fame, as two of the top U.S. military educators in the world, I say a monumental thanks, for all your assistance and guidance.

To Colonel (Ret.) Marcia L. Andrews, G1 of Human Resources, 9RRC and GS14 Human Resources Jaybee S. Obusan, U.S. Army Pacific, you were both wonderfully supportive!

Warmest thanks to Dr. Donna J. Duellberg, of the U.S. Coast Guard, who mentored me, as we assisted military personnel and their family members throughout the Pacific and Asia regions. For over a decade, we successfully collaborated on numerous education fairs in Saipan, Guam, Hawaii, and spoke nationally in America and internationally in Australia. Dr. Duellberg, a former doctoral professor of mine and dissertation chairperson provided the idea of using Pearls of Wisdom for my Books 1 and 2.

I want to especially acknowledge Dr. Carole Freehan, of Freehan & Company, Spokane, Washington, for guiding me through the writing process for Book 1 as Senior Editor, and again, for assisting me as Senior Editor for Book 2. As the Pandemic surged, your encouragement to me never waivered. Earlier, you served as one of the most excellent professors I had when I was on my doctoral journey, teaching, supporting, encouraging, indeed, urging me to continue my research and writing. I want to especially thank you for your fantastic attention to detail!

To Dr. David C. Cho, Dr. Michael K. Yamazaki, Dr. Yun Sun Lee, Dr. Siuling Y. Kwan, and Dr. David T. Lee – thank you for your continued excellence. And to Clayton George Hill of *Prudential,* thank you for your wonderful much needed financial advice.

To Samuel 'Sammy' Naah, from Accra, Ghana, a 21 year-old editor (who most courageously wants to venture into setting up a publishing company), I say a warm Aloha. You served as an excellent and professional Graphics Designer for my Education Essays Book 1 and Book 2 after taking online courses to perfect your skills in Microsoft Office Suite.

Finally, to John Waipa I of *Waimanalo, Hawaii*, Ivy R. Rivera of *Mililani Physical Therapy*, and Martha Osgood, retired owner of *BackWords Indexing*, Portland, Oregon, I say a hearty *Mahalo*!

INTRODUCTION

Readers – Why did I write this book, **_Education Essays from My Perspective: 50 Years as a Professional Educator Offering Pearls of Wisdom for Your Journey, Book 2_**? What value does is hold? May I share some pearls, some ideas with prospective and experienced teachers, administrators or managers, military and civilian? Will educators learn something new? I made many mistakes along the way. But I learned so much, too!

Education Book 2 is a continuation of Book 1 and includes the following major sections:

The first section, **Multiculturalism, Prejudice, Racism, & Lies,** includes chapters on gender inequality, racism and intolerance, sources of prejudice, elements in multicultural education, and diversity in society. In addition, I discuss evaluating books for bias, multicultural tokenism, special and bilingual education, cultural impact, role of religion, and much more. I also included two real tales of female genital mutilation when I worked in the Middle East.

The second section, **Change is the Only Constant,** includes chapters on how to manage diverse frames or viewpoints at 9th Regional Readiness Command, Army Reserve, ethical issues, change theories, and what exactly facilitates successful change in any organization – military or civilian. One soldier's real-life experience dealing with bigotry provides insight into recognizing racism in one's own family.

The final section, **Adult & Higher Education: Life's Challenges** includes chapters on adult learners and learning principles, Leeward Community College teaching contract and tenure issues, Fink's taxonomy of significant learning, diploma mills and fake degrees, graduate course preparation, challenges when pursuing a degree and my personal reflections.

I use my own experiences when discussing theories, procedures, processes, and programs, many times contrasting them with what noted authorities and writers stipulate.

Go to the Appendix and read more Pearls of Wisdom, to further your own journey Nothing made up or fabricated – no fantasies – just the real deal.

There is no central thread in my education book, no cord to bind chapters together chronologically or geographically. Each chapter stands alone. Each is merely a snippet. Each one is a pearl, from dozens of PEARLS OF WISDOM, if you will, which make up a strand of pearls.

Sometimes I wrote what professors assigned on my doctoral journey, but added the latest information on that topic. Other times, I provided some personal observations or included my own viewpoint or story. **I used my personal experiences throughout most of these 51 chapters.**

I wrote this education book to share with you my trials and tribulations in my journey – working full-time for 50 years as a professional educator at all levels, while raising a family, working for the military as well as civilian institutions.

From teaching at Hawaii Job Corps Center, a vocational-technical school, then Deaf and Hard of Hearing pre-kindergarten and first graders, to serving as a Title I & Title IV reading resource specialist in public elementary and secondary schools (in Guam for over eight years), I explored the educational arena. I enjoyed teaching also at University of Guam (undergraduate and graduate levels).

Returning to Hawaii in 1980, I loved teaching at *Punahou* Summer School. I became a Title I reading teacher at *Waipahu* Intermediate, a Department of Education (DOE) middle school in a very low-income area for a year, then a language arts instructor at University of Hawaii, Leeward Community College, and a DOE adult community school teacher, at night.

Subsequently, the Department of the Army, Department of Defense (in Hawaii) hired me as an adult military education counselor, and for the next 30 years moved me all over the world, to where the troops were stationed: Germany, Egypt, Panama, Honduras, back to Hawaii, Kuwait, Saudi Arabia, Japan, Korea, Puerto Rico, with extensive weeks-long temporary duty locations to include U.S. Territories of American Samoa & Guam,

Commonwealth of the Northern Mariana Islands (Saipan, Tinian, Rota), Korea, Japan, Alaska (Fairbanks and Anchorage), Maui, Big Island of Hawaii, Oahu, and all points in between.

Upon my retirement in late December 2012, I began working as a substitute teacher for the Hawaii State DOE (almost all grade levels and specialties); I witnessed the very good, the sometimes bad, and the wretchedly ugly. Many years ago, I attempted in vain to obtain a mortgage loan but an officious banker informed me at the time that "teachers earn too little to qualify." I succeeded in securing a house-loan immediately after beginning to work for the military, in 1983. It is never too late. I began my doctoral journey at age 60, concluding it at 65.

My first book, **(Book 1)** if you are interested, covers **Teaching – Heaven or Hell,** a section of articles on **Professional Development: Truth or Consequences**, another group on **Test, Evaluate, Plan: Does It Work?** and finally **Communication and Leadership: Is It Possible?** These 72 chapters in **Book 1** open the reader to many diverse ideas, practices, and questions!

I hope you will love reading about solutions to problems, challenging yourself, exploring ideas and new methods, as you continue your academic education journey.

Aloha, Dr. Marsha Diane Akau Wellein, of Mililani, Hawaii

My Pearl of Wisdom: Gotcha Now!

Education would be much more effective if its purpose was to ensure

that by the time they leave school

every boy and girl should know how much they do **not** know,

and be imbued with a lifelong desire **to know it.**

William Haley

PART A: MULTICULTURALISM, PREJUDICE, RACISM, AND LIES

My Pearl of Wisdom: Accept the Challenge

If somebody is different from you,

that's not something you criticize,

that's

something that you appreciate.

Barack Obama

CH 1 Racial Tracking, Prejudice, and Segregation at Hawai'i Job Corps

My Pearl of Wisdom: Know Your Value

Keep exploring. Keep dreaming. Keep asking why.

Don't settle for what you

already know.

Never stop believing in the power of your ideas,

your imagination, your hard work to change the world.

Barack Obama

THE DEFINITION OF THE TERMS **racial tracking, racial prejudice, and curricular segregation** are important to understand; educators might accept these (Diaz, 2001; Noel, 2000) concepts, using Job Corps as an example. Sargent Shriver founded Job Corps nationally in 1964, for low-income males. Hawai'i placed one large center (all males) at Koko Head on Oahu, later moved the highly successful residential program to *Waimanalo* (and subsequently opened it to females as well), and built a second one on Maui (U.S. Department of Labor, Careers begin, 2017).

By 2020, Job Corps (the largest, federally funded nationwide residential career vocational training program in America) was annually serving 76,359 males and females ages 16-24, at 123 centers in the U.S. and Puerto Rico, training them in 81 career paths (U.S. Department of Labor, Career training, 2017). Some centers even offered childcare plans, recognizing the desperate need to assist young, single parents (U.S. Department of

Labor, Parents, 2017). But I digress. In 1969 in Hawai'i Job Corps was only five years old.

Racial Tracking

This term refers to assembling ethnic or racial groups of students together in a school situation. This means that educators place students from one racial or ethnic group together, with instruction or testing/assessment geared towards them because they are from a particular race, as opposed to placing students of all racial backgrounds together, due to their grade level, age, skill levels, interest, or other aspects.

At Hawai'i Job Corps Center in 1969, the director integrated all classes; there was no racial tracking in school. Students were Samoans and Guamanians (CHamorus) from the U.S. Territories of American Samoa and Guam, Hawaiians (all racial extraction) from the state of Hawai'i, Micronesians from the Federated States of Micronesia i.e., 607 islands, including Chuuk, Pohnpei, Yap, and Kosrae together with others from the Marshall Islands including Kwajalein and also Palau and the Northern Mariana Islands (Saipan, Rota, Tinian) atolls. All students from all islands with different heritage and backgrounds were totally integrated in all academic and vocational classes.

Almost all needed a high school diploma, self-discipline, good work habits, and certification if possible in a vocational trade (automotive, welding, painting, culinary arts, etc.). Ages were integrated as well, so everyone 16-21 was placed together in various classes, both academic and vocational. Later, Job Corps expanded its programs up to those 24 years of age with over 80 vocational trades and academics to include English Language, Science, and Writing (U.S. Department of Labor, Parents, 2017).

Thus, every two weeks, students rotated from academic to vocational training during their one - to two-year stay at the Koko Head center with approximately half in school, half in training. Juvenile court authorities in Hawai'i regularly released a few local students to Job Corps from Hawaii's *Koolau* training center (an all-male reformatory for Oahu's delinquent youths), where the state had incarcerated them as juvenile offenders. These young adults from Hawai'i had the advantage of speaking

English, but were the most difficult to teach, in addition to a sprinkling of others whose lack of English language abilities was a detriment to their learning. Most of the 'local' youths from Hawai'i were totally unmotivated!

However, many of these **young men from *Koolau*** segregated themselves **by their own request** when it came to dormitory living, usually six to eight in a dorm. So did those from Guam. CHamorus occupied several hooches, and spoke their native language, CHamoru, with each other when they had finished with academic or vocational training for the day. So, these young men from Guam preferred to dorm together with those from Northern Mariana Islands who also spoke CHamoru.

Many Micronesians wanted to live with their own native islanders also, so that they could speak their own native language and share their own cultural way of doing things. If they were from Pohnpei, Marshall Islands, or Palau for example, they asked to live together with their own 'native group' and speak Pohnpeian, Marshallese, or Palauan,

So, after school and hands-on vocational technical courses ended for the day, students voluntarily practiced racial tracking by living in their segregated living quarters.

I questioned one of the instructors when I first began working at Job Corps around Thanksgiving, 1969, "Why does Job Corps administration separate the dorms by 'origin' or island'? He explained, "These guys fight too much if they are mixed with others." I discovered later that might not be the whole truth. They liked speaking their native language, especially if their English was quite deficient, and they enjoyed talking about their own island's issues, sharing friends, family, and culture. They liked segregated living. But they still had physical brawls among their own dorm mates and with others.

Several of the youths from Hawai'i wanted to dorm with other locals as well as non-locals. Remember that the Hawai'i youths were generally of mixed ethnicity, so for example, one student might be half-Japanese and half-Korean, another a quarter Hawaiian, Filipino, Chinese, and White, and another boy Hawaiian, White, and Puerto Rican. Occasionally one youth might be all Japanese, or all Okinawan, but I never saw a

100% Hawaiian as there were few left in Hawai'i. (Several sources indicate that there are about 5,000-10,000 'pure Hawaiians' now living in the state together with over 150,000 part-Hawaiians.)

Job Corps hired Residential Advisors (adult males who lived on campus and maintained peace and order) to prevent any fighting. Sometimes, fights indeed broke out, but interestingly, **I rarely heard about fights when students were in their vocational training areas**, such as automotive repair, painting, or welding, or especially when handling their specialized equipment.

Fighting (physical fistfights, practiced leg kicks, and shoving matches) mainly occurred inside and outside of dormitories, near the base's cafeteria, and occasionally, outside the classroom areas. And of course, there were many loud raucous arguments with much swearing daily.

Racial Prejudice

This term refers to bias an individual feels towards a person or group based on their race, color, national origin, or ethnic heritage. Sometimes, the government or agency can regulate behavior by policies, laws, common practices, or other regulatory documents. However, it is difficult to regulate feelings and beliefs. At the Job Corps Center, **there appeared to be a great deal of racial prejudice, with one racial group taunting another every day.**

On several occasions, I would hear about fistfights that broke out among the young men, on or off campus when they took the Job Corps bus to shop at a local mall or anyplace they ended up drinking! (Yes, the legal drinking age was 21, and there were a few corpsmen who were indeed, that age. And who is to say they did or did not buy liquor for those younger in their group?) **Again, personally, I only witnessed this negative behavior (fighting) in the school area,** where I taught GED Preparation, and Reading but of course I heard about the other incidents from both corpsmen and instructors.

Curricular Segregation

This term refers to school or instruction curriculum based on group characteristics, such as language. For example, if a teacher places all non-native speaking English students together for a class, this is an example of such segregation. Job Corps center classes (GED Prep, World of Work, Mathematics for Shop, etc.) were all conducted in English although many students (especially from Micronesia, American Samoa, and Guam) spoke and read English as their second language. In vocational courses, schools designated which students took the basic (such as Automotive Mechanics I), before the advanced course (such as Automotive Mechanics II).

Segregation by subject area and level, of course, is used throughout most middle or intermediate and high schools in most classes in America, thus the designation 'I' or 'II,' or 'III' for example.

Racial Prejudice Experience

I would like to share one incident of racial prejudice, although unfortunately, I have experienced several similar incidents. This particularly disturbing event occurred when Job Corps first hired me as an instructor of the local Center at Koko Head, on Oahu. The racial prejudice stemmed from the **adults working there**, and not the young corpsmen. Only local male instructors (from Hawai'i) worked there, although previously the director had hired two female U.S. mainland Caucasian instructors, each lasting not more than three or four months.

I look Caucasian or White (*Haole*, in Hawaiian) so many of the students and other instructors simply assumed I was indeed, a *Haole* from the mainland. The director of the center (a part-Caucasian, part-Hawaiian, with a master's degree in social work) hired me to teach at this all-male student facility following a lengthy interview. Perhaps he hired me because he believed that instructors should be both male and female. Perhaps he wanted to give a teaching opportunity to a part-Hawaiian female, who came from a prominent local family, spoke perfect English, and could relate to local youths, although over 40% were males from other Pacific or Micronesian island sites. Or perhaps he discovered I was a young single mom, with two toddlers under the age of three and desperately needed a job. I do not know. However, the first four months working there were sheer hell.

The worst remarks came from the other instructors, and not the male students. I often overhead loud remarks about me (from one instructor to another) such as: **"Hey! What can a F***ing *Haole* girl do here?** Those corpsmen will eat her alive." Another instructor actually said to me: **"I wouldn't want to work here if I was a woman. The last woman dated so many corpsmen that she should have opened up a whorehouse."** I tried to maintain my composure and said nothing. A student overheard this particular comment and said to me after that instructor left the room, "Wow, that wasn't such a nice thing to say to you. **Don't worry. He's just a F***ing Jap, anyway." I was speechless.**

About three-four weeks later after I was first hired, there was a staff meeting where Director James Bacon introduced new staff members. Mr. Bacon **said to the group** (and yes, I remember this entire incident as if it happened yesterday and not decades ago):

> I want you to meet our new GED and Reading instructor. She is part-Hawaiian, Chinese, Portuguese. Her dad is from Hilo, the Big Island, her mom is a well-respected educator and one of the five main writers of the 1950 Hawai'i territorial constitution used in 1959 so Hawai'i could become a state. She graduated from the University of Hawai'i at Mānoa three years ago. Please welcome her.

The staff members looked around at each other in stunned silence. I smiled and said nothing, stood up, looked around the room, and sat down quietly, but always remembered how terrible these instructors had treated me. Much later, the center director told me that I was the first female instructor to remain working there (for over two years by the time I resigned), because the previous two only worked there for less than four months before quitting. (Was their departure due to the harassment from the students **or** the other instructors? Who knows!) Racial prejudice was alive and well!

While at Job Corps, I had spent two years, after work (on my own at 5 p.m., each weekday, 12 months a year), completing coursework towards a teaching certificate (20+

semester hours) and I was the first instructor (the director told me) whom everyone respected – instructors, residential advisors, job corpsmen, parents. Absolutely no one had made any complaints against me, and I had not made a single complaint against anyone!

Subsequently, I left to teach on Guam under a two-year contract, which provided free airline transportation to Guam and housing for my two sons and me. Furthermore, teaching special education on Guam meant I could attend late afternoon university courses and spend summers, at the University of Guam working towards a master's in education. What was there to lose? Almost everything I was familiar with including my own Hawai'i *Kai* house, and my entire family support system! But I would be able to obtain a master's in education, and to stretch my wings, professionally! Nothing ventured – nothing *gained*.

So, with $150 (my entire savings) in my handbag, two youngsters under the age of five in tow, a lot of mettle, spirit, and tenacity, we spent three weeks on Continental Air Lines traveling through the Marshall Islands, Chuuk, and Pohnpei (free stop-overs), staying with families of Job Corpsmen, before arriving on Guam, Christmas Day. The Department of Education (DOE) representative forgot to meet me at the airport (due to the holidays), but unbelievably, a former Job Corps student of mine from Guam saw me at the arrival section, by accident. When he learned that no one was helping me from the DOE, he took me to his mother's house for the weekend. It took a few days to get things sorted out, but I never forgot the graciousness of that wonderful lady and her family.

CH 2 Multicultural Terms to Understand

My Pearl of Wisdom: Words Can Be Demons

It is time for parents to teach young people early on that in diversity

there is beauty and there is strength.

Maya Angelou

WHAT DO TERMS USED in any discussion of multiculturalism actually mean? Is racism the same as anti-diversity? Is one term used synonymously with another, such as 'ethnic' vs. 'nationality'? Merriam-Webster Dictionary (n.d.) provides the **following definitions of relevant words or terms** used when discussing multiculturalism:

Terms - General

Culture: social traits, features of a shared people, values, practices.

Diversity: the condition, instance of being diverse, variety.

Ethnic: relating to large groups of people based on common racial, national, tribal, religious, linguistic, cultural origin or background; being a member of an ethnic group which retains the culture, customs, language, or social views of the group.

Ethnos: race, people, cultural group.

Ethnocentric: characterized by or based on the attitude that one's own group is superior (to others).

Multicultural: relating to, reflecting or adapted to diverse cultures.

Nationality: citizenship or nation, that is, people can share the same nationality or citizenship but be of a different ethnic group.

Racial: relating to, or based on a race; existing or occurring between races.

Racism: a belief that race is the primary determinant of human traits and capacities, and racial differences produce an inherent superiority of a particular race.

Lynch (2015) has a detailed definition of multicultural education:

a progressive approach for transforming education based on educational equality and social justice. The components required . . . [include] content integrations, prejudice reduction, empowering school culture and social culture. These all relate and all require attention as they relate to the efforts of conflict resolution in today's world. What kids learn in their classroom environments when it comes to interactions with those who are different from them translates into how well they will manage life in the global marketplace. (p. 1)

In the last century, there has been an increase in global mutual acceptance of opposing views and different cultures – though arguably, there is still a long way to go. Specifically when it comes to America, it is crucial that multicultural education exist with the increasing number of students who speak a second language and come from somewhere else. Diversity exists even within mainstream society and students need to have the communication life skills that multicultural education promotes. (p. 1)

Terms for K – 5th Grades

However, there are many additional terms such as **inclusion and exclusion** that should be defined, so I shall continue the list, below. **Elementary School level vocabulary words** related to bias and bullying are very important to students, teachers, and administrators, as explained in the **Anti-Defamation League [ADL] Glossary, No Place for Hate** (ADL, Glossary, 2021, p. 50):

Allyship: An action where someone helps or stands up for someone who is being bullied or who is the target of bias.

Bullying: When a person or a group behaves in ways—on purpose and repeatedly—that make someone feel hurt, afraid, or embarrassed. **Behavior is not considered bullying if it occurs once with no intention of gaining power** (e.g., bumping into someone by accident, telling a joke once, not playing with someone, etc.); still, it is important that all mean behavior be addressed in a timely and appropriate way.

Bystanding: When a person or a group sees bullying or prejudice happen and does not say or do anything.

Culture: The patterns of daily life that can be seen in language, arts, customs, holiday celebrations, food, religion, beliefs/values, music, clothing and more that a group of people share.

Discrimination: Unfair treatment of one person or group of people because of the person's or group's identity (e.g., race, gender, ability, religion, culture, etc.). Discrimination is an action that can come from prejudice and can often be illegal.

Inequality: An unfair situation when some people have more rights or better opportunities than other people.

Injustice: A situation in which the rights of a person or a group of people are ignored, disrespected or discriminated against.

Multicultural: This refers to including many different cultures.

Name-Calling: Using words to hurt or to demean a person or a group.

Nonverbal Communication: Aspects of communication (such as gestures and facial expressions) that do not involve speaking; these can also include nonverbal aspects of speech (tone and volume of voice, etc.).

Prejudice: Judging or having an idea about someone or a group of people before you actually know them. Prejudice is often directed toward people in a certain identity group (color, economic class, gender, etc.).

Stereotype: The false idea that all members of a group are the same and that they think and behave in the same way.

Teasing: Laughing at and putting someone down in a way that is either friendly and playful, or mean and unkind.

Terms for 6th – 12th Grades

Some middle and high school terms are important to understand, and although some of the terms (indicated with an *) are the same as those listed for Elementary School level, **the definitions are more detailed and explicit.** The terms are as follows (ADL, Glossary, 2021. p. 51):

Anti-bias: An active commitment to challenging bias in oneself, others, and institutions.

Bias: An inclination or preference either for or against an individual or group that interferes with impartial judgment.

Bigotry: An unreasonable or irrational attachment to negative stereotypes and prejudices of individuals or groups belonging to one or more social identities.

*Culture: The patterns of daily life learned consciously and unconsciously by a group of people, as seen in governing practices, arts, language, customs, holiday celebrations, food, religion, relationships, family roles, clothing, etc.

*Discrimination: The denial of justice, resources and fair treatment of individuals and groups (often based on social identity) through employment, education, housing, banking, political rights, etc. In America, laws can protect those discriminated against in many cases.

Diversity Different or varied; the population of the U.S. consists of people belonging to diverse groups characterized by culture, race, ethnicity, nationality, gender, sexual orientation, ability, etc.

*Multicultural: Many or multiple cultures; the U.S. is multicultural because its population consists of people from many different cultures (unlike some countries which are monoethnic such as Japan, and China).

*Prejudice: A premature judgment or belief formed about a person, group, or concept before gaining sufficient knowledge or by selectively disregarding facts.

Scapegoating: Blaming an individual or group for something based on that person or group's identity when the person or group is not responsible. Bias, prejudicial thinking, and discriminatory acts can lead to scapegoating.

*Stereotype: An oversimplified generalization about a person or group of people without regard for individual differences. Even seemingly positive stereotypes that link a person or group to a specific positive trait can have negative consequences.

Find a full list of terms at ADL's Glossary of Education Terms at:

https://www.adl.org/sites/default/files/documents/glossary-of-education-terms

Terms for All Levels

I have defined additional terms used in this brief discussion, so important when understanding multiculturalism and the challenges involved in our schools, other institutions, companies, organizations, the military, indeed, all of society, (ADL, Glossary, 2021, pp. 51-54). These terms are as follows:

System of Bias: The specific, pervasive systems of oppression and marginalization described below are upheld by **institutionalized, cultural and historical ideologies, and discrimination.** These systems exist simultaneously, compounding the harm to individuals with multiple marginalized identities. Individual acts of prejudice and discrimination perpetuate these systems, which exist **regardless of individual** prejudices and interpersonal acts of bias.

Ableism: The marginalization and/or oppression of people who have disabilities, including temporary, developmental, physical, psychiatric and/or intellectual disabilities.

Ageism: The marginalization and/or oppression of older people based on the belief that older people are inferior, incapable, or irrelevant. Ageism also describes the marginalization and/or oppression of people who are too young to have social independence.

Anti-Immigrant Bias: The marginalization and/or oppression of people who are of immigrant origin, transnational, or outside the dominant national identity or culture. Other related terms include xenophobia to describe a fear to anyone or anything that is perceived to be foreign or strange.

Anti-Muslim Bias: The marginalization and/or oppression of people who are Muslim based on the belief in stereotypes and myths about Muslim people, Islam, and countries with predominantly Muslim populations.

Anti-Semitism: The marginalization and/or oppression of people who are Jewish based on the belief in stereotypes and myths about Jewish people, Judaism, and Israel.

Anti-Trans Bias: The marginalization and/or oppression of people who are transgender and/or non-binary (identifying as neither a man nor a woman) based on the belief that cisgender (gender identity that corresponds with the sex one was assigned at birth) is the norm.

Bullying is a behavior: Bullying is usually directed to those who might have less power or status. Because of this, ADL encourages educators to use language that describes **students' behavior** rather than the student themselves (e.g., "the student who bullied" rather than "the bully;" "the student who was targeted" rather than "the target"). By focusing on behavior, we avoid sending the message that a student's behavior cannot change, and we acknowledge that one person can exhibit multiple behaviors in different bullying situations. **Below are the behaviors individuals may exhibit in incidents of <u>bullying</u>.**

Bystanding: Many students observe bullying behavior without supporting or confronting it out of fear of being bullied themselves or because they do not know how to support the one who is being bullied.

Classism: Marginalization and/or oppression of people who are from low-income or working-class households based on a social hierarchy in which people are ranked according to socioeconomic status.

Cyberbullying: Intentional and repeated mistreatment of others through the use of technology such as computers, cell phones, tablets, and other electronic devices.

Heterosexism: Marginalization and/or oppression of people who are lesbian, gay, bisexual, queer and/or asexual based on the belief that heterosexuality is the norm.

Name-Calling: Use of language to defame, demean, or degrade individuals or groups.

Racism: Marginalization and/or oppression of people of color based on a socially made racial hierarchy that White people are privileged.

Religious bigotry: Marginalization and/or oppression of people who belong to one or more religious groups or no religious group, based on the belief there is 'just one' correct or sanctioned faith system.

Sexism: Marginalization and/or oppression of women based on the belief in a natural order based on sex/gender that privileges men over women.

Weightism: Marginalization and/or oppression of people who are larger than the 'socially accepted' norm for body size.

Carlos F. Diaz, a well-recognized pioneer, educator, and writer about multiculturalism, in *Multicultural education for the 21ˢᵗ century* (2001) states that multicultural involves "restructuring the curriculum to reflect multicultural perspectives" (p. 4) so that the White culture is not dominant. Diaz reports that "students of color make up over 33% of the public-school population, although 90% of the teachers in American self-identify as White and middle class" (p. 4). (This has changed!) The curriculum, textbooks, and teaching practices, explains Dr. Diaz, also seem to reflect the fact that there is mainly a European/American culture present in the schools. Indeed, the entire education system in many parts of America seems to ignore the minorities.

Understanding multicultural 'vocabulary' is important for all students, teachers, administrators, and especially important for the military, law enforcement officers, government officials, and elected lawmakers.

More recently, however, the federal government documents a different picture:

Schools that had more racial/ethnic diversity in their student populations also tended to have more racial/ethnic diversity among teachers. The percentage of minority teachers was highest at schools that had 90 percent or more minority students and lowest at schools that had less than 10 percent minority students. (NCES, 2019, p. 1)

Final Thoughts

I do not believe that the term 'multicultural' means the same as 'racial' or 'ethnic.' Many writers clearly point out that multicultural includes not only a variety of races and ethnic groups, but includes gender, exceptionalities, color, culture, and even multiple elements of intelligence (diversity). In addition, race involves the physical appearance such as skin color, hair texture whereas ethnicity includes cultural factors, tribal-affiliations, religion, and language.

Educator Matthew Lynch (2015) says that multicultural education really cannot be learned from a textbook but must be developed in the classroom based on a "particular student group" (p. 2). He states that teachers must learn their students' learning styles, be proud of their own heritage, be aware of their own biases, and create classroom assignments that celebrate multiculturalism and ethnic backgrounds.

Writer Ronald Takai (2000), in *A different mirror: A history of multicultural America*, mentions that writers have historically defined 'Americans' in America as 'White' but that minorities are 'fast becoming the majority.' Takai does not use the terms 'racial' or 'ethnic' interchangeably. When he discusses diversity, he refers to large groups of people who have their own culture, heritage, race, color, religion, or language.

In 2018-2020, teachers in America self-identify as follows (NCES, 2019):

> The majority of public elementary and secondary school teachers were White in both 2003-04 (the first year for which teacher data for all racial/ethnic groups were available) and 2015-16. However**, the percentage of teachers who were White was lower in 2015-16** than in 2003-04 (80% vs. 83%). The percentage of teachers who were Black was also lower in 2015-16 than in 2003-04 (7% vs. 8%). In contrast, the **percentages of teachers who were Hispanic, Asian, and of two or more races** were higher in 2015-16 than in 2003-04. The percentages of teachers who were Pacific Islander in these two years were not measurably different, nor were the percentages who were American Indian/Alaska Native. (p. 1)

Apparently, **schools that have more racial or ethnic diversity among its teachers may have a positive effect on minority students, in terms of achievement, motivation, attitudes, and behavior.** Obviously, the experienced teacher of any age (no matter what the color, religion, nationality, gender, or ethnicity) might be able to offer maturity of judgment, passion, best teacher practices, technology skills, and organizational/management experience in the classroom as well. Students deserve no less.

CH 3 The Most Important Education Law Ever in U.S. History

My Pearl of Wisdom: The Time is Now

Every time we turn our heads the other way when we see the law flouted,

when we tolerate what we know to be wrong,

when we close our eyes and ears to the corrupt

because we are too busy or too frightened,

when we fail to speak up and speak out,

we strike a blow against freedom and decency and justice.

Robert Kennedy

WHAT WAS THE MOST IMPORTANT event in the history of multicultural awareness in American and what direct effect has it had on education?

Joel Spring (2000) in *The great civil rights movement and the new culture wars* discusses the 1954 Supreme Court decision **Brown v. Board of Education of Topeka** (Kansas) that overturned the separate but equal doctrine of the Fourteenth Amendment to the U.S. Constitution. The National Association for the Advancement of Colored People (NAACP) which prepared the case, stated two goals: "to show that the climate of the times required an end to segregation laws **and** to show that the separate but equal doctrine contained a contradiction in terms, i.e., that separate facilities were inherently unequal" (p. 14).

Discussion

Brian Willoughby (2004) discusses the significance of this historic 1954 Supreme Court decision. Willoughby quotes Chief Justice Earl Warren: **"We conclude that in the field of public education, the doctrine of "separate but equal" has no place"** (p. 2).

In an article about this famous ruling Allen (2004) states the following:

> Although the *Brown* decision struck down public school segregation laws, the Supreme Court could not, of course, control where people chose to reside. So de facto segregation based on neighborhood demographics continued – in both the South and the North. Court-ordered busing in places such as Cleveland and Boston attempted to redress this situation in the 1970s. One group that closely monitors the legacy of *Brown* is the Harvard Civil Rights Project; their report, "Brown at 50: King's Dream or Plessy's Nightmare" shows many unsettled issues. (p. 2)

An Education Week, 2014 article, *Data: Race and ethnicity in U.S. schools today* states:

> in the six decades since the U.S. Supreme Court handed down its decision in Brown v. Board of Education of Topeka, the racial and ethnic landscape of the United States has evolved, and the nation's schools along with it. The U.S. population is much less dominated by non-Hispanic whites than it was in the 1950s. By 2060, the U.S. Census Bureau predicts, the United States will become a 'plurality' nation, with no one race in the majority. (Whites will still be the single largest group, with Hispanic Americans the next largest group.) (p. 1)

The National Center for Education Statistics (NCES, 2020) reported in 2019-2021 that Whites make up only 49% (down from 61%) of public elementary and secondary school students, and Black students decreased from 17 to 15%. However, **Hispanic students increased** from 16 to 26%, and **Asian/Pacific Island students increased** from 4 to 5%.

Over a dozen years later NCES (2020) discussed the funding problem (to implement this 1954 decision) seen in many states with high minority populations:

> Nationally, school districts serving the **most Black, Latinx, and Native American** students receive significantly less state and local funding than districts serving the fewest [and as a result] families and education advocates are still

suing to compel states to uphold their education funding obligations. (p. 1)

My Personal Beliefs

I believe that this court decision, **Brown v. Board of Education of Topeka** in 1954 was the most significant event in the history of multicultural awareness even though it took years for the actual implementation. America, now nearly 67 years later, is **still** attempting to deal with this momentous Supreme Court decision (see *Sixty years after Brown v. Board of Education*, 2014).

In December 1955, 42-year-old Rosa Parks refused to give up her seat on a public bus in Montgomery, Alabama, and the city jailed her for violating the city's racial segregation law (Rosa Parks, Biography, 2021; Rosa Parks, History, 2021). A young Baptist minister, Martin Luther King Jr. organized the Montgomery Bus Boycott, following the historic act of civil disobedience, and the rest is history.

America has experienced a first Black American president, 2008-2016 (Obama, born in Hawai'i, half-White, half-Black); as of January 2021, and America has a first Black, female American vice president (Harris, half-Indian from India, half-Jamaican). Newly elected U.S. President Joe Biden has appointed a diverse, multicultural group of directors, managers, administrators, and cabinet members, with respect to age, gender, race/ethnicity, and experience in government and private industry. Let America finally fulfill 'her promise' – separate is not equal. The time is now!

CH 4 Declaration

of Independence, á la 2021

My Pearl of Wisdom: Freedom is Everything

The content of a book holds the power of education and it is with this power

that we can shape our future and change lives.

Malala Yousafzai

WE HUMANS OF PLANET EARTH and throughout the solar system hold these truths to be self-evident and accepted by beings and species of all ages, races, colors, national origins, religions, faiths, physicality, mental/emotional abilities, ethnicities, cultures, languages, educational levels, traditions, income levels, belief systems, economic status, skills, abilities and disabilities, legal systems, political beliefs, abilities/disabilities, creed, genders, sexual orientations, societies, governments, continents, planets, solar systems, islands, nations, countries, communities, work and societal groups, families, individuals and societal organizations (Diaz, 2001; Noel, 2000). That all living beings/species located on all planets throughout the solar system are created equal, and that they are endowed by their Creator, Nature, God, Higher Power, Individualistic Power, Family or Group cultures or values to include those who question or refuse to believe in any higher power and wish to have freedom from such beliefs, with certain unalienable rights and privileges (ADL, Religion, 2021); that among these are life, liberty, and the pursuit of happiness, health, cultural beliefs, individual pursuits, education, recreation, work, home, social, psychological, economical, political, emotional, and family life. Such pursuits should not be hurtful or harmful in any way to others (Gal, Kiersz, Mark, Su, & Ward, 2020). Freedom really is everything.

CH 5 Culture and Its Effects on Gender in School

My Pearl of Wisdom: Cinderella vs. Cinderfella – Why Does Society Continually Treat the Sexes Differently

Be yourself. Everyone else is already taken!

Oscar Wilde

MERRIAM-WEBSTER DICTIONARY (n.d.) **defines Culture** as first, the "integrated pattern of human knowledge, belief, and behavior that depends upon man's capacity for learning and transmitting knowledge to succeeding generations" and secondarily, culture as the "customary beliefs, social forms, and material traits of a racial, religious, or social group" and finally, the "set of shared attitudes, values, goals, and practices that characterize a company or corporation" or group.

Edward T. Hall (2000) defines culture as a "form of communication," and as a total summary of a people's "learned behavior patterns, attitudes, and material things" (p. 81). Hall mentions that the most important reason for the common person, that is, student, teacher, homemaker, blue- or white-collar worker, techie, food server, etc., to learn about culture is that it allows the individual to learn new ways of perceiving ideas, things, people, events, and to learn more about him or herself. Henry T. Trueba (2000) further explains that Hall says that the essence of culture is "socially shared norms, codes of behavior, values, assumptions, etiquette, and world view . . . and is made up of the concepts, beliefs, and principles of action and organization" (p. 85).

Educators have written a great deal in the past about culture and its effects on gender within the school system.

Good Articles to Read

Educator Joseph Cimpian expressed his ideas in *How our education system undermines gender equity and why culture change - not policy - may be the solution* (Cimpian, 2018). He discussed gaps in academic achievement between males and females from kindergarten through college, including paying particular attention to science, technology, engineering, and mathematics (STEM) courses.

Cimpian (2018) pointed out that teachers need to recognize personal prejudices about female abilities in STEM. Also, teachers may believe that girls need to work harder to achieve well, compared to boys, and finally, that it is difficult for teachers to change their attitudes if standardized test scores show gender achievement differences. However, "state standardized tests consistently show small or no differences between boys and girls in math achievement, which contrast with somewhat larger gaps" (p. 3).

Ten Examples to Ponder

A disturbing article by Carolina Sherwood Bigelow (2014) provides *10 examples of gender inequality in the world* as follows (pp. 1-3):

1. **Lack of Mobility:** A male family member must accompany any female member who is going from one place to another; husbands have a right in some countries to stop their wives from leaving the country; in other countries, wives must obtain written permission to travel. (Think of Saudi Arabia!)

2. **Freedom of Marriage:** Some children in sub-Saharan Africa or South Asia are married well before they are 18; they have no choice of partnership. In Pakistan, society expects females to accept arranged marriages; 'honor killings' are uncontested by several governments in the Middle East, if a daughter dishonors her parents by going against their wishes.

3. **Discriminatory Divorce Rights:** In much of the Middle East, males believe they are superior to females; some can divorce their wives easily; in Lebanon, for example, usually abused women do not have the right to file for divorce.

4. **Citizenship**: Many women in the Middle East cannot pass their citizenship to their children; men can do so and to their non-national wives.

5. **Frontline Combat**: In some countries, women cannot serve in front line units; in United Kingdom, this inequality continued as recently as 2016 while

women in U.S. combat units were integrated in 2017 or so, depending on the service branch.

6. **Custody Rights:** In some countries, the courts grant custody of minor children to their fathers; mothers are left with no means of financial support; some family laws allow courts to deny mothers custody of their children, depending only on judges' decisions; judges are predominantly male.

7. **Violence:** Spousal rape, especially in countries like India, does not apply to wives; society and many women themselves believe sexual subjugation in marriage is normal.

8. **Professional Obstacles**: Women earn about 77% of what men earn for the same work. (It will take an estimated 45 years to see this gender inequality end according to Bigelow.)

9. **Restricted Land Ownership:** Despite constitutional provisions in some countries, customary or religious laws prohibit land ownership by females; females sometimes must obtain approval of husbands to buy or inherit land.

10. **Access to Education:** Women are more than 2/3 of the adult illiterates of the world. In some countries like Afghanistan, many females do not even understand that they have the right to attend school, read, and write. (Bigelow, 2018)

Bigelow updated her 'list' in 2018, as seen in Chapter Six.

Discussion

I believe that many individuals believe that there are an extraordinary number of factors that may affect students at all levels in education and learning in addition to 'gender.' Samuel Bowles (2000) stipulates several sociological and anthropological factors affecting student performance in school. **These factors include** social-class status, income levels, occupational types, immigration status, age, educational levels of the parents, students' race, color, creed, cultural, and ethnic heritage, minority or majority group status, religious affiliation, and sexual orientation (Soken-Huberty, 2020).

Other factors are athletic or academic skills and abilities, financial and actual physical condition of the facilities, plant, building, school, grounds, amount and type of parental support given to the school, inner city or urban school vs. country school and location, as well as teacher background (race, color, cultural/economic and educational background).

In addition, I have found that variables such as the linguistic background of students, parents, teachers, and school administrators are important as well. Other factors involve citizenship status, living conditions of both students and staff (i.e., if extended or multigenerational families are the exceptions or the norm), number of parents holding part-time or and full-time jobs, overall division of labor in the community, crime rates, and high school drop-out rates. Let us not forget the obvious factors: physical, emotional, psychological, and economic variables, in addition to disabilities of all kinds.

However, the role of gender cannot be underestimated especially the effects of gender in school! School as an institution of society represents its culture, and thus gender discrimination is a factor affecting performance in school including the following:

- **Lack of job equality**: Females have only 75% of men's employment rights.

- **Job segregation**: The best paying jobs go to men, because 'men are simply better equipped to handle' them.

- **Lack of legal protection**: More than one billion females lack legal protection against domestic sexual or economic violence.

- **Lack of bodily autonomy**: Over 200 million women who don't want to get pregnant are not using contraception.

- **Poor medical care**: Women more than men lack good doctor-clinic care as there are more women living in poverty.

- **Lack of religious freedom**: Georgetown University and Brigham Young University conducted a study showing a connection between religious intolerance and females' ability to work in good paying jobs.

- **Lack of political representation**: Females governed only 11 nations.

- **Racism:** Pay inequities between white women and women of color continues.

- **Societal beliefs**: Gender beliefs remain an on-going problem, one which society cannot solve in a generation, and certainly not without addressing systematic discrimination in each country and school system.

- **Uneven access to education:** One-fourth of young women 15-24 will not complete primary school. (Soken-Huberty, 2020, pp. 1-6)

Two Famous Women of Color

Many minority women – Black-Americans, Asian-Americans, Hispanic Americans, American Indians – could be discussed here, but I will mention only two, both Asians, representing Hawai'i.

The first individual, a trailblazer in politics, is **Mazie Keiko Hirono, Japanese born, the first Buddhist and the first Asian immigrant to serve in the U.S. Senate** from Hawai'i, 2012 to the present. Senator Hirono initially served in the U.S. House of Representatives earlier (2007-2013), and elected Lieutenant Governor of Hawai'i (1994-2002) as discussed by Gregory Lewis McNamee (n.d.) and Richard Mertens, (2012).

Another role model for gender equality was Patsy Mink, an extremely important individual in the history of women's rights, whom my mother considered a friend. U.S. Congresswoman Patsy Takemoto Mink (born on Maui), represented Hawai'i, and who as a young woman, applied to dozens of medical schools after her bachelor's degree (Hawai'i News Now, 2007). All institutions denied her admission **because she was a female**. So, she earned a law degree from University of Chicago Law School (University of Chicago, n.d.) instead, but when firms refused to hire her because she had a small child, she began a private practice.

She was the first Japanese-American woman to practice law in Hawai'i (Stringer, 2018). When she served in the U.S. Congress (1990-2002) as **the first woman of color elected, she authored the Title IX legislation, mandating**

equal treatment for women and men in education After 45 years, the law has led to dramatic progress: Now 11.5 million women attend college, compared with 8.9 million men. Before Title IX, just 300,000 girls nationwide participated in high school sports every year, versus the 3.5 million who do today. The fields of medicine and law that first excluded Mink are now almost equal in their enrollment of male and female students. (p. 1)

After Mink's success with Title IX, she helped pass the Women's Educational Equity Act in 1974, which provided funding to prevent discrimination in education programs (Mertens, 2012). **Congress eventually renamed Title IX as the Patsy Mink Equal Opportunity in Education Act, and in 2014, President Barack Obama posthumously awarded Mink the Presidential Medal of Freedom, the nation's highest civilian honor** (Stringer, 2018).

> In addition to her work on education issues, Mink promoted numerous laws that dealt with other issues important to women. These included the <u>Consumer Product Safety and Equal Employment Opportunity Acts of 1972</u>; the <u>Equal Credit Opportunity Act of 1974,</u> and various bills dealing with discrimination in insurance practices, pensions, retirement benefits, social security, survivor's benefits and taxation; equitable jury service; health care issues; housing discrimination based on marital status; and privacy issues. In 1973, she authored and introduced the <u>Equal Rights for Women Act</u> (H.R. 4034), which never made it out of committee, and she supported the ratification of the <u>Equal Rights Amendment</u>. (Patsy Mink, 2021, p. 7)

Personal Note

I am proud that my youngest son, Nicholas Wellein, served as a volunteer 'Honorary Page' for Patsy Mink in Honolulu, for several weeks toward the end of his high school years at Mid-Pacific Institute.

Presently, my family and I live about four miles from the massive, recreational, **'Patsy T. Mink Central Oahu Regional Park,'** which has lovely tennis courts, spacious soccer and softball fields, an archery range, an Olympic size swimming pool, meeting room, snack bar, running trails, several restrooms, huge parking lots, and children's' playgrounds complete with slides. In 2007 the City of Honolulu celebrated renaming the park in honor of Senator Mink (Hawai'i KHON 2, 2012; Hawai'i News Now, 2007).

"From these parks will come many more scholar athletes, from these parks will come many more champions who will represent the state of Hawai'i in many areas," said Mayor Mufi Hannemann (Hawai'i KHON 2, 2012, p. 1; Hawai'i News Now, 2007, p. 1). Mayor Hannemann, an American Samoan educated at Harvard University and a Fulbright

Scholar explained, **"Mink was the driving force behind 'Title Nine' which prohibits gender discrimination within federally funded educational institutions"** (Hawai'i KHON 2, 2012, p. 1; Hawai'i News Now, 2007, p. 1).

In January 2020, the city held a groundbreaking ceremony for a 13,000 square foot expansion space for a dog park at the ocean-end of the Patsy T. Mink Central Oahu Regional Park. She remains a magnificent inspiration to us all even long after she passed away.

Summary

America has come a long way in the past 50 years. We have walked on the surfaces of the moon. We have found cures for all types of disease, although we still do not have one yet for COVID-19. But America and other nations of the world are desperately working on a cure as the COVID-19 pandemic rages across the globe. Vaccinations by a large majority of the populace will most certainly help.

In *Our view* (Sept 3, 2020), the United Nations states that "the COVID-19 pandemic has deepened gender inequality and could reverse decades of progress on women's rights" (p. 1). The article explains that women are seriously affected as many health care workers, teachers, including essential hospital and clinic staff left jobs and careers to stay at home and care for their young children when the pandemic forced offices, businesses, schools, and other entities to close for over a year. Women are thus less represented in decision-making roles (Our View, 2020).

So, Americans, why can't we stop gender inequalities? What is preventing us from recognizing society's gender discrimination, especially in schools and other institutions? If not now, when? If not us, who?

CH 6 Gender Inequality Issues

My Pearl of Wisdom: We Can Do It Together

Don't ever let anybody tell you that your efforts don't matter

or that your voice doesn't count.

Don't ever believe that you can't make a difference.

You have.

Barack Obama

GENDER INEQUALITY ISSUES today are an interesting topic among many of the cultural and legal issues in American society today. **Multiculturalism** includes such topics as race, religion, national origin, color, language, social class, sexual orientation, transgender, gender identity, human rights, physical ability, class, prejudice, ethnicity, veterans' status, disability, and age. Our discussion continues with its focus on **Gender** in this chapter.

Gender Inequality in Schools

Educator Rebecca Alber (2017) defines gender discrimination in school when girls are treated differently than boys, not just by their peers but also by their teachers. "Education research has found that the stereotypes of assertive male and passive female are often reinforced in our schools and in very classrooms" (p. 2).

In *How to encourage gender equity and equality in the classroom* (2020), an article posted by Waterford, a 501(c)(3) organization, the writer states "Gender is defined as a student's social identity as male, female, or non-binary. . . Gender definitions also include transgender students who identify as a gender that is different from their biological sex" (p. 2). The writer further stipulates that "Gender equality involves empowering all students and providing them with the same human rights" (p. 2) as everyone. Emphasis regarding gender equality "as the end goal and gender equity as the means to get there" (p. 2) is clear. Finally, "Gender equity refers to promoting fairness in education, as well as confronting stereotypes and biases that have historically limited a student's potential" (p. 2). These are powerful words, indeed very powerful ideas, and aptly expressed!

Problems – a Discussion

In another article, (Teachers reduce, 2018) the author reviewed a highly publicized report that "found that America's schools 'shortchanged' girls" (p. 1). Specifically, the author charged that females fell behind males in mathematics and science scores, teachers called on males more than females, and females were not represented in proportion to males in the school curricula.

However, many articles dispute these findings, and state that the difference between boys' and girls' standardized test scores **are small**; the teacher makes the difference (Alber, 2017; Cimpian, 2018; How to encourage, 2020; Schools may perpetuate, 2019; Seigfried, 2019).

The *How to encourage* (2020) article states that children at a very tender age (four) already show signs of discriminatory ideas. "Children learn to think about themselves and others from the messages they hear in society. And often, these messages include stereotypes about gender that stick with them for the rest of their lives" (p. 3). For example, "more than 50% of all women in STEM ultimately leave their field due to hostile work environments. Also, 75% of all transgender students report feeling unsafe at school, which affects their academic achievement in very serious and harmful ways" (p. 3).

Two websites support these findings: *Strategies to promote gender quality in the classroom* (2018, https://www.elesapiens.com/blog/strategies-to-promote-gender-equality-in-the-classroom/) and Roy (2017), *Why we need gender equity now* (https://www.forbes.com/sites/ellevate/2017/09/14/why-we-need-gender-equity-now)

Finally, *How to encourage* (2020) lists four ways teachers can promote gender equity and equality in education (pp. 4-5):

- Be a Role Model for Your Students, showing that Gender is a strength, never a weakness.

- Don't Connect Gender to an Ability or Personality Trait; individual's ability, profession, or personality is never based on Gender

- Include Gender Equality in Your Curriculum; this includes avoiding tokenization, stereotyping, and gender 'myths'.

- Teach students to be Aware of Personal Biases; we all have some. A person's abilities are not linked to their gender.

This article lists nearly a dozen websites identifying and discussing gender issues and methods of dispelling biasness.

How to Reduce Gender Inequities

The U.S. Agency for International Development [USAID] (2021) article mentioned the following actions schools may take to reduce gender inequities: ensure that posters and other classroom displays do not show gender stereotypes or bias; avoid challenging females against males in games, spelling bees, or other similar types of activities; call on all students equally (rather than just those who raise their hands); review the types of books introduced to students (to ensure that stories and characters do not stereotype by gender). If stories do use stereotypes, discuss changes in gender roles in the decades following the publication of the books. Be aware of gender biased vocabulary or expressions, such as 'boys will be boys' or using 'he' instead of 'he or she' pronouns.

If cultural practices or attitudes influence students to show chauvinistic or demeaning behaviors, educators must discuss the importance of respecting all individuals (females and males). **Encourage all students** to enroll in courses (such as home economics or woodworking) which educators have traditionally designated for only females or males, respectively, and encourage all students to participate in sports without regard to gender if possible (Teachers reduce, 2018).

Personal Point

In my high school, the counselor would not allow me to enroll in Wood Shop because after all, it was only for boys! My oldest brother however, took Home Economics because although it included sewing (only for girls, right?) it also involved cooking for someone who wanted to be a chef at a fine hotel. That, of course, would be great. After all, only males could be excellent chefs, right?

Other Strategies

School administrators and teachers additionally may use the **following list of strategies to reduce or eliminate gender inequities**: be aware of body language, gestures, voice; do not 'talk down' to female students; call on males and females equally; ask higher-order, open-ended questions equally of males and females; accept and encourage educated guessing, and questioning. Additionally, group females with females to avoid male dominance in group activities; use cooperative techniques and avoid competition-only projects; mention female as well as male leaders and scientists; encourage females to take higher level coursework; avoid gender bias in group names, colors, careers, daily living tasks, etc. (Alber, 2017; Schools may perpetuate, 2019).

Joseph Cimpian (2018) in *How our education system undermines gender equity and why culture change – not policy – may be the solution* discusses that

> the overall picture related to gender equity is of an education system that devalues young women's contributions and underestimates young women's intellectual abilities more broadly. . . . [Furthermore], in order to improve access and equity across gender lines from kindergarten through the workforce, we need considerably more social-questioning and self-assessment of biases about abilities. (p. 1)

Cimpian (2018) writes that "it is the 'beliefs that teachers have about student ability" (p. 5) which are important; teachers underrate female students from K-grade three, which "accounts for about half of the gender achievement gap growth in math. If teachers believed that girls were just as good as boys in math for example, the so-called gender gap might be much smaller" (p. 2). Some standardized test scores show no or only small achievement gaps between the sexes, although other tests scores such as those from the PSAT, SAT, and ACT sometimes do show gender discrepancies. **Cimpian asks if these discrepancies are due to boys' confidence levels or the devaluing of girls in general.**

Finally, Cimpian (2018) states that if "fields that were perceived to discriminate against women were strongly predictive of the gender of the students in the field . . . women are less likely to enter fields where they expect to encounter discrimination" (p. 4). Educators, indeed education systems must stop viewing females as less intellectually capable in all fields, but especially in the areas of Science, Technology, Engineering, and Mathematics (STEM). Thus, **societal changes are needed**: teacher's attitudes and behavior in the classroom, textbook authors (to prevent stereotypical use of words and examples), cultural beliefs that somehow females are less innately talented in particular fields than males, and all educators must examine their own biases.

Teacher Training Programs at Colleges

Education professors in teacher training programs may train their students to deal with this topic of gender inequality, and other agencies can assist this noble pursuit, by noting the following ideas, and recommendations from several sources, including those mentioned in this book.

First, organizations including large groups and charities, businesses, and the state and federal government should establish large postsecondary scholarship programs for females who wish to enter traditionally male-dominated STEM fields. The scholarships should be substantial to help entice females to obtain degrees in these areas and include not just tuition and fees, but textbooks and housing costs as well.

The American Association of University Women (AAUW, n.d.) already awards fellowships and grants in 2021-2022 worth $5 million to over 260 women and community projects worldwide. However, there is much to be accomplished; other private groups and governmental agencies need to increase their sponsorship of women attempting to enter STEM fields.

Second, postsecondary institutions dealing with teacher education should require students to take a unit in gender inequality, along with other units or sub-units dealing with race, ethnicity, religion, color, sexual orientation, and other possible bias areas throughout their college years. Additionally, these institutions should require all professors to take similar units, **because the problem is that some of the professors promote their bias, themselves**.

Some professors appear reluctant to call on females or those exhibiting gender-orientation issues. Some professors might unconsciously down-grade papers, if students are of a minority class: Black, White, Oriental, Asian, Micronesian, Polynesian or students from a certain part of the country, or a non-native speaker of English, or disabled, or from a 'poor section' of town, or Muslim, or . . . the list is really endless. The point I am making is that students as well as professors need to examine themselves to ensure that they recognize their own biases; we all have some.

Third, both students and teachers in the field of education could also benefit from participating in hands-on activities (**sensitivity training**) perhaps when introducing any of the topics mentioned above. When doing this, teachers need to design appropriate-level activities for those under age 18.

Fourth, all students in teacher-training programs, including those without certification, current teachers working on recertification, emergency hired teachers needing additional credit, principals, counselors, and other administrative staff at schools, need to participate in appropriate sensitivity training on an on-going basis. This also includes current teachers, as well as professors at postsecondary institutions. This means such training is continuous and requires regular, systematic evaluation.

These four suggestions are important to implement immediately. However, I do not feel that these suggestions will work completely, without holding braining-storming periods at schools of all levels everywhere, asking everyone to come up with other ideas on how to fight gender bias as well as other kinds of prejudices (ADL, Handbook, 2020). Seek specialists to visit your agency and provide hands-on training throughout the year!

More Information

In *Gender inequality in education* by Stephanie Seigfried (April 12, 2019):

> Gender inequality cripples a nation's economy at the expense of women. According to UNESCO, an average of 130 million girls between the age of 6 and 17 are out of school and 15 million girls of primary-school age will never enter a classroom. The most common explanations for this gender gap are poverty, geographic remoteness, violence, disabilities, lack of infrastructure, or belonging to a minority ethno-linguistic group. The highest rates of gender inequality in education [are in] Africa, South Asia, and the Middle East. (pp. 1-2)

> Advancing girls' secondary education is one of the most transformative development plans countries can invest in. Completion of secondary education brings substantial benefits to girls and societies which includes increased lifetime earnings . . . ending poverty and boosting a nation's economy. (pp. 5-6)

In a recent article in U.S. Agency for International Development, "What We Do – and Women's Empowerment: Reducing Gender-Based Violence, author Morgana Wingard (2020) cites some horrifying statistics:

> 1 in 3 women will experience gender-based violence in her lifetime. In the Developing word, 1 in 7 girls is married before her 15th birthday. And between 1998 and 2008 alone, sexual violence against females was noted in reports on 25 conflict-affected countries. (p. 1)

In a recent article, *Gender-based violence prevention and response,* the U.S. Agency for International Development (USAID, 2021) discusses the meaning of gender-based violence (GBV). For a more extensive review of this issue see U.S. Department of State (2016), *U.S strategy to prevent and respond to gender-based violence globally.*

More Specifics

Another striking article in World Economic Forum by Kate Whiting (2019) discusses '7 Surprising and Outrageous Stats About Gender Inequality' from https://www.weforum.org/agenda/2019/03/surprising-stats-about-gender-inequality/ *Facts and figures: Women's leadership* (2021) provides extensive data on the global lack of women in leadership positions, highlighting the widespread gap in gender inequality.

In addition, a striking article in World Economic Forum by Kate Whiting (2019), discusses *7 surprising and outrageous stats about gender inequality* from (https://www.weforum.org/agenda/2019/03/surprising-stats-about-gender-inequality/)

Another factor demonstrating gender inequality is that women in Africa's rural areas spend about 40 billion hours each year collecting water. Whiting's 2019 chart (p. 1) shows the countries of Guinea, Madagascar, Malawi, and Sierra Leonne (statistics from 2000-2004); gathering wood and water is 'women's' work. She estimates that it will take 108 years to close the gender gap in many of these countries.

A significant variable in female inequality is shown by the fact that "only 6 countries give women equal legal work rights as men" (Whiting, 2019, p. 3). The World Bank's recent Women, Business and the Law report measures such discrimination in some 187 nations; only Sweden, Denmark, Latvia, Luxembourg, France, and Belgium scored the highest.

The Whiting article (2019, p. 3) lists the following statistics in underdeveloped countries: "only 22% of professionals are female, due to a lack of confidence in their own abilities, mainly in the mathematics and sciences fields." **(Personally, I can relate to that.** I wanted to take the Law School Admissions Test at age 40 but lacked the confidence in my own abilities; I wanted to work on a doctorate too, but believed I did not have the skills needed at that time. This is a **true example of self-doubt** without a logical explanation.) Whiting cites a Cornell University study, and the Forum's Global Gender Gap Report to support her findings.

The last statistic is often overlooked. For "every female film character, there are 2.24 men" (Whiting, 2019, p. 4). Whiting states that the Geena Davis Institute "analyzed 120 theatrical releases between 2010 and 2013 in 10 countries – and found that of the 5,799 speaking or named characters, less than a third (30.9%) were female and more than two-thirds (69.1%) were male" (p. 5). Obviously, some characters in many roles were children or adolescents. (See also Woolhouse (n.d.), *Geena Davis*.)

In *Schools may perpetuate gender inequality without realising it* (November 14,

2019), British authors stated, "gender stereotypes affect children's views about their abilities and aptitudes to their potential achievements" (p. 2). Teachers in school talk about nurses as females and bus drivers as males. There are 'girl toys' and 'boy toys' (think dolls vs. tiny trucks); girls are nice while boys are clever; girls behave nicely and properly while boys are rough and aggressive. "Gender stereotypes limit children's futures when they see certain careers as 'girl jobs' and 'boy jobs' (p. 3).

Moreover, males have entered the engineering and mathematics fields in vast numbers while girls have studied teaching and social service fields. "Gender stereotypes are unintentionally reinforced in school through the curriculum, books, language, staff assumptions, and daily interactions with adults and peers" (p. 3) and this must change, say the authors.

More Details

You can find some of the most important ideas in ending gender inequality in another fascinating article, *10 important examples of gender inequality happening today*, by Carolina Sherwood Bigelow from the Borgen Project, **who updated her 2014 report by the same title. Bigelow writes, on July 11, 2018,** that more recently, gender inequality is becoming a topic more openly discussed, more transparent, where on her blog, she provides an updated list of 10 examples of gender inequality happening today, and not just in schools! These include poor infant mortality, pregnant women's lack of access to good medical care, education favoring males, the majority of illiteracy by females, economic independence where females earn significantly less than men, violence against females at twice the rate of males, female genital mutilation (200 million alive today), child marriages, human sex trafficking, and poor female representatives leading governments (pp. 1-5). I offer only a few websites here, as there are many:

1. **Infant Life Expectancy**: In China, girls have a 7% higher mortality rate than boys; in India (2000 - 2010), risk of death between ages of 1-5 was 75% higher for girls than boys.

2. **Access to Prenatal Care and Maternal Mortality:** In 2017, of the 1.6 billion

woman of reproductive age in developing countries, and of some 127 million who gave birth, only 63% had 4 prenatal care visits; only 72% gave birth in any sort of health facility; only 1 in 3 received care they or their newborns needed, of those experiencing medical complications.

In 2017, 308 thousand women in developing countries died from pregnancy-related causes and 2.7 million babies died in the first month of life. See *Investing in sexual* (2020): https://www.guttmacher.org/fact-sheet/investing-sexual-and-reproductive-health-low-and-middle-income-countries

3. **Education:** Less than 40% of nations offer girls and boys equal access to education; only 39% of countries have equal number of genders enrolled in secondary education. By helping both genders, some 420 million people could attend school. See *International Women's Day (2014):* http://www.unesco.org/new/en/unesco/events/prizes-and-celebrations/celebrations/international-days/international-womens-day-2014/women-ed-facts-and-figure/

4. **Illiteracy:** About 774 million adults worldwide are illiterate; 2/3 are females. 123 million youths are illiterate and 61% are females.

5. **Economic Independence**: In 2013, male employment was 72.2% compared to 47.1% women; women earn only 60 -75% of men's wages. See *Facts and figures: Economic empowerment* (2018, July). https://www.unwomen.org/en/what-we-do/economic-empowerment/facts-and-figures

6. **Violence Against Women, Sexual Assault and Rape:** Women who have been sexually or physically abused by their partners are twice as likely to have an abortion, almost 2 times more likely to be depressed, and in some countries, 1.5 times more likely to get HIV. Worldwide, 120 million girls had experienced forced intercourse or some sexual violation in their lifetime.

7. **Representation in Government**: Only 22.8% of national leaders were women.

8. **Child Marriage:** Almost 750 million females alive today marry before they are 18, and many are years younger. Child marriage is one of the most devastating examples of gender inequality, as it limits women's opportunities and their ability to reach their full individual potential.

9. Human Trafficking: Females account for 71% of all such victims, globally with 3 of every 4 trafficked are young girls.

10. Female Genital Mutilation: At least 200 million females alive had had this surgical abomination, with the majority before age 5. Poor or no use of anesthesia, later chronic or severe bacterial complications, increased Caesarean sections, hemorrhages, etc. are common.

Female Circumcision

In a 2019 article from the U.S. Agency for International Development, *International Day of Zero Tolerance for female genital mutilation cutting* (Jhunjhunwala, 2019), girls who are first generation – in Kembata, and Durame Woreda, **Ethiopia,** and in 29 other countries might not have to face this egregious act of violence towards their person. However, some estimated 30 million girls still are at risk, the majority before age 5, in many parts of Indonesia, Malaysia, the Middle East, Latin America, and the Russian Caucuses.

Personal Note

I find it difficult to believe that we have completed one fifth of the 21st century, and we must continually confront these terrifying statistics, mentioned above. **Americans, do we believe in equality for both genders?** If the answer is decidedly **yes,** what are we doing about the draconian situations described in these chapters?

Let me give you a very specific, compelling example of my experience with just one gender 'practice' or rather, abomination, that of female (forced) genital mutilation, i.e., surgical circumcision.

I worked as the Education Director in El Gorah, Sinai Desert, Egypt, under the Multinational Peacekeeping Force (MFO) from early 1987 through Christmas 1989. The U.S. State Department controlled the 11 military contingents of some 3,700 personnel; I was the only Army civilian federal employee stationed in North Camp with the second one (a male) at South Camp.

There were 11 nations taking part in this Camp David Accords-initiative overseeing the terms of the peace treaty between Egypt and Israel. At North Camp, in the Sinai Peninsula, Colombians contributed Infantry soldiers, as did the Fijians and Americas; the French provided fixed wing aircraft i.e., two 18-seat twin otters to fly to Cairo or South Camp. The Uruguayans were the bus drivers, driving 45-passenger buses many hours to and from Cairo, South Camp, or North Camp. The Canadians provided helicopter units, and Netherlands provided military police; New Zealand, Australia, Italy, and Norway also provided a different unit, even a base commander. The medical doctors and dentists were mainly from the U.S. and Canada. South Camp was filled with mainly American infantry troops.

A rather well-educated Egyptian bartender with a bachelor's degree in business from Cairo University asked me a searing question one night while I nursed a Jack Daniels and Coke after a grueling day at the El Gorah North Camp Education Center (which I converted from an Israeli kindergarten building complete with low toilets and gun-sights). Drinks were 50¢ – beer, wine, whiskey, soda – and each military contingent had its 'own' club. Crazy, right?

"My custom is that when my little girl-child is six or seven, she must be cut, you know, down there," he stammered, gesturing to his netherlands. My eyes widened. "My wife – she does not agree. She says it hurts too much. But if not, the girl will be too hot-blooded." I was totally dumbfounded.

"No - Please, do not hurt your child," I blurted out. "It is against the law. You cannot cut her genitals."

"But if I do not, she will get married, then she might be unhappy (I think he meant sexually dissatisfied) and then want to leave her husband for another man. I cannot have that!"

Readers – beware: genital 'cutting' means female genital mutilation (FGM) i.e., surgical circumcision, barbarically cutting off the female's clitoris and surrounding sensitive areas of skin (i.e., the labia), so that sexual intercourse is extremely painful. FGM is the partial or total removal of external female genitalia or other injuries to the female genital organs for non-medical reasons. Many times, the surgery leaves the child with urinary and vaginal injuries and issues throughout adulthood. FGM may cause infections, severe bleeding, problems urinating, cysts, childbirth complications, and tremendous pain.

Somalia, Sudan, Eritrea, Djibouti, Egypt, Sierra Leone, Mali, Guinea are just a few of the dozens of countries which practice this surgical abomination. This atrocious ritual is often performed by a female relative without regard to sanitation, use of antibiotics, anesthesia, or detailed knowledge of female anatomy. In America, the STOP Female Genital Mutilation Act of 2020 was signed into law on January 5, 2021 by the 116th U.S Congress (H.R. 6100) because certain immigrant communities were practicing this barbarism right here in the U.S.A.! FMG was alive and well in America! Horrors!

I stumbled out of the bar that night, not from too much drink but from too many barbaric pictures swimming around in my head. How could an educated father profess to love his little daughter and even consider such a monstrous, mutilating act? How could such a medieval custom continue well into the 21st century? And if you reread earlier pages in this chapter, some 200 million females have had this abomination done to them!

Another True Tale

On another occasion, **I was stationed at Khobar Towers compound in Saudi Arabia** and Beth (not her real name), an American, whose husband worked for an oil company (Aramco) nearby served as a University of Maryland (UMD) representative. Our education office was above the building's Patriot Missile Battery section. It was 1993, and we had a very revealing conversation one day.

"What did you do before this job?" I asked Beth, curious as to why UMD was so lucky to have a well-spoken counselor.

"Oh, I am a Registered Nurse, so I worked for a female doctor at the local hospital." "My goodness," I replied. "What made you leave a good paying nurse's position?" (I knew that a RN made a great deal more than a college representative. Indeed, most jobs paid more than a college registrar.)

"My boss wanted me to help surgically circumcise her own daughter. I could not do that – it is abuse."

I gasped. "But your boss is female! And she is a medical doctor! And it is illegal!"

"Yes," Beth replied. "These medieval ideas are drilled into them all their lives. Their grandmothers, aunts, mothers, sisters, and now their daughters . . . it never stops. It is pure evil. It is child abuse, mutilation."

Beth saw how ashen I had become and quickly changed the subject. But I never forgot this conversation when I think about Saudi Arabia, Kuwait, Egypt – all places I have worked!

Americans do not practice surgical abuse on our children, but we do indeed practice all sorts of discrimination. We must act now, by becoming informed about gender discrimination, the issues mentioned in this chapter, and **then making our individual and collective voices heard.** We can move forward, as a nation, to improve gender equality together. Let **that** be our legacy.

CH 7 Impact of Multicultural Education Curriculum -

Anglocentric & Male-Dominated

My Pearl of Wisdom: How Do You Like It?

I am different. Not less.

Temple Grandin

MULTICULTURAL EDUCATION has greatly impacted the Anglocentric, male-dominated curriculum common to most schools prior to the 1960s. **Schools reflected societal concerns and beliefs**, and thus many educators believed that **male students** were generally brighter, more intelligent, better skilled, quicker to learn, more capable, better athletes, and future leaders of America. **Females** did not need to further their education because society assumed that most would marry and if not, they would enter traditional fields such as teaching, nursing, and the secretarial arenas (National Association for Multicultural Education [NAME], Advancing, 2021).

The landmark Supreme Court decision, Brown v. Board of Education (Topeka, Kansas, 1954) changed the laws regarding separate but [not] equal but it took decades before busing and other government actions forced desegregation (Sanders, 2019). "Families and education advocates are still suing to compel states to uphold their education funding obligations" (p. 1).

The **following two article**s may provide additional insight into multicultural education and its effect on modern schools.

Articles

First, the National Association for Multicultural Education is a group based in Washington, D.C. whose members write about the different aspects of multicultural education. In an article (NAME, Definitions, 2021) **covering the definition of multicultural education**, the author states that schools which teach the value of cultural differences and pluralism allow students to enter and reinforce a democratic society. Multicultural education is a process that allows for the development of student confidence and self-esteem, while simultaneously preparing students to value others who are different from themselves.

The article concludes by stating that for schools to accomplish these goals (tolerance and understanding for those who are different from themselves), **schools must have instructors who are themselves able to be sensitive** to the needs of the linguistically, racially, and culturally diverse population (of students and community members). Multicultural education must flow throughout all aspects of the curriculum at all grade levels, all subjects, and all students and staff members (NAME, Advancing, 2021; NAME, Position, 2021).

COVID-19 pandemic just added greater challenges in schools (NAME, Supports, 2021), and the Anti-Defamation League Handbook (2020) offer much information for educators and parents, too.

Second, educator Rebecca Alber (2017) offers educators the following guidelines:

- Gender Disparity: **Participation** – allow boys and girls equal time and attention during classroom discussions and that "starting in grade school, teachers engaged less frequently with female students, asking them fewer questions, while at the same time providing males with more feedback" (p. 2). Furthermore, in terms of teacher time and attention, male students receive more than do girls.

- Gender Disparity: **Curricular Materials** – U.S. schools seem to have male-dominant curricular materials. Less than 30% of the textbook authors were female, for example, in the Los Angeles United School district study. Also, male characters appear to outnumber female characters in curriculum materials.

- Examining Practices and Curriculum: **Hidden Gender Biases** – dealing with race, class, gender, age, sexual orientation, physical appearance, ability or disability, national origin, ethnicity, religious belief must be recognized. Alber (2017) asks educators the following questions (pp. 3-6):

    1. Do any texts I use omit girls and/or women, or tokenize their experiences? How are boys and/or men stereotyped?

    2. Are females or males presented in stereotypically gendered roles in any texts I have selected? If these are historical texts, how might I teach students to be critical of the limitations in the gender roles presented in these texts?

    3. Do I encourage empowering and nonsexist behaviors among my students? Do I discourage both female and male gender stereotypes?

    4. If I have a classroom library, is there a balance in male and female authors? Are there plenty of books with strong female protagonists? Do the nonfiction books feature notable women and girls?

    5. In what ways do I encourage gender equity of voice and participation?

    6. Do I ask girls as well as boys complicated questions? During discussions, do I inquire as diligently and deeply with female students as I do with male students?

Strategies to Improve Practices and Curriculum (Alber, 2017, pp. 5-6):

Here are some ideas for improving gender equity in your classroom.

    1. Use wait/think time deliberately. Instead of calling on the first or second hand, choose the fourth, fifth, or sixth.

    2. Be aware of the number of female students you call on. Be incredibly proactive in making sure that all students (regardless of gender, ethnicity, language, or learning ability) are equitably included in discussions and participation.

    3. Call out sexist notions or terminology in texts used in the classroom – for example, a textbook, magazine article, poem, research report, or blog post. You can also highlight any gender stereotypical language used by students in the classroom and use it to invite broader discussion.

    4. Videotape your classes (with administration approval) and review your

interactions with students. You could also invite a colleague to watch you teach and note which students are being asked questions, and what type of questions.

5. Design a lesson or unit of study based on exploring with your students' issues of gender, self-image, and equality. In partnership with USA Today, the Geena Davis Institute on Gender in Media offers eight lessons that explore media and bullying in the context of gender equality.

Disrupting Gender Inequities (Alber, 2017)

Female physicians and surgeons earn 38% less than their male counterparts, and female lawyers earn 30% less than male lawyers. Education is a vital tool in helping close this wage gap. For teachers, continued monitoring of gender bias is necessary to minimize its impact on students' opportunities for learning and for achievement. (p. 6)

We all need to work to become more aware of any gender-biased tendencies. We need strategies to help us reflect and change any biased practices, and we need to commit to combating gender bias in educational materials. (p. 6)

Another article by Daniele Moore, Maureen Hoskyn, and Jacqueline Mayo (2018) *Thinking language awareness at a science centre* in International Journal of Bias Identity and Diversities in Education, support the above theories, because there is much discussion about discrimination beginning at a very early age.

Will America recognize these important issues raised in multicultural education? Is the assimilation of different cultural groups different from cultural integration while we still recognize specific components of each culture, race, group? So, teachers – what are YOU doing to promote multiculturalism in YOUR classrooms? **Important questions continue**.

CH 8 Teachers' Greatest Challenges in Multicultural Classrooms and Why?

My Pearl of Wisdom: Trying is Everything

Too often we enjoy the comfort of opinion without the discomfort of thought.

John F. Kennedy

IN *Prejudice, discrimination, & stereotypes* (2014; see also Multiculturalism lesson plans, 2020; Seifert & Sutton, 2009) the authors discuss some of the greatest challenges (both philosophical and pragmatic) that a teacher faces in a multicultural classroom in an ever-changing world. The writers agree that students need to respect those different from themselves and this dissonance is the crux of the problem.

Chapter 4 of *Educational Psychology* by Kelvin Seifert and Rosemary Sutton (2009) covers a myriad of subjects dealing with student diversity, such as culture, diversity, values, morals, ethics, social justice, stereotypes, discrimination, social justice projects, genocide, nationalism, human grouping, institutional racism, ethnocentrism, culture shock, and self-identity.

In addition, the U.S. public-school population is changing, as reported in *Data: Race and ethnicity in U.S. schools today* in Education Week (2014):

By 2060, the U.S. Census Bureau predicts [the U.S.] will become a 'plurality' nation, with no one race in the majority.

Where students live affects where they go to school, and different racial groups tend to be concentrated in different types of communities. White students are concentrated in suburban and rural communities. Black, Hispanic, and Asian students are most often found in urban and suburban communities. White and Hispanic students in the U.S. tend to go to schools where they are in the racial majority, and White students only rarely attend schools where they make up less than 25% of the enrollment. By contrast, Asian students are usually in the minority in schools. (pp. 1-2)

Important Questions

How do teachers handle racial, religious, class, gender, language, color, social, regional, and ethnic discrimination in the classroom, when negativities are pervasive in society (ADL, Handbook, 2020; Schultz, 2005)? **For example,** how do teachers deal with the violence students see daily on their computers, tablets, laptops, television, You Tube videos, in the newspapers, and magazines if teachers want to institute major changes in the classroom dealing with this subject of violence? Indeed, how do teachers instill cultural pluralism, ideals of social justice, the ending of discrimination and prejudice, the endearing and understanding of minority cultures and customs, and the academic excellence which is a needed ingredient, into the classroom learning environment?

The Anti-Defamation League has a detailed booklet on **Lesson Plans** (2020), designed for teachers: https://www.adl.org/education-and-resources/resources-for-educators-parents-families/lessons or anyone may contact the ADL at: www.adl.org/contact

Important questions continue. How do teachers persuade school administrators to allow them to use varied, innovative, multicultural education techniques and processes in the classroom, perhaps not part of the 'approved curriculum' at the moment? Must the teachers' unions get involved? How do teachers raise their students' confidence, and feelings of pride and respect in their own unique cultural heritage, so that teachers and students can critically examine the textbooks and lessons presented and ask what is "our role in creating a truly democratic and multicultural society – fair, just, and inclusive?" (Schultz, 2005, p. 33).

How do teachers learn enough about their students' traditions, ethnic backgrounds, religious beliefs, and other ethnicities, so that teachers may use that information to help students become more positive learners, active listeners, better able to function in the classroom and society?

Factors for Teachers from the Anti-Defamation League (ADL) Handbook (2020)

Teachers should focus on student equality in the classroom, empowering students to understand various cultures, develop a multicultural perspective, and value cultural pluralism. Finally, and most difficult, teachers should respond positively to linguistic diversity. Those students learning English as a Second Language face tremendous frustration when they only have textbooks in English!

Guiding Principles to Use

In addition, teachers should read the ADL Handbook (2020) and other **ADL** materials (books, coordinator course, curriculum guides, glossary of terms, lesson plans, manuals, etc.) that includes a great deal of information about inclusiveness, social justice, diversity, and anti-bullying techniques for all grade levels and all subjects.

Personally, I have seen or participated in the following activities at the elementary and secondary school levels: celebrate all regular holidays; discuss why these days are holidays; bring resource speakers and movies about the subject to class; draw or paint some aspect of what students learned (or do something artistic, to include writing an article, creating a poster or flyer. Involve the librarian as a literature resource too.

Over a two-week period, a teacher may divide the class into small groups, with each group covering one aspect of the "celebrated" event or person. The class may write stories about what they have learned and present the group's findings to the rest of the class. The class may also enjoy ethnic foods together.

The class can discuss the various ethnicities present, to include placing students into smaller groups, researching about a culture, ethnic, or religious group different from their own, and sharing their findings to the class. Groups can bring in their own guest speakers, videos, YouTube movies, regular movies, pod-casts, etc. and all these activities are quite stimulating and exciting. Whereas **previously** celebrating an important person or event consisted of perhaps a one-day event i.e., watching a movie and then discussing it, the idea is to incorporate the celebrated person or event into the curriculum so learning is on-going and systematic.

A Department of Defense School, on a Military Base

At the beginning of the school year in Kitzingen, Germany (on a U.S. military base, several years ago), the teachers held a parent-student night. The school asked parents and students of all cultures, colors, beliefs, military ranks, and socio-economic classes, to share something about themselves, their heritage, their foods, and customs. Some families brought in special dishes of food, with the recipe and history of those dishes written out to distribute. Other families brought colorful posters, depicting special events from their own culture. Still others shared dances and songs that night, with everyone.

The teachers had spent several weeks with their students in preparation of this night, and proceeded to take pictures of the parents and students. They displayed the colorful photos and other items in their classrooms throughout the remaining months of the semester, which brought great joy to the students and families.

This event was at a Department of Defense Education Activity (DoDEA) school in Germany, and teachers called this curriculum unit, **Understanding Self and Others**. My daughter, in fourth grade at the time, wrote many stories that revolved about that unit on multiculturalism, and read library books about various cultures throughout the year. She told me that learning about others was most exciting.

Tokenism vs. Realism

What are the differences in the teaching process in a token multicultural classroom compared to a truly inclusive multiculturalism classroom? What are the characteristics educators would like to have in their classrooms?

Tokenism – to Avoid

A **token classroom, compared to an all-inclusive one**, would have the following characteristics: a multicultural holiday would be celebrated as a single one-day event, without spending more than a few hours in the classroom discussing the reason for the celebration (societal concerns). No attention would be paid to the linguistics of the children because after all, they all must function in an American society where English is required (and the home language is ignored). **Teachers: does this sound familiar? Horrors**

Moreover, in this 'token' classroom, historical references are European – White dominated, because that is the main culture (not questioned by many teachers); any bias seen in the media, text or work books, or other classroom materials remain unrecognized (aren't these just curriculum concerns?), and the teacher views differences in students' learning styles as a waste of time and does not address students' self-esteem and empowerment issues. (School counselors can sort these issues out, right?) The teacher does not recognize students' "cultures or use them to help students understand the world, and give meaning to lessons covered in class" (Schultz, 2005, p. 33). The author summarizes these factors as curriculum reform, multicultural competence, equity pedagogy, and society equity.

Total School Environment

In an article by Dr. Nakieta Lankster (2020), *The importance of multicultural education in American schools*, he discusses the total school environment as playing an important role in addressing prejudice and empowerment.

> Integrating multicultural education into the existing curriculum, instead of making it a separate content area, relieves the burden of creating separate lessons, units and courses in an already-overburdened curriculum. Content integration encourages the teacher to provide additional opportunity for higher learning skills, such as inquiry and problem-solving. Using ethnic demographics for mathematical concepts allows students to consider the ethnic and racial distributions in their own classroom.

> When students can propose solutions about social events, such as civil rights movements, they are learning to think analytically and critically. (p. 2)

When students from different racial groups work collaboratively together on common issues, the teacher and students see a reduction in school bullying, exclusion-behavior, and ethnic slurs.

Teachers should seriously consider the issues raised by Dr. Lankster (2020) and discuss them at staff meetings. Then, act! Involve both administrators and school staff – clerical, custodial, educational aides, and all others. Get the entire school involved. Brainstorm. Bring speakers from nearby universities to discuss how to implement multiculturalism in the classroom. Talk – then do the walk! Make it happen!

CH 9 Misconceptions about

Multicultural Education and

Systemic Racism

My Pearl of Wisdom: Falsehoods – Past and Present

The things that make me different are the things that make me.

Winnie the Pooh

MANY MYTHS PERVADE THE TEACHING of multicultural education, and this article explores fifteen of them most succinctly. The authors Aldridge, Calhoun, and Aman (2000) list each major myth, comment on each fallacy after citing examples, and list various educational specialists and authors who have written about this topic. Although the article, *15 misconceptions about multicultural education,* was published in the Focus on Elementary Journal several years ago, it remains relevant and thought provoking even today, in 2021. I conclude this chapter by examining systemic racism in an article by Gal et al. (2020).

15 Misconceptions

Guidelines for including multicultural education in the school curriculum at all grade levels have surfaced over the past twenty years, gaining momentum and prominence (Aldridge et al., 2000; Multiculturalism lesson plans, 2020; Nkabinde, 2017). Educators and curriculum specialists are genuinely interested in incorporating such guidelines into school curriculums (ADL, Handbook, 2020). However, there appears to be several widespread myths about multicultural education that need our attention, because these fallacies are hindering the movement forward. **These fifteen erroneous**

beliefs (Aldridge et al., 2000, pp. 1-5) are:

1. People who are from the same nation or geographic region, or speak the same language share a common culture. **NO**. Teachers should understand that Spanish-speaking inhabitants of Puerto Rico, Mexico, Cuba, and Argentina have different cultures; the French Canadians are quite different from other Canadians.

2. Families from the same culture share the same values. **NO**. The authors disagree, and state that there are four ways people view their own culture: **mainstreamers, bicultural individuals, culturally different individuals, and culturally marginal individuals.** Sometimes, an entire range is found within a single family, such as the grandmother may maintain her original culture and language, while her grandchildren may be bicultural or mainstreamers.

3. Children's books show authentic culture. **NO**. This is not necessarily true. **Sometimes, authors take great liberties to publish a colorful, best-selling book.**

4. Multicultural education only includes ethnic or racial issues. **NO**. However, other factors are also important, such as socioeconomic diversity, gender, culture, age, language, sexual orientation, and religion. The authors state that others have written extensively about the promotion of strength and value of cultural diversity as well as acceptance of alternate life styles, respect for human rights of others, equality, social justice for all, and equal distribution of income and power among groups.

5. Teachers should use the Tour Approach. **NO**. The tour approach **(a quick visit to the new culture)** and the detour approach **(activities only dictated by the holiday, month, or season of the year) are not appropriate for teachers** in some instances. Both methods patronize, trivialize, use stereotypes of other cultures, and avoid the true picture of everyday existence, adding even more myths and biases.

6. Teachers should teach multicultural education as a separate subject. **NO**. The authors disagree, and cite **four curriculum approaches**: contributions, additive, social action, and transformational approach, stating that this last approach is powerful and should be used.

7. Multicultural education is already an accepted part of the curriculum. **NO**.

8. Multiculturalism is divisive, rather than unifies. **NO**.

9. Further study of other cultures is unnecessary, as there are only Whites, Blacks, and Latinos, and these three groups form the mainstream of the American populace. **NO. This myth is pervasive in a monocultural or bicultural society.** [Asians and other minorities are ignored.]

10. Educators know that multicultural education is only for older children, who are less egocentric or ethnocentric. **NO.**

11. If teachers teach multicultural education, then commonality is lost. **NO.**

12. America already acknowledges its cultural diversity, so students do not need any further instruction.**NO.**

13. Historical data always suffers when dealing with multicultural educational curriculum. **NO.**

14. Because most individuals identify with only one culture, multicultural education is a waste of time and effort. (Just which culture is the 'one' culture?) **NO.**

15. There are simply not enough resources for classroom teachers and curriculum specialists, to add multicultural education to the school**. NO.**

The journal article concludes by stating that there are many other fallacies about multicultural education, too numerous to mention.

Systemic Racism Documentation

In another, rather lengthy U.S. Business Insider article, authors Shayanne Gal et al. (2020) discuss some **26 facts documenting why racism remains such a massive, pervasive problem in America**. It is **not** enough to mention the common myths about diversity and multiculturalism. **It is important** however, indeed vital in this conversation to list the following statistically significant facts showing why multicultural education is so difficult to achieve in America. **Racism is systemic because it is "ingrained in nearly every way people move through society in the policies and practices at institutions like banks, schools, companies, government agencies, and law enforcement"** (p. 3). The authors offer 45 pages of charts and explanations, as follows (pp. 1-45):

1. **Percent of population with a job** in America: Black, 49.6%; White, 53.4%.

2. **Unemployment rates** of Black and White Americans: Black, 16.8%; White, 12.4%.

3. **Employed management, professional, and related occupations**: Asians, 54%; Whites, 41%; Blacks, 31%; and Hispanics, 22%. If Blacks 'whitened' their résumé with American or White sounding names, they got more callbacks for corporate interviews: 25% of Black candidates received callbacks from their 'whitened résumés' while only 10% got calls when they left ethnic details on their résumés.

4. **CEOs of companies**, by race and ethnicity: only 8.7% of the 675 companies in the study had CEOs of color; the remaining CEOs were White. Only four Fortune 500 companies in 2020 had Black CEOs: Lowe's Home Improvement; Tapestry, a fashion holding company; TIAA, an insurance company; and Merck & Co, a pharmaceutical company.

5. **In the 116th U.S. Congress** (after the 2018 midterm elections): 57 of the 535 members were Black (10.6%), the highest number ever.

6. **Black annual income:** the average Black worker earned only 62% of what the average White worker earned.

7. **Per capita income:** Blacks earned about one-half of what Whites earned; $24,700 vs. $42,700; the poverty rate therefore for Black families is over twice that of White families.

8. **Aggregate wealth:** There are about six times as many White Americans as Black Americans, but Whites have about 17 times the aggregate wealth as do Blacks.

9. **Black women's annual earnings vs. other races**: The average Black women earned just 66% of what the typical White man earned, with Asian women and White women ahead of the Black women; only Hispanic women were below Black women.

10. **Number of days women have to work into the next year** to earn as much as White **men:** Asian women must work 42 extra days; White women must work 100+ extra days; Black women must work 226+ days (i.e., it would take the median Black woman worker 226 extra days or more into a new year to earn what a median White male worker made in the previous year).

11. **Household income ranking of children** born into the 25th income percentile, by state: New York, the highest; Los Angeles, the middle, with Detroit, the lowest on this chart. This means that children of White households in the bottom quarter of the income distribution were much more likely than children from Black households at the bottom to **move up** into a higher income bracket over their lifetime.

12. **Advanced Placement or International Baccalaureate credit**: in 2013, Black high school students were only a bit more than half as likely as White students to have any Advanced Placement or International Baccalaureate credit, and only about a third as likely to have AP/IB credit for mathematics.

13. **College completion**: only 15% of Black students from less-educated households went on to finish college, well below the 25% of White children who earned a degree.

14. **Schools**: Even though the U.S. government desegregated schools 66 years ago, about half of students in the U.S. still attend either predominantly White or non-White schools. Poor White school districts receive about $150 less per student than the national average – an injustice all to itself. Yet they are still receiving nearly $1,500 more than poor-nonWhite school districts.

Other Facts

Other facts documenting systemic racism in America (Gal et al., 2020) include the fact that home ownership is lower among Blacks than other racial groups; access to health care is proven more difficult (and expensive) for Blacks than many other groups; Black Americans are nearly twice as likely as Whites to lack health insurance; and during the 2020-2021 COVID-19 pandemic, Black Americans get sick and die at a higher proportion than others due to lack of health care and access to health clinics and hospitals.

Furthermore, the current coronavirus pandemic thus has had a disparate impact on people of color; Black Americans have higher rates of underlying health conditions like diabetes and hypertension, which put them at a higher risk for developing complications from the coronavirus

Finally, Black prisoners are overrepresented in U.S. prison populations compared to others by population (Gal et al., 2020). This means that Black inmates made up roughly 33% of the country's prison population, yet just 12% of the U.S.'s total population. (In Hawai'i, there is a disproportionate number of Hawaiians and part-Hawaiians in jails and prisons, compared to their numbers in the island's population figures. This population, to include other Pacific-Islanders from Micronesia and elsewhere also shows a higher percentage of those infected with the COVID-19 virus, when compared with the state's population figures.)

Last Thoughts

When will racism end? I do not know. But I am glad I live in Hawai'i, where there is no majority race, no majority religion, no majority color, no majority ethnicity, and no majority culture. However, please do not think even a state such as Hawai'i has no racial problems. **Hawai'i has many problems**! And the fact that the majority of the voting populace is Democratic and mostly all elected politicians are Democratic does not really help at all! Life on Oahu is not just one of sea breezes and sunshine.

Many residents have not visited the beach in years – there is very little parking available close by the shoreline. Many 'locals' have not frequented restaurants or entertainment areas as many hold two and even three part-time jobs because the minimum hourly wage is below $11. Still others find that their wages cannot catch up with the escalating costs of basic living: utilities are sky high with an electrical kilowatt hour 29¢ (the national average is under 12¢ a kilowatt), gasoline in 2021 for vehicles averaged $3.65 a gallon (surging to $4.70 on neighbor islands at times), and food costs much higher than the U.S. mainland norm.

Of the one million people living on Oahu, the majority of multiracial island residents say that they are some sort of combination of Asian, White, Native Hawaiian, or Pacific Islander. About 25% self-identify as White, while 38% self-identify as Asian, but 20% consider themselves to be 'mixed' with a smattering of Hispanic (9%), Black (2%) and Other (10%) (Data: Race & ethnicity, 2018, p. 1).

But when you add elements of income/economic·disparity, immigration status, education/skills, and 'class,' together with the **high cost of living** where the average house of 1,300 square feet costs over $980,000, you are bound to have significant problems. (Is there any wonder that many of the 7,000 homeless, marginalized individuals here simply cannot survive Hawai'i's housing costs?) **Race is just one of these problems, magnified by the other issues, mainly economics.**

We need to first recognize systemic racism in our country. Then **secondly,** we must elect officials at the local, state, and national levels of government who reflect inclusiveness, diversity, tolerance, and stand on these principles. Only then will we **finally**, as a nation, begin to change this egregious and pervasive racism in our society to one of justice, tolerance, equality, and economic fairness for all. Our schools reflect our society and its culture, beliefs, and behaviors. Let us go forward, renewed in our joint efforts to improve ourselves, our communities, indeed our entire society.

CH 10 A Real - Life Example of

Racism and Intolerance in Hawai'i

My Pearl of Wisdom: Challenging Times for All

Diversity: the art of thinking independently together.

Malcolm Forbes

"HE'S FALLING. SHIT. SHIT. OH MY GOD" one teacher screamed, to no one in particular. Students were running hither and yonder, craning their necks, pointing to the sky; others were crying, gesticulating towards the ground. And on the emerald green freshly cut grass lay the student, unconscious.

"What is going on?" demanded another teacher, pushing her way through a throng of students. She rushed over to the inert figure, lying so still. This was around 1981 – before ubiquitous cellular phones, before instant videos of any and all life events, before….

"Call an ambulance" one teacher told another. "No, only the admin can do that," the other teacher replied.

Kawananakoa Intermediate school, located in lower *Nuuanu* Valley on the island of Oahu was a school for 7th-8th grades; 6th grade was added much later. My two sons were in the Summer School Program there, having left the island of Guam and their regular school permanently behind.

At Dinner that Night

When we all had dinner together that night, I asked each boy about their day, as I normally did, never dreaming I would hear a tale about a fight, and possible death.

"So, mom, I saw one boy throw another boy off the second floor of my building today," Nick replied, as he helped himself to a glass of ice-cold tea.

"What did you say, dear?" I exclaimed, thinking I had not heard correctly.

"Yeah, one boy just threw another boy off the top of the school building, you know, the second floor. The kid went over the railing!"

I looked closely at him, from across the table. My breathing slowed as my pulse raced.

"I told you we should have said something earlier to mom," his older brother, Geoff blurted out. "Is it kill *Haole* (White) day or what?"

I breathed deeply. My head started to throb. "Are you telling me that a student was attacked by another and he landed on the ground from the second story? From the top of the building?"

"Yep" Nick paused, as he ate his desert cookie slowly.

"Why? Did someone call an ambulance? Is he dead?" I asked these same questions several times, in rapid succession.

Geoffrey frowned; "I told you it was a rough school. These kids don't like *Haoles* and with blue eyes, they don't believe Nick and I are part-Hawaiian. But when dad picked us up from school last week, they finally stopped picking on us. (Their step-dad was a dark-skinned CHamoru from Guam.)

"Why didn't you say something to me," I demanded. "You know I would have gone straight to the principal!"

"Yeah, and the bullying would have just continued, but in 'private,'" stated Nick.

Hawaiian-Style Racism

Kill *Haole* Day was something that happened once a year at local schools (usually the last day of school before summer) in the 1950s through 1970s, as I recalled, before it was finally stamped out. **Or so I thought.** I asked some students in 2020 about this abomination (Kill *Haole* Day) and they said no, that they did not really hear about that. But then one girl smiled, and said, "I am Japanese. So, I don't care about Kill *Haole* Day. Only Kill Japanese Day." The other girl laughed and explained, "I'm part Chinese and

H*aole*, but I don't look *Haole* so it's ok. I heard that there are fights in some schools in other parts of the island." I just rolled my eyes and walked away. (There never was any other racial group targeted I recalled, except for Caucasians.)

When I grew up, local students would gang up on students from the U.S. mainland (mainly military) and there would be a scuffle, a shouting match, or fistfight **only because of race**. I heard the words 'Kill *Haole* Day' when I was in high school, but never saw a fight. I attended the University of Hawai'i Laboratory School, which was not a public school but not quite a private one either. Students' racial background reflected the island's racial background, so if for example, 12% of Hawaii was Chinese, then 12% of the Lab School's students were too. Many students had parents who were either educators (from the nearby university, public, or private schools), professionals such as doctors, dentists, lawyers, architects, engineers, or business directors and managers from large corporations on the island.

The Lab School (as we called it) had an academic entrance exam, and required a small annual tuition fee. It was a small, insular school of two classes per grade level and I was in the first to graduate when the school increased in size to three classes per grade level! I dated a few young men from some of the nearby public and private schools and yes – Roosevelt High and Punahou were two of them. But I honestly believed that by the 1980s and 1990s, 'Kill *Haole* Day' was just an old, ignorant idea, a ghost from the past.

The U.S. Department of Education (DOE) on December 31, 2008 released a sizzling report (Office of Civil Rights [OCR], 2008) validating harassment based on race and sex at a particular island school in Kona, Big Island: Civil Rights authorities stated that "substantial evidence [proved] that students experienced racially and sexually derogatory violence and name-calling on nearly a daily basis on school buses, at school bus stops, in school hallways and other areas of the school" (OCR, 2008).

Specifically, students were called names such as **F***ing** *Haole* and other derogatory terms, and that a racially and sexually hostile school environment existed from 2003-2005. Students were subjected to retaliation if incidents were reported to school officials, and that DOE did not enable parents to utilize grievance procedures. In summary, Hawai'i DOE did not comply with Title IX, Title II, and Section 504 (OCR, 2008).

Story Ending

This is a true story that my sons talked about at dinner that night in 1981. A boy did indeed get pushed off the second story of a DOE building. DOE failed to substantially change many student behaviors in some schools, which led to the 2003-2005 civil rights case in question, detailed above. And incidents described by OCR were not isolated ones although certainly, most fights did not end with a second story fall! Certain schools had negative reputations. It did not help that many Hawai'i public school teachers sent their own children to private schools. Indeed, almost 20% of all island students attended private schools, including my own (Wellein, 2021), a costly undertaking.

Was the physical fight at *Kawananakoa* School that day about race? That information was never released. Later, in the newspapers, there was some mention about the incident; one student was Filipino and the other, Samoan. They were both enrolled in that summer school. The neighborhood was lower-middle class, and both were new arrivals from their respective countries, the Philippines, and Samoa.

However, I quickly enrolled both of my boys in two fine private schools, Mid-Pacific Institute and Our Savior Lutheran, both in Mānoa that very next week for the coming school term, where they thrived and developed into two great sons, academically and emotionally! (I asked the school to provide academic scholarships for both youngsters, and they agreed, noting that **I earned very little as a full-time teacher**! Sad, but true!)

Finally, in a truly you cannot-make-up-this-article in the Honolulu Star-Advertiser on June 3, 2021, *There is no racial discrimination in Hawai'i, Blangiardi's [Mayor of Honolulu] police commission nominee says,* nominee Larry Ignas told City Council members that he has "never witnessed racial discrimination in Hawai'i and that **he doesn't believe it occurs here**" (Boylan, 2021, p. 1). Perhaps this individual was misquoted, I do not know. The police department has been strictly scrutinized this past year for the racial disparities in officers' use of force, pandemic rule enforcement, and disproportionate arrests of minority groups in Hawai'i. But if quoted correctly, all I can say is thank goodness this nominee was not accepted to be on the Police Commission.

This chapter is real. The incidents are real. The Office of Civil Rights Report (OCR, 2008) is real. Private schools flourish in many states; in Hawai'i, about one-fifth of the children under 18 attend such institutions, including private and religious-affiliated ones. What does that say about education in Hawai'i, knowing that the cost of living makes teacher-salaries here among the lowest in the nation?

CH 11 Multiculturalism in Education at All Levels: How to Integrate this Concept into the School Curriculum

My Pearl of Wisdom: Hurry Up and Wait

We must learn to live together as brothers or perish together as fools.

Martin Luther King, Jr.

CAROLYN S. WARD (2003), in discussing how to best integrate multiculturalism into the discipline of education, mentions that college teachers must incorporate multicultural education into their college classes, so that individuals who are preparing themselves to enter the world of teaching learn. She gives an example of college students who are asked to discuss and think about such issues as "racism, classism, sexism, homophobia, ableism, and misunderstanding of language minority students" (p. 76).

Educator N. Lankster (2020) also talks about ways to integrate.

College Students Prepare for Teaching

College students, upon their education degree completion, and prior to teaching, should be able to do the following (ADL, Handbook, 2020; Gal et al., 2020; Lankster, 2020, p. 1; Multicultural lesson plans, 2020):

- **Demonstrate an understanding** of multicultural education, role of culture in the educational process, and how to infuse the curriculum throughout the year with information on diversity, etc.

- **Explain how individual viewpoints** are affected by various cultural and ethnic backgrounds including exclusivity and inclusivity.

- **Explain and describe** political, economic, cultural, social, and demographic trends that have a real effect on schooling and American society.

- **Discuss present and future** issues of diversity, and its impact on schools and society.

- **Analyze educational reforms needed**, based on community and student needs.

- **Evaluate possible curricula and presentation methodologies**, to meet the diverse students' needs.

- **Demonstrate** how teachers can make a positive difference.

Personally

As a former reading specialist, this article was especially provocative, because part of my job (when I was at the school level) was to provide Guam's classroom teachers with recommended reading lists for the summer period. **It never dawned on me to check on racial balance, finding books with minority characters in them, checking for stereotypes, and so forth**. I was searching for well-recognized books, such as those written by Dr. Seuss. Many of these famous children's books deal with everyday issues: finding a lost cat, getting ready for the first day of kindergarten, learning how to swim, or shopping for a birthday gift.

The Guam school population (indeed, the island's population) was about 70% *CHamorus*, 20% Filipinos, and 10% "others" who were Caucasians, Micronesians, and Orientals from Asia. Most were bilingual and a significant portion, trilingual. Most of the literature I reviewed did not have any characters who were *CHamoru,* Filipino, Micronesian, or Oriental/Asian, as these were all minority groups.

My Own Novel

In response to needing a master's degree project as well as finding something appealing to Guam's students, I wrote a children's hardback chapter-book in English, but used some *CHamoru* vocabulary; I published it in New York in 1976. Specifically, **I believed that there was a lack of such literature in Guam** (Wellein, 1976).

First, I asked the Scholastic Book Company (yes, that massive publishing giant) to publish my novel. I was delighted to learn that the company was seriously interested in doing so – provided I removed the 66 *CHamoru* words in my novel. **I explained that I could not do this, as language is very much a part of the culture. And my book reflected that culture in the language used and actual cultural topics I wrote about**. The Scholastics representative said no deal. I was disappointed, to say the least. I ended up self-publishing *The endless summer: An adventure story of Guam.*

The Guam Department of Education used my hard-back novel (77 pages) for many language arts teachers, elementary through high school. (I provided teachers who used my book a complimentary list of 10 questions and answer key for each of the novel's 15 chapters, so that they could use the book in any part of their language arts lesson plans.)

Teachers in the University of Guam's Creative Writing courses also used my chapter-book. But perhaps the details of my book's success are best saved for another time. Suffice to say, I enjoyed writing this children's book, and seeing it read by thousands of youngsters. And I kept all the *CHamoru* words and expression intact. I plan to republish my novel soon, as it is currently out-of-print.

Final Note About Teachers Unions

Multiculturalism can be reflected and integrated in school K-12 and postsecondary educational classes, if teachers recognize the need to do so, and district, school administrators and curriculum specialist agree. Teachers' unions are quite powerful and must be concerned with topics such as teacher salaries, duties, rights, promotions, vacancies, class size, and duty days vs. training days (Augenblick, Palaich, & Associates, 2020).

However, perhaps teachers' unions need to also take a stand on **important educational issues** because these compelling subjects reflect societal ones. Unions, working together with the various education departments and Education Boards can institute real change. Multicultural education at all levels is an important mandate that all can agree to and implement.

CH 12 Evaluating Children's Books

for Bias in School

My Pearl of Wisdom: Grab a Righteous Read

No Matter WHO you are,

No matter WHERE you come from,

You are BEAUTIFUL.

Michelle Obama, First Lady

UNIVERSITY OF NORTHERN IOWA in their In Time discussion online mentions *Evaluating children's books for bias* (2020). The Anti-Defamation League (ADL, Assessing literature, 2021) also offers readers much information as they produce several handbooks and guides about race, bullying, discrimination, and biasness (including ADL, Books matter, 2021).

Frances Ann Day's *Multicultural voices in contemporary literature: A resource for teachers* (1999) discusses **eleven factors to review for bias in children's literature,** still accurate **today.** Author Day states that 'Guidelines for Selecting Bias Free Textbooks and Storybooks,' by the Council on International Books for Children, New York, NY was also important in writing about bias in children's books.

Eleven Factors

These **11 factors include** stereotypes, exclusion of certain groups or minorities, incomplete story lines, lack in authenticity of cultures and lifestyles, and difficulty in showing accurate relationships between characters from different cultures. Other factors include depicting heroes and heroines inappropriately, damaging children's self-concept by negative portrayal of minority group members, author's or illustrator's lack of backgrounds in cultures depicted, author's or illustrator's inaccurate perspective, book's use of sexist language, and finally, books written prior to the 1960s. It becomes readily apparent, however, that the last generalization in the article, about books written before the 1960s, might not be totally accurate. Let us review Day's 11 factors combined with information from the ADL Handbook 2020 and other ADL booklets.

Factors in Evaluating Children's Books for Bias

Omission appears to be the largest problem in literature for children today. Day (1999) explains that while some racial or ethnic groups are seen in a stereotypical fashion, other groups are totally excluded, sending a silent but psychologically unhealthy message that the group is so insignificant, so unimportant as to merit complete absence. (The next three pages in this chapter are based on F.A. Day's writings and ADL 2020 resources.)

Illustrations sometimes show **stereotypes** defined as a generalization (usually false) about a particular group or culture. The implications are usually negative and derogatory. Stereotypes in illustrations, paintings, or photographs can be considered **tokenism** (one person from the race or culture has positive qualities while all others from that same group possess negative traits), or role-playing. Another example is if a company hires one minority person in order to be able to say they hire minorities – when in reality, this individual is a 'token,' and hired just to demonstrate that the company has valid, non-discriminatory hiring practices.

Role-playing is when members of the **minority group** are shown to be in **subservient** roles, either by color (Whites being dominant) or by gender (males being dominant) or by age (young people being dominant over those considered 'old' or elderly).

The **story line and characters** might show biasness, and it may be subtle or direct. What are the standards for success in the story? Is the White male the only person who can reach those standards? Do females and minority characters need to show extraordinary strengths and special characteristics, while the White males do not? How are the story line problems or areas of conflict created, shown to the reader, and then resolved? Are minorities, the very old and very young, as well as women considered to be part of the problem or part of the solution? Do these individuals tend to be passive or active characters?

What is the **relationship between characters** in the story? If it is about a man and a woman, who makes the decisions, assumes the leadership role, or handles the finances? Who acts as the pacifier in a family when there is indirect or direct conflict between family members? Do women need men to define them as whole human beings, or must they rely on the males for role definitions and approvals? For **teenagers and older students**, does the story show people who are homosexual, lesbian, transgender, elderly, or disabled only in submissive or non-dominant roles? (It would extremely **rare** for characters in children's books to be labeled in this manner, except for the term 'elderly'.)

What **roles do females** play in the story? Does the story show the traditional view of women (i.e., they grow up and marry, have children, and assume the role of the homemaker), or does the story allow the reader to see non-traditional aspects of female roles i.e., assume the responsibilities as head of the household in some instances, or have important professional duties such as a scientist, banker, doctor, engineer, or computer specialist? Are females central to the story line? Are females considered important only if they are physically beautiful? Can main female characters be described as plain, older, or commonplace? Do male heroes always rescue the females because they are helpless?

Is the story authentic? Is the description of foreign cultures, customs, and lifestyles realistic? Are all Asians (i.e., Chinese, Korean, Japanese, Vietnamese) grouped together, no matter what their origin? Do all American Indians celebrate birthdays in the same manner, regardless of tribal affiliation? If the book mentions recent immigrants to America, does the author categorize these people as holding the same customs and cultural practices as those of previous generations?

Is the **hero or heroine** in the story shown as having little or no conflict with males who are perhaps White, physically healthy, sexually oriented in society's approved, appropriate ways? Such heroes or heroines are considered safe, non-controversial, and appeal to a wide audience.

In addition, note such factors as omitting groups, presenting stereotypes, restricting story lines, describing inaccurate cultures and lifestyles, and misleading readers about the relationships between story characters. Are heroes and heroines limited to those who are 'acceptable' by White, Middle-Class standards? Educators must watch for books showing that sometimes, individuals from minority groups are portrayed as being weak, negative, having low self-esteem with poor self-image. These characters have **poor self-concept.** Are heavy-bodied characters shown as slow thinkers, for example? Are Asian Americans always shown as better-behaved minorities than Black or Latino Americans?

Another factor to check for in literature bias **is a review of the author or illustrator's background.** What are their qualifications to deal with the subject? If they are not part of the minority group discussed in the book, is this considered cultural thievery (i.e., writing about a culture one is not a part of)? Can an author write authentically about a group, race, religion, or ethnic group without experiencing any of these factors personally?

If authors are White, Middle-Class, heterosexual, physically fit, and Protestant, then can they really write accurately from the perspective of a lower socio-economic class member, who is Latinx, limps, or a Buddhist?

Sexist use of language should be checked. Are negative terms used for females, the old, infirm, and members of minorities? Are **gender-neutral terms**, such as firefighter instead of fireman, chairperson instead of chairman, synthetic instead of manmade fiber, and ancestors rather than forefathers used?

Finally, Dr. Day (1999) states that teachers should check the copyright date of the book. Many times, books written prior to the 1960s did not reflect society accurately.
Discussion

These factors are quite provocative. However, I believe that a good writer does not have to be an integral part of the culture described in the story or book. Logically, an accurate description of the wonderful, mouth-watering Chinese food from Canton need not come only from a Cantonese writer. But the writer must have prepared and consumed Cantonese food for years. One does not have to be paralyzed and in a wheelchair, to write authentically about the experience. Perhaps the author was a full-time caregiver to his paralyzed mother for decades, carting her to various physicians, psychologists, physical therapists, or picking up her medications, etc.

However, it is a fact that a **good writer must have some connection, some real experience with what he or she is writing about! Otherwise, how can you write authentically?**

The factor of checking the copyright date (to check for bias) seemed to be a gross generalization. Thousands of books written for children prior to the 1960s are **not culturally biased**, do not demean females or the elderly. Indeed, many are about animals, or objects that 'speak' and thus are not about female or male, old or young. These stories deal with universal themes of good and evil, life and death, hunger and plentiful, and so forth. It is not clear why the issue of copyright date seemed important at all except that I agree that prior to the 1970s, it was not common to see females dominate, the disabled win over others, or dark-complected characters triumph over the lighter-skinned ones.

Finally, we need to be clear about defining the term, **children's books**. For example, are children's books (often referred to as picture books) for young children under the age of six? Or perhaps children's books are assumed to be for those under the age of 12? Generally, chapter books are considered by many teachers to be designed for those at least in third grade and higher. (Homosexual and lesbian orientation concepts **might** be mentioned in some literature, but usually, these subjects **are not found** in young children's books especially for those under the age of 12.) Nevertheless, I believe that the factors mentioned above in this chapter are thought provoking and stimulating.

I Wrote My Own Book

When I wrote a children's hardback novel (Wellein, 1976), my two main characters were CHamoru children, but I based many of the episodes on what my own two boys (at the approximate ages of the characters in the book) experienced while growing up on Guam. **I used my children's real experiences, and other adults' trials and tribulations**, when writing this chapter book. For some events, I filmed it (such as killing a pig), so that I could carefully and accurately recreate the event in the book.

There was not much literature available about Guam for children, and certainly not chapter books. After consulting with several CHamoru language experts, I proceeded to write this book to fill a void! What is extremely important is that the author must thoroughly and accurately research the subject, culture, location, specific island, food dish, or whatever is discussed in the book to ensure total accuracy and authenticity. **If you live through the experience – then you can really write about it.**

As I said earlier in this chapter, I think it foolish to write about a subject you know nothing about. **Authentic writing is just that, writing about what you have experienced**, or at least witnessed first-hand.

Additionally, I recently read the Coordinator Handbook & Resource Guide 2020 - 2021 by the ADL (2020), (https://www.adl.org/media/11295/download) which discusses **No Place for Hate** anti-bullying activities for all schools throughout America. I believe the information is terribly significant, because racism usually begins at an early age, and so I am including much of the last few pages, here, in this chapter on children's books. The following resources are listed in ADL (2020, pp. 48-49):

> **11 Ways Schools Can Help Students Feel Safe in Challenging Times -** Prevention, intervention and educational strategies that help to promote inclusive school environments where young people can learn and thrive.
> https://www.adl.org/education/resources/tools-and-strategies/11-ways-schools-can-help-students-feel-safe-in-challenging
>
> **Anti-Bias Tools and Strategies Tips** - Tools, strategies and discussion guides for K–12 educators and students in order to promote anti-bias and culturally responsive learning environments.

https://www.adl.org/education/resources/tools-and-strategies/anti-bias-tools-strategies

Bullying and Cyberbullying Prevention Resources - Collection of expert advice about bullying and cyberbullying for educators, administrators, students, parents and families. https://www.adl.org/education/resources/tools-and-strategies/bullying-and-cyberbullying-prevention-strategies

Books Matter (Book of the Month) - A collection of 800+ children's and young adult literature on bias, bullying, diversity and social justice. Each month, a featured Book of the Month includes two discussion guides: one for teachers and one for families. https://www.adl.org/books-matter

Calendar of Observances - A tool to increase awareness and sensitivity about religious holidays, observances as well as ethnic and cultural festivities that may affect students, colleagues and neighbors in your community. https://www.adl.org/education/resources/tools-and-strategies/calendar-of-observances

Empowering Young People in the Aftermath of Hate - A discussion guide for educators and families that provides the tools necessary to help young people engage in conversations and actions in the aftermath of hate-motivated violence, extremism or other incidents in their community or society. https://www.adl.org/education/resources/tools-and-strategies/empowering-young-people-in-the-aftermath-of-hate-en

Lesson Plans - A collection of K–12 timely lesson plans and multi-grade units that promote critical thinking and assist educators in teaching current events topics through a lens of diversity, bias and social justice. https://www.adl.org/lesson-plans

Rosalind's Classroom Conversations - Written by best-selling author and bullying prevention specialist Rosalind Wiseman, these essays explore bullying, current events and the social and emotional development of children. https://www.adl.org/rosalinds-classroom-conversations

Table Talk: Family Conversations About Current Events - A resource that provides parents and families with the tools they need to engage in conversations about important news stories and other timely discussions about societal and world events. https://www.adl.org/table-talk

What We're Reading This Week - ADL Education recommends weekly articles and blogs that highlight stories about anti-bias topics, social justice and general education. https://www.adl.org/education/resources/tools-and-strategies/what-were-reading-this-week

Winter Holidays: December Dilemma or Teaching Opportunity? - Suggestions for how to approach the winter holidays with sensitivity and care so that they can be fun and festive without some students feeling excluded and marginalized. https://www.adl.org/education/resources/tools-and-strategies/winter-holiday

Finally, once more, the Coordinator Handbook & Resource Guide (No Place for Hate) stipulates 12 activities teachers, counselors, administrators – indeed everyone can do, to create an Anti-Bias Learning Environment for children (ADL, 2020, pp. 54-55):

Talking with Students about Diversity and Bias: It is important for teachers to think about how they can most effectively raise the complex issues of hate, bias, scapegoating, and exclusion with their students. To prepare to raise issues of diversity and bias in the classroom, teachers should attempt to integrate the following practices into their classroom curricula:

Self-Exploration: Provide students with opportunities for the examination of personal cultural biases and assumptions.

Comprehensive Integration: Integrate culturally diverse information/perspectives into all aspects of teaching.

Time and Maturation: Allow time for a process to develop. Introduce less complex topics at first and allow the time it takes to establish trust.

Accepting environment: Establish an environment that allows for mistakes. Assume good will and make that assumption a common practice in the classroom.

Intervention: Be prepared to respond to intentional acts of bias. Silence in the face of injustice conveys the impression that prejudicial behavior is condoned or not worthy of attention.

Lifelong Learning: Keep abreast of current anti-bias education issues and discuss them with students.

Discovery Learning: Avoid "preaching" to students about how they should behave. Provide opportunities for students to resolve conflicts, solve problems, work in diverse teams and think critically about information.

Life Experiences: Provide opportunities for students to share life experiences; choose literature that will help students develop empathy.

Resources Review: Check materials so that classroom displays and bulletin boards are inclusive of all people.

Home-School-Community Connection: Involve parents, family members, and other community members in the learning process.

Examine the Classroom Environment: What is present and absent in the school classroom provides children with important information about who and what is important.

Summary

A good children's book still must have all the elements of a good story: vivid characters and character development, style, theme, plot, significant incidents, conflict, conflict-resolution, point of view, interesting location and illustrations, in an age-appropriate setting. The goal of course, is to provide children with such books minus the biasness mentioned in this chapter. The story should make use of authentic language, expose children to different perspectives in the story, ensure that characters articulate their cultural values, explore various universal themes, and that the settings include urban, suburban, rural or inner city, magical, forest, desert, or any number of possible locations.

Writer Linda A. Santora's, *Assessing children's literature* (2013), said it most succinctly:

> Selecting good multicultural books involves an anti-bias approach, an active commitment to challenging prejudice, stereotyping, and all forms of discrimination; good multicultural children's books challenge stereotypes, provide a realistic glimpse into the lives of diverse groups of people, help children learn to recognize unfairness, and provide models for challenging inequity. (p. 1)

The ADL recently published Coordinator Handbook and Resource Guide 2020-2021 (No Place for Hate) and the other articles and books mentioned in this chapter provide excellent information for anyone who wants to know more about this topic and who evaluates children's books for bias in schools. I hope that reader considers many thought-provoking ideas.

CH 13 A Demographic Revolution in American Schools

My Pearl of Wisdom: When Will This Happen?

Diversity in the world is a basic characteristic of human society, and also the key condition for a lively and dynamic world as we see today.

Jintao Hu

THERE IS A DEMOGRAPHIC revolution in America now (Data: Race and ethnicity, 2014; Rabinowitz, Emamdjomeh, & Meckler, 2019).

Statistics

To bring this problem into perspective, it is interesting to note the following **American** public-school **K-12th grade** students 2017 statistics: 48% are White, 15% are African American, 27% are Hispanic, 6% are Asian/Pacific Island, 1% are American Indian/Alaska Native, and 4% are two or more races (NCES, 2020).

Racial characteristics of **postsecondary** students in America in fall, 2018 (NCES, 2021) who self-identify include 19.7 million total enrollments, with 16.6 million undergraduate students: 8.7 million White, 2.13 million Black, 3.35 million Hispanic, 1.09 million Asian, 44,700 Pacific Islander, 120,200 American Indian/Alaska Native, 647,000 two or more races, and 567,000 Nonresident alien.

Graduating from colleges in fall 2018 includes a total of 3 million students, of which 1.64 million were White, 365,400 were Black, 292,400 were Hispanic, 215,000 Asian, 5,800 Pacific Islander, 13,600 American Indian/Alaska Native, 81,300 two or more races, and 425,400 nonresident alien (NCES, 2020).

The impact of this problem is that many teachers do not 'match' let alone understand their students. Many middle-class teachers speak English as their first language and they are instructing students who are bilingual - 10% of the public-school students (NCES, 2020). About 7 million (14%) public-school students in 2018-2019 school year received special education (SPED) services (National Association of Special Education Teachers [NASET], 2021). But there is also a vast need for SPED teachers because over 90% of school districts in America report SPED teacher shortages.

What to Do

First, the recruitment procedures of teachers in America need to strongly focus on making the recruitment of teachers of color a priority. This means school district administrators need to purposefully act. Obviously, however, a good qualified SPED teacher of any race must be a top priority.

Secondly, the local colleges and universities in the area need to recruit more teachers of color into educational doctoral programs, so that they may be hired to teach at America's colleges and universities. This means postsecondary institutions must offer generous scholarships and grants to prospective graduate students.

Third, it is imperative that educators address this very real issue of diversity (students and teachers) to deal with the dissonance that exists; students of color need more teachers of color.

Specifics

There are two problems. There are not enough SPED teachers, **and** there are not enough SPED teachers of color. There are several methods of dealing with the problem of **increasing the number of SPED teachers and also attracting more minority teachers into the SPED field.** Put most succinctly, **teachers need to reflect the ethnic diversity of their students.**

Some Methods

One method is to increase the number of state and even national scholarships minority students have available to them at postsecondary institutions from various governmental agencies. In addition, increase the number and size of scholarships and grants specific **university departments** offer students. If the college of education wants to graduate more teachers majoring in SPED, they need to make that an attractive option.

Another method is for colleges to give special presentations at various public sessions of Board of Education meetings several times a year to attract more students into the SPED program. The Board of Education needs to become aware of how important the issue is to colleges and universities. Bring in stimulating speakers; **offer door prizes;** have drawings such as 15% off any book up to five. Ask local businesses to donate solid prizes, like $50 worth off food at a local food market. Make attending such meetings exciting! These meetings should be well advertised. [How many of you reading this chapter have ever attended a Board of Education meeting?]

Other methods include asking those responsible for pre-service, professional development, or new teacher programs to write grants to provide staff development and **offer special incentives to teachers already in other fields to enter SPED**. The Board of Education in various cities and states (over 13,000 school districts nation-wide) might offer teachers a bonus ($10,000) for going into the SPED field, as Hawai'i did (Hawai'i State Department of Education, Salary modernization, 2020).

Other writers have suggested holding a series of forums inviting speakers about the topic (i.e., needing more SPED teachers) to lecture **on campus** during college registration and instructors in education courses may invite a speaker to their own classrooms as well. Still others have written about the role that power plays at postsecondary institutions. Identifying how to maintain and increase the sources of power from ethnically diverse student populations is important (Rabinowitz et al., 2019).

Emma Garcia and Elaine Weiss (2019) state in their excellent report, *The teacher shortage is real, large and growing, and worse than we thought,* that the current conditions are becoming intolerable, with high-poverty schools suffering the most.

Summary

In a Washington Post article, Rabinowitz et al., (2019) project that in 2020 "there will be more children of color than white children in America" (p. 1). In 2017 some 66%

of students "attended school in diverse districts, up from 45% in 1995" (p. 6). Furthermore, this represents 11 million children attending highly integrated schools. However, the picture is uneven. For example, Chicago continues to have the "least integrated school [system] in the country" (p. 10). Continuing, Rabinowitz et al., explain that "Most newly diverse communities remain majority White, and research suggests Whites may be comfortable with diversity as long as they remain the largest group. Once that flips, White may start to leave" (p. 11).

The article ends with the term diversity defined as "the proportion of students in the dominant racial group. . . . **Diverse districts** are places where fewer than 75% of students are the same race . . . [and] **undiverse districts** are where 75 to 90% of students are the same race" (p. 12).

Some of the elements in a strong multicultural program include school culture and attitude towards diversity, language spoken and taught, curriculum used, and types and methods of instruction (such as teaching basic and advanced skills). Additionally, using varied methods of student participation, experiential and theme-based activities, academic support services such as after school hour programs, tutorial and mentoring assistance, guidance counseling, college preparatory help, and community-based support are also important.

These community-based support features resource centers, summer and vacation programs for students, free or reduced-cost health clinics, language and Basic Skills courses for adults, good quality but affordable children's day care centers, and so forth.
Note

One element not fully addressed here is **if students come from different cultural, racial, religious, economic, social, and educational backgrounds when compared to teachers,** what specifically can administrators, school superintendents, Board of Education personnel do, if anything**?** This factor of diversity in faculty and student population is probably one of the most important factors in making any multicultural education program successful. Just what is a school district to do? Any ideas?

Now, readers: decide what **you** can do. It is now 2021, but there are still major problems with a teacher's culture being out of touch with their students' culture – think language, learning style or modality, physicality, athleticism, ethnicity, color, religion, socio-economic class, travel experiences, immigration status--it is a very long list! As we approach the third decade of the 21st century, there will be increasing numbers of students who are minority members of society. The time is now to support diversity in your educational system.

CH 14 Key Factors in Sources of Prejudice

My Pearl of Wisdom: What are You Going to do?

Two things are infinite: the universe and human stupidity;

and I'm not sure about the universe.

Albert Einstein

PREJUDICE IS FORMED in many ways. Sources of bias and prejudice in individuals and societal groups appear to stem usually from more than one source. In Sociology (2010), "prejudice refers to a set of negative attitudes, beliefs, and judgments about whole categories of people and about individual members of those categories, because of their perceived race and/or ethnicity" (p. 2). This textbook also stipulates that racism is the belief that "certain racial or ethnic groups are inferior to one's own. Prejudice and racism are often based on racial and ethnic stereotypes" (p. 2).

It is important to understand that **prejudice is a feeling**, a belief that laws cannot change; whereas **discrimination is an action** and thus can be litigated. Prejudice and discrimination include the following factors: age, race, sex, gender identification and expression, religion, color, national origin, ancestry, citizenship, disability, genetic information, marital status, breastfeeding, income assignment for child support, arrest and court record (except as permissible under state law), sexual orientation, domestic or sexual violence as victim status, national guard (or reserve) absence, or status as a covered veteran (ADL, Handbook, 2020; Whiting, 2019).

Sources of Prejudice - Theories

The **first** source of prejudice is based on the **Authoritarian Personality theory** (Sociology, 2010), which appears to be due to parents who practiced harsh discipline, forced children to obey without question, and made them follow strict rules.

A **second** source of prejudice, called **Frustration or Scapegoat theory,** is when people faced with a myriad of problems become frustrated and want to blame their problems on groups of people they dislike to begin with, that is, ethnic, racial, and religious minorities (Sociology, 2010).

The **third** source of prejudice, **Social Learning theory,** is when "prejudice is the result of socialization from parents, peers, the news media, and other various aspects of their culture" (p. 4).

Next, the **Group Threat theory** (also referred to as **Ethnic Competition theory**) is based on "competition over jobs and other resources and from disagreement over various political issues" (Sociology, 2010, p. 4). People who are fearful over jobs, housing, and other life issues subscribe to these ideas that their group is best, and that the 'other groups' cause problems.

Also, traditional or old-fashioned racism which previously was evident in the South (when segregation was accepted) has now been replaced by a "more subtle form of racial prejudice, termed *Laissez-faire,* **Symbolic, or Modern racism**" (Sociology, 2010, p. 4). This is a belief that because certain races are culturally inferior, they bring poverty and problems to themselves, and are responsible for their own issues with homelessness, crime, poor education, low pay, etc.

In the **Eclectic theory** that accepts a multifaceted approach, an individual's personality and socialization (family, school, neighborhood, city, and region) greatly determine an individual's acceptance of bias – or not. More educated people seem to be less racist than less educated ones. (This is of course, a generalization!) News media with biased news reporting certainly can hurt people's acceptance of legal changes on the state and federal levels.

A Historical Review of Six Sources of Prejudice

The first source of prejudice, according to Allport (2000), is historical. This source includes such factors as colonization, segregation, imperial expansion by certain city-states or nations, the exploitation of individuals, groups, countries, and regions, genocide, dominant vs. sub groups, economically ruling classes vs. lower classes, etc.

The second source of prejudice, identified by Allport (2000), is sociocultural. This source includes the movement towards greater urbanization, centralized vs. decentralized governments, multibillion-dollar corporations vs. the small businessperson, domination of finance and politics, and European-American vs. immigrant culture, (and mainly from poor countries located throughout the world). Newer immigrants spoke various languages, spoke little or no English, and had a more difficult time "fitting in" to American society.

The third source of prejudice discussed in Allport's chapter (2000) is situational. This theory includes the **atmosphere theory** (i.e., bias is a reflection of what an individual was taught as a child), the **employment theory** (the haves and the have-nots), the **social mobility theory** (some individuals and groups can increase or decrease their social status), and so forth. Basically, prejudices occur from various situations, and the possibilities are endless.

The fourth source of prejudice Allport mentions is the psychodynamic or frustration theory, which emphasizes that bias can come about by individual and group deprivation, frustration, hostility, and human instinct. This is also called the **scapegoat theory**. Allport (2000) concludes, "Only certain types of people develop prejudice as an important feature in their lives. These seem to be insecure and anxious personalities who take . . . authoritarian and exclusionist way(s)" (p. 99).

The fifth source of prejudice is the phenomenological theory, whereby an individual "attacks members of one group because [he] . . . perceives them as repulsive, annoying, or threatening" (Allport, 2000, p. 99). **Myths and stereotypes** about the person's race, religion, sexual orientation, color, and so forth play an important role in the development of this type of bias.

The sixth and final source of prejudice Allport (2000) discusses is the earned reputation theory. Namely, that **there may be actual differences between groups** (color, financial, appearance, and other types of differences) and **these differences form**

the base of the prejudice.

Although Allport wrote about these theories in 2000, they remain valid today, as documented by many writers in these chapters (in Book 2).

Discussion

Sociologists, psychologists, educators – indeed many researchers and authors discuss the concept of prejudice endlessly. You only need to Google the term, 'prejudice', if you wish to locate thousands of recent articles. One stimulating piece by author Ellie Mulcahy (2017), in *What can schools do to reduce pupils' prejudice?* discusses how children as young as three can demonstrate prejudice and how they might have developed it at such a tender age. "Multicultural education involves explicitly teaching about the history and culture of specific groups" (p. 1).

Mulcahy (2017) warns however, that simply celebrating a historically important person once a year at a birthday event will **not** work, without extensive class discussion, writing, and other inclusive curriculum. Perhaps more thorough examinations, books, movies or podcasts, YouTube videos, regular videos, and art projects might prove helpful. (For example, students could create thought-provoking posters about the famous person or event, for display in their classroom, library, school building walls, school cafeteria, etc.)

Writer Mulcahy (2017) also notes that celebrating special events and people involves "teaching pupils about historic and current events rooted in prejudice and discrimination, such as the Holocaust or the Slave Trade" (p. 2). (Note that in some school districts, this discussion about the killing of six million Jews, or the economic greed of slave owners might be considered controversial.) Her article is extensive, and provocative.

Notes

I have personally seen many different prejudices stem from many different sources. Some, in fact, are based on real differences, such as appearance. One group of people might naturally be slight of build and rather short, while another group may be generally tall, and sturdy. I also have seen one group of people feel threatened by a new group of immigrants because they actually feared economic loss of jobs. How do prejudices affect immigrants and how to mitigate these effects? That is the million-dollar question. **I do believe that once prejudice is present, it is most difficult to eradicate. Education is the key.**

Moreover, education must be persuasive through all grades, all subjects, everywhere. For example, if you explain to a group that they will not suffer job loss in their community because of new arrivals (immigrants), that will help sometimes. (I believe an informative chart might assist in demonstrating these ideas.) I agree, however, with the people who state that while **laws can be used to change behaviors, they may not necessarily change feelings. Nevertheless, without these laws, there is absolutely no chance that behaviors and feelings will ever change.**

So, the sequence, I believe, is this – education at all levels followed by reinforcement of learning and educational matters (K-12, undergraduate and graduate levels) then legislative (legal) changes continue, resulting in behavioral changes due to the enforcement of the enacted laws imposing stiff penalties for non-compliance. **Finally, once laws are full enforced, eventually beliefs will change, over several generations. This means steady progress although it is a long-term process. We must begin now!**

CH 15 Special Education and Multiculturalism, Hawaiian Style

My Pearl of Wisdom: All is Not So Sweet in Paradise

A lot of different flowers make a bouquet.

Muslin Origin

THE RELATIONSHIP BETWEEN special education (SPED) and multicultural education is somewhat different in Hawai'i, compared to the continental U.S.

Christine E. Sleeter and Rodolfo Puente (2001), in *Connecting multicultural and special education,* say "So many students of color are in special education, and most teachers are White. . . . [But] most special education teachers continue to plan their teaching around students' disabilities, with little consideration to students' cultural and linguistic backgrounds" (p. 111). **This statement is not true in Hawai'i**, as many teachers are Japanese - 25%, White - 24%, Mixed two or more races - 24%, Filipino - 7.2%; Chinese - 3.3%; remainder (American Blacks, Indians, Hispanic, Korean, Pacific Islanders) - about 16.6% (Hawai'i State Department of Education, Employment, 2019; Hawai'i State Department of Education, Teacher modernization, 2020), which I believe helps both regular and SPED students.

However, in many parts of the Continental U.S., teachers who are White are still in the majority in many school districts.

Special Education (SPED)

What impact does racism have on multicultural SPED students? Unfortunately, in many parts of the continental U.S. as well as in Hawai'i, **racism might still be prevalent**, in both regular as well as SPED classes. (However, generalizations must be avoided.) If, however, racism occurs, the impact is horrific in these situations, because SPED students already may have significant levels of low self-esteem and little self-confidence. This low self-esteem may have originated at a young age and have little or nothing to do with racism; sometimes, it is almost impossible to identify the source.

More on SPED

The term **SPED** includes "Minority students with special needs in urban schools [who] have triple-layered problems: that of being culturally different, linguistically different and having special needs" (Nkabinde, 2017, p. 1). SPED is used by educators, to separate the 'normal students from the special students,' namely gifted and talented, physically disabled, emotionally and/or mentally challenged, learning disabled, autistic, and linguistically different.

A Discussion

Benedict, Brownell, Griffin, Wang, and Myers (2020) discuss how to prepare general and special education teachers in today's society to deal with diverse educational issues.

Sometimes, parents are not included in **all** school decisions concerning their child. The method of SPED instruction (pulling out students from their home base SPED classroom, and placing them into various classes i.e., mainstreaming them throughout the day) might have increased ethnic and racial prejudice or other situations within the school system in some school districts. Again - we must be careful to not make broad assumptions. However, to make SPED truly multicultural, the Department of Education (DOE) in each school district might assist in the following:

- **Include the parents in all conferences and conversations** regarding their child. This means even at the beginning, **when the classroom teacher provides a basic referral to the counselor**. If conferences are inconvenient, ask parents or guardians to sign letters, stipulating which are the best times and dates for such meetings. If the subject of the meeting is not critical, and there is no disagreement, ask the parents or guardians to show their agreement by signing the SPED forms. (Oftentimes, single parents who work long hours may find it difficult to take time off from work to simply sign forms where everyone agrees.)

- Offer a **bonus for teachers** who teach SPED, at all levels. **Indeed, I do see that a bonus is needed to encourage any certified teacher wanting to go into SPED classrooms to do so**.

- I also believe that all regular **teachers (all subjects and levels) need to get a significant salary bump ($5,000-$12,000) now**, because teachers are professionals and should not be working at or below the poverty level of that city or town. Every two years, add another significant bonus to maintain and attract additional certified teachers. Why should plumbers, electricians, and certified carpenters earn more than teachers? What does society's acceptance of teachers working side jobs on the weekends or evenings tell you?

- Develop a **special** pamphlet for students entering the teacher education program at the local colleges and universities, stating advantages for teachers entering SPED or mathematics field, and whatever the DOE is looking for, in terms of teacher qualifications. In Hawai'i, the DOE needs Hawaiian language instructors in addition to SPED, mathematics and science teachers. Michigan, New York, California, Texas, or Illinois may desperately need other kinds of certified teachers. Update this sort of pamphlet annually, and include a list of special incentives and how to apply to include source of grants or scholarships, amount of stipend, who to contact, deadlines, e-mail addresses, etc.

- Ensure that an adult educational aide or skills trainer is placed in every SPED classroom whenever possible, especially when dealing with severely handicapped students.

Pay Issues

In a review of the newly released 72-page *Hawai'i teacher compensation study and recommendations* (Augenblick et al., 2020) which compares several similar school districts in the U.S. to Hawai'i's, it **documents teachers' pay disparity of between $8,000-$26,000**, per year. Because the poverty level in Hawai'i is listed at approximately $67,000 per annum for a family of four (Augenblick et al., 2020), and it takes 10 years for an average teacher in Hawai'i to go from $49,000 (starting pay) to around $67,000 a year, it is no wonder that the department has a terrible time in recruiting and retaining many of its **teachers of any subject and grade level.**

> According to the U.S. Department of Housing and Urban Development, individuals earning less than $67,500 per year, in the urban Honolulu area, qualify as low income. The starting salary for teachers who completed a state approved teacher education program (SATEP) with 0-5 years of experience is $49,100, and it could take them over 10 years to earn more than the $67,000 (Augenblick et al., 2020 p. 2)

Vacancies

In the Hawai'i Department of Education Teacher Salary Modernization Project of 2020, regarding its salary increase proposal for SPED teachers, it shows that 1,820 SPED teachers currently work in Hawai'i's public schools, out **a total of 2,184 positions**. In total, **some 364 positions – all grades, all subjects – are vacant yearly.** (SPED needs 364 teachers, Hawaiian language needs 74 teachers, and other hard-to-fill positions also need teachers.) There are usually 850 vacant positions annually for the public schools in Hawai'i. These vacancies are filled with Substitutes, Emergency Hires, Long-Term Substitutes, or those who do not have a State Approved Teacher Education Program (SATEP) degree or certificate.

Pay Differential

The education department in Hawai'i has proposed (with legislative approval, but **unfunded**) a $10,000 pay differential for SPED teachers, an $8,000 pay differential for Hawaiian language immersion teachers and Hawai'i School for the Deaf and the Blind instructors, and lesser amounts for other hard -to-fill positions (Teacher Salary Modernization Project, 2020).

As of January 31, 2020, Salary Differentials (Augenblick et al., 2020) in Hawai'i will cost **$10.2 million** in School Year (SY) 2019-2020, **$30.7 million** in SY 2020-2021, and **$46.0 million** in SY 2021-2022 to pay for general teachers due to Equity and Compression problems. This last issue discussed on the report, is as follows:

> The current distribution of teachers on each step of the salary schedule is **inconsistent and compressed,** contributing to senior teachers leaving the profession. In some cases, teachers on the same step can have a difference of 10 years of service.

> Current data show that 5,942 teachers with between 0 and 24 years of service are clustered between steps 9 and 11. This phase will provide the Department with a strategic basis to initiate a discretionary pay adjustment to existing teachers where it is determined through analysis that a teacher's salary is less than and/or equal to less experienced teachers in comparable or similarly situated teaching positions.

> The desired effective date to implement the compensation adjustment(s) for certain eligible teachers is the first day of the 2020-21 school year. (p. 2)

> Finally, the Compensation Study (Augenblick et al., 2020) states "as long as teachers are being paid below the poverty level, Hawai'i will continue to see escalation in the teacher shortage crisis" (p. 1). The Hawaii State Department of Education needs to "adjust the number of classes and steps in the salary schedule to better compensate for teacher experience and increasing stipend levels" (p. 3). Recommendations also include alternative teacher pay plans focused on four basic parts:

- Performance pay or bonuses for increased student performance; most teachers did **not agree with this.** (SPED, Hawaiian Immersion, and English as a Second Language students may not show 'normal' progress through no fault of anyone – teachers and students.)

- Professional growth pay for professional development.

- Assumption of additional responsibilities such as mentorship, instructional coach, etc.

- Market-based incentives, for teaching in hard-to-fill subjects, or at hard-to-staff schools.

> Additional pay may be a substantial one-time bonus or an amount added to the

teacher's regular salary on a permanent basis. Many education districts in most states participate in the Federal Teacher Incentive Fund grant program (p. 5).

The *Compensation* (Augenblick et al., 2020) report also promotes a cost-of-living increase yearly and proposes that teachers must be treated and paid as professionals to attract and retain top educators and support top high school and college students to the teaching field. Dr. Linda Darling Hammond, of the Learning Policy Institute mentioned in this Compensation Study (Augenblick et al., 2020) uses Maryland as an example. She discusses data from the international research supported by National Center for Education and the Economy in this important, definitive report.

Now, it is up to the Department of Education and Hawai'i Legislature to ensure that they provide sufficient funds to implement these sound suggestions. Experts such as Dr. Hammond have already made their recommendations. Action please, now.

Hawai'i Racial Make-Up

Everyone in Hawai'i is a minority; there is no majority race or culture. Yes, it might be true that Hawai'i's SPED program may be unique because the teachers are quite culturally, racially, and ethnically diverse, as are the students. Many teachers and students who live in Hawai'i are racially mixed by as many as up to eight race categories. There is no one predominant, majority race. But if you visit a SPED classroom, you will notice a lack of bilingual books for students who are both SPED and speakers of a language other than English. You will not usually see classroom books in Tagalog, *CHamoru*, Mandarin, Vietnamese, Cambodian, Marshallese, or Yapese, with English translations. So many students with no or limited English remain frustrated.

However, the reason for Hawai'i's teachers leaving the profession has everything to do with the extremely high cost of living (Augenblick et al., 2020**). In SY 2018-2019, fully 755 teachers of all levels and subjects resigned, and 274 retired**. Reasons for **resigning** are as follows: leaving Hawai'i (375), entering non-teaching jobs (106), accepting non-DOE teaching jobs (65), family/personal issues (139), and problems with the work place environment (70).

Thus, due to the low pay and other negative conditions, many teachers (general and SPED) move, relocate, or leave the Hawai'i Department of Education at any given time. Hawai'i's children suffer because of this continual teacher-shortage. In 2020, the COVID-19 virus hit the world and Hawai'i schools shuttered, students and teachers stayed home, adding to the teacher vacancy issues. In school year 2021, some schools **partially** reopened nationwide, including Hawaii.

Hawai'i appears to be the only school district not funded by property tax. When will Hawai'i's citizens stop talking about annual teacher shortages and do something about the dire situation (Baker, 2018)? Over 850 vacancies each school year in Hawai'i will never be permanently filled without an infusion of dedicated funding. Parents – don't you think your children deserve a better learning outcome? Our children are our future!

CH 16 Culturally Relevant Teaching at the Elementary Level

My Pearl of Wisdom: Start with the Young

There is only one way to avoid criticism:

do nothing,

say nothing,

and be nothing.

Aristotle

CULTURALLY RELEVANT TEACHING for students at all grade levels should include their need to experience academic success in school, maintain positivity and value of their own culture and language while learning English, and simultaneously integrate into a new (American) culture.

Academic Success

Academic success is important to all students (Noel, 2000), because all need to learn skills in numbers, literacy/reading, technology, political, and social arenas. Such academic success is especially important to the marginalized student, the one with low self-worth, poor English language abilities, and who may be socially ostracized or not easily accepted. With increasing school success, these marginalized students obtain positive recognition by their peers, praise from their parents, and academic, scholastic, athletic honors, awards, and such from their teachers and the school (Diversity Lesson Plan, 2016).

Cultural competence is important in that teachers can use students' home languages, cultures, and value systems as a bridge to school learning, according to

Ladson-Billings (2000). **The students can demonstrably see their own culture being valued by others** (Koppelman, 2017; Lankster, 2020).

In *Linguistic imperialism in the United States*, by Margery Ridgeway and Cornel Pewewardy (2005), the authors state that "A person's first language defines who that person is, from what culture that person . . . comes, and the mental and spiritual framework that person uses to perceive the world in which he/she lives" (p. 218). Ridgeway and Pewewardy explain that "when a person loses his/her first primary language he/she loses a part of him/herself. When a person is degraded because of his/her first language, it is a degradation of the whole person" (p. 218).

Two Elements

Personally, I believe that these two elements, **native language loss and degradation of the native language, can affect a student's self-esteem**. Loss of one's own language and seeing that language devalued are extremely important factors in a bilingual individual.

Personal Note

My dearly departed husband, Daniel Navarro Atoigue, did not learn English until his early teens. Daniel spoke only *CHamoru* to his grandmother on Guam (and she spoke **only** *CHamoru* to everyone); he spoke only *CHamoru* to his family and extended family, as well, although they all spoke **some** English. When Daniel began to learn English in school, it was a difficult period in his life.

World War II had ended in 1945, but the Japanese had occupied Guam with ferocious brutality since the early days of December 1941. Although Daniel was born in 1948, the island remained in a spasm of neglect after the war and for many years after that. His family had survived those awful years of deprivation, starvation, enforced hiding in caves and later, moving from one area of the island to another mostly without shelter, weathering the elements, and relying only on themselves and the goodness of relatives and friends for food. When the Americans came to liberate Guam, Daniel's mother had already lost her newborn son (the first Danny) to exposure and disease. So,

95

my mother-in-law (Agnes) named my husband (her third son) in honor of her dead baby.

The years between 1945-1960 were 'bartering' and 'sharing' years. CHamorus and those calling Guam home farmed, raised vegetables, chickens, pigs – anything they could eat, with which to feed their families. Jobs were scarce following the war. The U.S. military controlled Guam during those after-war years, providing much needed stability, basic medical and dental care, food, and shelter.

When Super Typhoon Karen hit Guam and the Mariana Islands in November 1962, it was the most powerful storm in decades, with winds gusts exceeding 180 miles per hour. Another super storm, Pamela, struck Guam in May 1976, with wind gusts over 150 miles per hour, so government assistance was invaluable! The wind was so powerful that it broke the 'wind meter' at the International Airport in Tumon. (I lived through Typhoon Pamela, seven months pregnant at the time, but that is a tale for another time.)

It was subsistence living for many. Youngsters climbed coconut trees, twisting the heavy fruit loose, with those on the ground scrambling to retrieve the wonderful life-savers. Families used coconut milk for drinking, cooking, and shredded the sweet coconut meat for meal-toppings. Coconuts were truly natures' miracles. Everyone fed any coconut leftovers to the pigs they raised. They used coconut husks as toothbrushes and if they burned the husks, the smoke would drive away pesky mosquitoes at night and flies during the day. Adults used large, coconut fronds as materials for thatched roofs and cut up *Hale Koa* (Hawaiian) or *Tangantangan (CHamoru)* trees for barbeque firewood and pig fodder. They picked banana leaves to wrap raw food in and bake them in the under-ground makeshift ovens for hours. Sharing with extended family members and neighbors was the norm.

You want your 'broken' car fixed? It will cost a young cow. Need a good present for a new baby? Slaughter one of your goats. What to bring to a funeral gathering for a dear relative? Bake two pigs (*lechons*). Neighbors routinely shared their cooking, meals, and supplies. Anyone hunting for wild pigs and deer? Everyone shared what they shot. Shrimp fishing in the fresh water streams in the mountains? Everyone shared in the catfish and shrimp caught. You want to see a doctor? See the Army volunteer medic (if lucky) available once a month or less. In the meanwhile, let Auntie Beatrice use some of her special herbs and medicinal teas on you. Do you need dental care? Brush your teeth with coconut husks and salty water or better yet, use Betel-Nut husks (Areca Palm Nut, called *Pugua)*. And Pray.

Life was in a survival, subsistence mode, but the island culture was one of deep sharing and respect for all life . . . families meant everything! Everyone knew who their relatives were, and if not, the typical greeting included the name of their village and their mother's and father's names. Youngsters bowed their heads to their relatives in greeting – to elders, indeed all adults as a sign of respect, almost kissing the adults slightly raised back of their hands in *manamko* which signified respect for elders' wisdom, family, and identity.

Daniel had no need to learn English until middle school. But instead of integrating English with *CHamoru*, the seventh-grade religious teachers stated they would allow absolutely **no *CHamoru* to be spoken in class, from Day One**. Furthermore, teachers and administrators severely punished students caught speaking their native language with corporal (physical) punishment. "Are you speaking *CHamoru*?" teachers asked. "Yes?" They would handily paddle students on the spot. The message was clear: speak ***CHamoru*** at your own peril. English must be spoken at this school, no matter what the cost. No other language would be tolerated.

Daniel tried to explain to his teachers that his grandmother who he was living with (because his parents had eight other children to care for) did not understand English at all, and **could not** sign her name on any of the school 'forms' he would take home for 'parent-signature'. **The teachers were not interested in excuses.** He had difficulty speaking English in school initially, but was better at reading and writing English. However, Daniel and his friends only communicated orally in *CHamoru*, even through high school.

Now, some 60 years later, I still remember my Daniel talking about how angry he was at his teachers for scolding and punishing him for speaking his own native language. He despised a nun at St. Jude's Middle School, Sister Merda who had escaped from Red (Communist) China, but to all the students, she was Sister Murda! Time may heal most wounds, but not all of them!

CH 17 Define Racism in Our Society

My Pearl of Wisdom: Talk is Cheap – Let's Act Now

So long as our relationship is defined by our differences,

we will empower those who sow hatred rather than peace,

those who promote conflict rather than the cooperation

that can help all of our people

achieve justice and prosperity.

This cycle of suspicion and discord must end.

Barack Obama

Racism has already been defined in earlier chapters. But let me provide some concrete examples proving that racism is still alive and well in the good-ole U.S.A. (Chung, 2021; Gal et al., 2020).

In Washington D.C., Hawai'i, California, Texas, Georgia, North Caroline, Maryland, Louisiana, Virginia, South Carolina, Alabama, Mississippi, Illinois, New Mexico, and New York (**all states, where huge numbers of minorities reside) students, teachers, administrators** – ask yourself the following questions (Gal et al., 2020):

Q. In school (all grades), when the teacher discusses our national heritage or about 'civilization,' I can see that people of my color really made significant contributions. **T or F**

Q. As a parent, I can be sure that school will give my children textbooks and other classroom materials that provide a positive example of their race/ancestry. **T or F**

Q. At a school, or business, I can be pretty sure that if I ask to talk to the person in charge, a supervisor, or manager, many times I will be talking with a person of my own race, color, ancestry, or ethnicity. **T or F**

Q. When I visit a drug store to purchase a Band-Aid or adhesive strip to protect a sore or blemish, I can purchase some that match my own skin color. **T or F**

Did you answer 'True' to any of these questions? I would be surprised if you did. Many would answer 'False' to at least half of them.

Presidential Action

The NAME (2021) *Advancing and advocating for social justice & equity* article states that it "condemns the Trump administration's action to cancel contracts that help to inform federal workers of 'white privilege,' 'critical race theory' and their long-standing effect on maintaining inequities in the U.S." (p. 1). The article continues, stating that President Donald Trump "instructed the White House Office of Management and Budget to restructure racial sensitivity training for federal agencies, saying such training is 'divisive, anti-American propaganda' (p. 1).

Personal Experience

The following true tale is an example of racism I have personally witnessed in an educational setting.

When I was a Hawai'i Job Corps teacher, I heard one Hawai'i local teenage male of mixed race say about another teenage male in my classroom: "**Oh look, another stupid F***ing Marshall guy" (referring to a student who was from Majuro, the Republic of the Marshall Islands, who spoke Marshallese and English.)**

How did I feel and respond? I did not approve of such remarks and told the part-Hawaiian youth, "Just because he is just learning English does not mean he is stupid. He is learning to speak and read English, which is his second language. **You only know one language.** So, don't make fun of him." The entire conversation was depressing to me.

Could I have prevented the situation from happening? Not really. There was no way to stop one student making negative or derogatory comments about another student. However, because students lived on campus, the residential advisors told me that they spent many nights discussing race relations, cultural heritage, and mutual cooperation.

I talked to the head dorm advisor about this incident and he explained that he would bring the issue of racism up with his staff and dormitory residents later that week. The subject of inappropriate and racial comments was not new; swearing (at each other), and fighting because of such insulting comments were also familiar to the dorm advisors.

Job Corps in America grew tremendously since its inception, later expanding to 123 centers, helping over 48 thousand female and males (U.S. Department of Labor, Parents, 2017). Racism was not confined to a few centers. However, I am writing only about my personal experiences as an instructor at the Koko Head Center.

So, even in Hawai'i, there is still much racism. Some of the locals dislike the mainlanders, called *Haoles*. Some light-skinned Hawaiians tend to look down on the more dark-skinned Hawaiians. Some Japanese tend to disfavor the Okinawans, calling them 'hairy." Some CHamorus who intermarried with Caucasians are shown biasness by those who consider themselves 'pure' CHamorus. Some mixed Black Americans dislike or look down on 'pure' Whites. Some Japanese look down on other Japanese who cannot fluently speak their native language. Some Chinese from Hong Kong look down on those from tiny country inlets and villages in mainland China, considering them to be 'just country rift-raft'.

Sometimes, it is just the reverse. Some Koreans dislike the Japanese and vice versa, due to lingering effects of the Korean Conflict. (Yes, I know that 'conflict' ended in 1953 but – wait for it – wait – **some Japanese are still hoping to see their relatives, soon in 2021-2025 if only these relatives can escape from North Korea**. And if the Pandemic 'allows' travel. Who knows!)

Some Polynesians look down on Micronesians as they are some of the last groups (think of Yapese, Palauan, Pohnpeian, Chuukese, Marshallese) to immigrate to the Hawaiian Islands. (Yes, assimilation takes time!) Some American Samoans show prejudice against the Yapese and Saipanese. Some light-skinned American Blacks do not associate with dark-skinned ones. (Notice that reporters from all over the world refer to President Obama as a 'Black American' and **never** biracial, half-White/half-Black, or in Hawai'i, *Hapa-Haole* or half-White. After all, his father was Black and his mother, White! So, apparently, he is considered just 'Black'.)

Some big-Manila City immigrants look down on the 'Filipino peasants' from poverty-stricken boroughs maybe because the city dwellers are light-skinned and think poorly of those with darker skin who have to perform manual labor in the sun. (Many country Filipinos work in the fields and thus have darker skin.) Some Portuguese in Hawai'i show prejudice to those of an oriental or Asian background. And many Pacific Islanders dislike or/and distrust *Haoles*. These prejudices are many times obvious, but other times, not.

Over the past several decades, as more people in Hawai'i (and in America) intermarry and thus more are of mixed races, society has the wonderful opportunity to reduce overt racism. However, in 2021, based on local television newscasts and the daily newspapers, blatant racism appears to continue.

Times Magazine writer Nicole Chung (May 27, 2021), a Korean-American, wrote *I'm tired of trying to educate White people about Anti-Asian racism,* a stirring article on not understanding Whites who remain silent when presented with blatant racism. She asks people of all races to engage in conversations about racism, even if it makes people uncomfortable.

Wayne Au and Moe Yonamine (2021) also wrote a stirring article, *Dear educators, It is time to fight for Asian America* on the website, **Rethinking Schools**, about the "deeply rooted history of white supremacy in violence against Asian people" (p. 1). They state that

> The racism, the devaluing of life of Asian and Asian Americans, the dehumanizing of immigrant workers, the fetishism of – and violence towards – Asian women have been perpetuated throughout U.S. history. . . . The white

supremacist model minority myth has perpetuated a fake hierarchy, pitting people of color against each other for an unattainable proximity to whiteness. (p. 2)

Authors Au and Yonamine (2021) speak directly to the "black, brown, indigenous, and white educator family," and ask them to do the following: **TEACH**

- about the long history of violence against Asian Americans, and how ignoring that history is itself a form of violence.

- about how pandemics have been used to justify anti-Asian violence.
- how Anti-Asian racism must not be ignored.

- about Asian Americans and important moments in people's history.

- the PBS Series Asian Americans and use the accompanying curriculum developed by Asian Americans Advancing Justice.

- a different Asian American timeline which places Asian American history in the context of race and capitalism in the U.S.

- about the incarceration of the Japanese Americans during WWII, from their imprisonment in local fairgrounds, to Japanese Latin Americans being rounded up internationally.

- about true diversity of Asians and Asian Americans, from indigenous Okinawans who have been colonized and resisted colonization by both Japan and the U.S., to Filipinos who have struggled against the . . . regimes of Spain and the U.S.

- that it is time to retire the term Asian Pacific America, because it marginalizes Indigenous **Pasifika** Island peoples

- across K-12 using books by and about Asian Americans. (p. 2)

The writers discuss over a dozen other actions that they want educators to take, for the rest of society to understand Asian-American hate and hate-crimes.

As we approach the first quarter of the 21st century, and more interracial children are born, race relations might not continue to be a serious problem. That is my fervent wish! And just think about this. If your mother is mixed-race Korean, and your father, Chinese, with Palauan and Filipino ancestry, and your four children grow up and intermarry with Japanese, White, Black, and Spanish mixtures, and your four grandchildren grow up and intermarry with Mexican, Polish, Okinawan, and Samoan individuals (who are also of mixed ethnicity), how in the world can overt racism still exist? And even if a White person marries a White person, can hatred continue when their children intermarry with those outside their race, religion, political party, language, color, socio-economic class, immigration status, or ethnicity?

CH 18 Multicultural Education -

Connecting Theory to Practice

My Pearl of Wisdom: Hurry Up and Wait

Don't listen to the person who has the answers;

listen to the person who has the questions.

Albert Einstein

SOME EDUCATORS DEFINE Multicultural Education as the time when teachers bring various materials to school, in celebration of special leaders or selected events, or adding innovative topics for discussion in the classroom. **Multicultural education** also refers to any form of education or teaching that incorporates the histories, texts, values, beliefs, and perspectives of people from different cultural backgrounds (Merriam-Webster, n.d.).

In 2018, approximately 50.7 million students in public elementary and secondary schools brought a huge variety of languages, cultures, perspectives, and cultures to the classroom (NCES, 2020).

Educators may also encourage students to have greater understanding of themselves and others, to preserve and value their native languages and cultures, by emphasizing the contributions of people who are **different from the White Anglo-Americans or Europeans** found in the common textbook.

Indeed, a true definition of **multicultural education must include an antiracist theme which runs throughout all grades and subjects,** and includes both student and teacher commitment to affirming positive differences in gender, age, sexual orientation, disability, ethnicity, religion, social class, citizenship, national origin, color, economic levels, and language (Sociology, 2010). There are four positive methods of implementing curricula changes and six specific suggestions.

Changing School Curricula to Incorporate Multicultural Education Practices

Educators must first define Multicultural Education, to know what changes they must make in school curricula, when incorporating an innovative multicultural education program throughout all grade levels and all subjects. Multicultural education is more than teaching about a special person in history, or celebrating a day or month in honor of a historical person or event.

The observances of Martin Luther King Day or Pacific-Asian Week are all too common and do little or nothing to teach tolerance for others. Any definition of multicultural education must include the use of a variety of themes, such as allowing the students to see society as it could be – a place that is tolerant of those who are in the minority, indeed, a place that celebrates the minority.

A second change is that multicultural educators must allow students to understand that they are valued, heard, feel important, and thus intolerant of bias and discrimination in school, work, home, and in society in general.

The third change of multicultural education is "not merely to promote human relations, to help students feel good about themselves, or to preserve students' native languages and cultures" (Cumming-McCann, 2005, p. 3) but **to help all students** of all races, ethnic backgrounds, religions, color, gender, and sexual orientation learn better, think more critically about all issues, and reject racism and all forms and appearances of discrimination.

Moreover, **the fourth change is that teachers must pay special attention to those students** who have been traditionally dismissed, undervalued, unrecognized, underserved, marginalized, and to positively accept and affirm such individual differences in the classroom.

Five Features to Include

Features of multicultural education should include the following (ADL,

Handbook, 2020; Cumming-McCann, 2005):

1. Schools tend to perpetuate bias unless teachers analyze ways how this bias is shown, so that the negative behavior can stop.

2. Teachers need to **become aware** of the background, history, causes, and examples of bias, sexism, and other forms of institutional prejudices. Once teachers are aware, they can make appropriate changes.

3. **All students,** not just those of color or who are from minority groups, **will benefit from these curriculum changes**. Discussions, readings, and activities will help students become more cohesive, unified, and knowledgeable, as they learn how people throughout history have fought against oppression.

4. **Teachers need to assist** their peers, principals, students, families and others in the community to learn about others who are different from themselves; they must embrace such differences.

5. **Teachers should** encourage learning opportunities individually or in groups, so that students and others can search for a future of promise, a society that allows, indeed encourages, differences.

Four Specific Approaches – a Historical Wrap-up

Educators would benefit if they are aware of distinguished scholar James Banks' writing. As a leader in multicultural education, Dr. Banks established a model that touched on these four ways or approaches, summarized by Cumming-McCann (2005) as follows:

The Contributions Approach: this is the "heroes and holidays approach" (Cumming-McCann, 2005. p. 7) – the most common form of multicultural education. There is no real curriculum change, and ethnic observances are limited to special holidays, events, and celebrations. **Unfortunately,** students and teachers pay almost no attention to the ethnic observance pre-or post and this Contributions Approach does not provide students and teachers the chance to see important roles of ethnic groups in American society. There are usually no discussions about racial inequality, ethnic struggles, economic challenges, or social oppression. Thus, **this approach actually reinforces and perpetuates ethnic myths and stereotypes**.

The Additive Approach: this is the **second type** of multicultural education, which takes very little time, effort, training, or creativity. The dominant viewpoint remains the White, European or American one, without reference to the minorities involved. The perspective remains that of the dominant culture "adding" information to the basic school curricula. Cultural and racial inequalities and social oppressions are not addressed (ADL, Handbook, 2020).

The Transformative Approach: this **third type** of multicultural education allows students to understand concepts from the perspective of various ethnic and cultural lenses. Students learn about the impact and importance of mainstream European or American events from the viewpoint of the minority groups involved. Unfortunately, this approach "requires a complete transformation of the curriculum . . . [and] a conscious effort of the part of the teachers to deconstruct what they have been taught to think, believe, and teach" (Cumming-McCann, 2005, p. 12). **Many teachers may not be willing to change how they think, what they believe, and the way they teach.**

The Decision Making and Social Action Approach: this fourth type of multicultural education involves all the ingredients of the Transformative Approach and in addition, includes the aspect of authorizing, indeed, demanding that students make informed decisions and take action, **by exploring the dynamics of historical events and then making decisions to change or alter the school system via social action.** This proposal states that students (and teachers) "develop and implement strategies to eradicate racism, sexism, or any other form of oppression in their schools, work environments, and personal lives" (Cumming-McCann, 2005, p. 14). Such a teaching method means that students must analyze and come to grips with their own beliefs and value systems, to decide what course(s) of action they should take, something very difficult to accomplish!

Educators can infuse multicultural education throughout all grades and subjects only through transformational means, where students must be informed about the existing inequalities and then genuinely empowered to make societal changes. (And teachers must first recognize these ideas!) In addition, educators must be encouraged to use a **blended approach**, beginning with the Contributions approach and then slowly making additional changes when both students and teachers feel ready to finally reach the Decision Making and Social Action Approach. Again, these actions are very difficult to accomplish, but must happen if multiculturalism is to flourish.

Six Ways to Implement Change - Lynch

Matthew Lynch (2015) discusses *6 ways to implement a real multicultural education in the classroom* and states educators and administrators should do the following:

- Agree upon a definition of multiculturalism; the "components required in educating a multicultural . . . [group] are content integrations, prejudice reduction, empowering school culture and social culture."

- Accept real-life experiences involving diversity over that presented in textbooks.

- Identify students' learning modalities.

- Promote students' heritage and difference in a positive way.

- Identify teachers' biases; all must identify what biases they have and then learn about other cultures, not in the most basic, elementary terms but really understand these cultures (language, customs, beliefs, art, religion, food, etc.)

- Writing assignments, to celebrate diverse, multiple cultural beliefs, should be numerous and flexible, involving "family stories and traditions [which] can play a significant role in unearthing information about a student's cultural heritage." (pp. 1-3)

Summary

Unfortunately, change takes time, and for the most part, the discussion above seems to ignore the important part textbooks, prepared curriculum, school administrators, district officials, indeed, especially parents play in putting multicultural education theory into practice (Ordway, 2021). Teachers are trained in teacher-education programs, at various educational institutions across America, and instructed by some of the most conservative professors in the country.

Present instructors of multicultural education courses seem to be a distinct minority. Thus, it may take decades to train new teachers with innovative ideas about how to implement a truly excellent multicultural education program. The conservative right seems to be increasingly interjecting their collective political opinions about textbook selections for all grades and subject areas. Politicians scrutinize school districts, and sometimes redistrict or divide them for political purposes, along economic lines. This is the reality. Nevertheless, as one educator stated most astutely, the **identification of the problems is half the battle**.

CH 19 Maintaining Diversity in American Culture

My Pearl of Wisdom: Together, Change is Possible

Our attitude towards immigration reflects our faith in the American ideal.

We have always believed it possible

for men and women who start at the bottom

to rise as far as the talent and energy allow.

Neither race nor place of birth should affect their chances.

Robert Kennedy

WHAT IS THE 'American Culture'? How do we maintain a diversity of cultures in America while keeping an American unity? How do we assimilate as one nation, but still maintain our personal identities as proud Native American Indians, or Russian Jews, or Filipino Americans or Nisei Japanese (i.e., second generation Japanese born in America)?

Problems

Many believe that there are **insurmountable problems in American *because* of the tremendous diversity:** diversity of religion, color, culture, skills, educational, sociological, economical levels and the list continues *ad nauseam*. **However, the diversity among its people is precisely what others say *accounts* for American's greatness.** America attracts immigrants from all over planet Earth, who search for a better life for themselves and their children, who want an opportunity to practice their own religion or to be free from a particular belief system, who want to be judged on their own activities, performance, and merit, not based on their skin color or social class.

It is this aspect of America, to remain one nation created by people from other islands, nations, territories, countries who are from racial, ethnic, religious, and cultural differences and yet, who strive, indeed demand, to live in an open, free society, a society which is indeed, based on tolerance, openness, opportunity, and hard work (Koppelman, 2017).

There are problems, of course. One need only open any American newspaper or view a television newscast to hear some of these convoluted, complex issues which many people see as divisive and dividing. American is a pluralistic society with a swelling number of immigrants. However, in 2021, America still remains a land of opportunity and hope to millions of people who leave their homes and countries, their possessions in foreign lands, to arrive in America legally (or in some cases, illegally) to better themselves. Millions of immigrants have passed through Ellis Island, seen the beacon of the Statue of Liberty, or enter America from dozens of access points, and strive to become American citizens.

Others come to America through a much more circuitous route – fleeing crushing poverty, murderous gangs, devastating typhoons and floods, enduring horrendous family separations – all for the opportunity America holds. They cross at 71 checkpoints including 33 permanent traffic stops, at the borders of Texas, New Mexico, California, and many other areas (Jimenez, 2021; U.S. Department of Homeland Security, 2021). America is the land of hope, and for some of these immigrants, it is their last hope!

I have worked in almost a dozen nations from one to three years, and worked or visited some 39 or more other countries from one to twelve weeks. Every time I return from overseas whether I am gone for six days or three years, I think how lucky I am. I would not trade America for any other place in the world! Even the poorest immigrants to American have access to clean water, social service agencies, hospital emergency rooms, and most probably, a better life for themselves and their children.

CH 20 Multicultural Tokenism

at All Levels:

Differences between Tokenism and

True Multicultural Education

My Pearl of Wisdom: Don't You Love to Hate This?

Education's purpose is to replace an empty mind with an open one.

Malcolm S. Forbes

"TOKENISM INVOLVES the symbolic involvement of a person in an organization due only to a specified or salient characteristic (e.g., gender, race/ethnicity, disability, age)" (Diversity lesson plan, 2016, p. 1). **It deals with practices or policies that seem to include minority** or underrepresented individuals, but in reality, it is misleading, because it does **not**.

> Psychological research suggests that **tokenism may occur** when members of the underrepresented group comprise less than 15% of the total environmental organizational context they are a part of. Furthermore, when there is only a single representative of a given group in an organizational environment, he or she is considered to have what is termed solo status. (p. 1)

Major Differences

There are several major differences between multicultural tokenism and true multicultural education (Lynch, 2015; Tokenism, 2021). A major difference is that tokenism **is simply lip service** educators pay toward accepting those different from themselves, **while in reality, there is no acceptance.** Therefore, nothing changes.

Discrimination continues, whether it is based on age, gender, race, color, religion, economic-social class, first language learned, geographical birthplace/home designation, disability, or any number of variables.

Eight Major Characteristics

Noted educator, writer, and **Father of Multicultural Education, James A. Banks** (2021), mentions eight major factors or characteristics of schools he would consider as truly multicultural educational institutions. These are as follows:

1. Both teachers and administrative staff have positive attitudes and high expectations for all students, and as such, treat them courteously, respectfully, and caringly

2. The official school curriculum incorporates varied experiences, ethnicities, and perspectives of a wide variety of cultural groups and both genders.

3. Teaching methods and styles are in sync with the motivational and learning styles of their students.

4. All staff members show respect for students' home or first languages or dialects.

5. The viewpoint of various cultural, ethnic, and racial groups is incorporated in the institution's events, activities, and curriculum.

6. Testing methods, techniques, and instruments are culturally relevant, resulting in students of color in gifted and talented classes, in direct proportion to their population numbers.

7. Both the curriculum – basic and hidden – as well as the culture of the school are relevant to the school's ethnic and cultural diversity.

8. School counselors expect high performance from all students of all races, ethnicities, languages, colors, etc. and assist them actively in establishing future career and academic objectives. (pp. 2-3)

Noted author Banks (2021) implies in this article that those schools that do not demonstrate these eight characteristics are really demonstrating only multicultural tokenism.

Four Approaches-a Quick Summary

Banks (2021) in his seminal work also identified four approaches to the multicultural curriculum reform and integration of multiculturalism in schools covered in earlier chapters. First, the **Contributions Approach**, - think of heroes and holidays. The second, **Ethnic Additive Approach**, which integrates some ethnic content into the classroom curriculum, but from the viewpoint of mainstream White culture. For example, the Westward movement of settlers is from the standpoint of White settlers, and not the Lakota Indians or other tribes, who were already in the West.

The third, **Transformative Approach** uses the studying of various perspectives such as studying the Revolutionary War from the viewpoint of the White settlers, Indian tribes, British government, soldiers, and colonialists, emphasizing how various groups made up this new American Society. Banks (2021) finally discusses the fourth, **Decision-Making and Social Action Approach,** which combines all the three earlier discussed approaches, asking students examine the various groups' beliefs, values, and perhaps alternative courses of action. Students then make decisions on how to reduce prejudice and discrimination in today's society and institutions, such as their own schools.

Best Practices

The Anti-Defamation League (ADL) Coordinator Handbook and Resource Guide, **No Place for Hate** (ADL, 2020) suggests that schools follow best practices to prevent tokenism and encourage kindness among students. These practices include the following:

1. Survey students, to amplify students' voices and make students feel that they are active participants in creating a school culture where everyone feels welcomed and supported.

2. Implement anti-bias curriculum: https://www.adl.org/education/resources/tools-andstrategies/anti-bias-curriculum-guides

3. Host an ADL workshop (anti-bias – bullying prevention workshops) to train entire school communities.

4. Take the **No Place for Hate Online Course**: at http://bit.ly/NPFHCoordinatorCourse a self-paced 45-minute course for administrators and coordinators, which provide helpful information, tips, pitfalls

to avoid, best practices, and additional resources. (p. 11)

Additionally, the ADL (2020) suggests schools ask students to take a pledge, as follows (p. 15):

For Elementary School Students – DO

- I promise to do my best to treat everyone fairly.

- I promise to do my best to be kind to everyone—even if they are not like me.

- If I see someone being hurt or bullied, I will tell a teacher.

- I will help others to feel safe and happy at school.

- I will be part of making my school No Place for Hate.

For Middle/High School Students – DO

- I will seek to gain understanding of those who are different from me.

- I will speak out against prejudice and discrimination.

- I will reach out to support those who are targets of hate.

- I will promote respect for people and help foster a prejudice-free school.

- I believe that one person can make a difference—no person can be an "innocent" bystander when it comes to opposing hate.

- I recognize that respecting individual dignity and promoting intergroup harmony are the responsibilities of all students.

Six More Ideas

In a Washington Post article, Laura Meckler and Kate Rabinowitz (2019) provide a welcome addition to Dr. Banks' work. The six important points are as follows (Meckler & Rabinowitz, 2019, pp. 1-4):

- The U.S. is becoming more diverse each decade; in 2020, Whites will no longer represent a majority of American children. In fact, the Census Bureau projects that by 2060, just 36% under age 18 will be non-Hispanic

- There will be a huge number of diverse school districts (two-thirds in 2017), across America.

- These diverse districts used to be mainly White.

- Schools in these newly diverse districts have high levels of integration.

- However, schools in historically diverse districts are much more segregated.

- More students are now attending schools which are diverse, and in highly integrated school systems.

It appears obvious to most that we all need to avoid tokenism at all costs, in schools, organizations, civilian and military institutions – indeed everywhere if we are to work towards a better tomorrow (Ordway, 2021). Everyone must contribute to this effort.

We are now into the second fifth of the twenty-first century. Can we welcome diversity and embrace our commonalities? **Who** are we fearful of, and **when** can we open our hearts and minds? **What** will **you** do? **How** will you do it? **What action** will you take **now – today – tomorrow?**

CH 21 Multicultural Lesson Plan Sample

My Pearl of Wisdom: Can You Try This?

You can teach a student a lesson for a day;

but if you can teach him to learn by creating curiosity,

he will continue the learning process

as long as he lives.

Clay P. Bedford

Background Information

THERE ARE LITERALLY hundreds of sample lesson plans, if one does a Google search for Multiculturalism Lesson Plans, or lessons dealing with prejudice, discrimination, and stereotypes. One recent online search included a fascinating article about introducing the concept of racism to school age youngsters (Multiculturalism lesson plans, 2020; Prejudice, discrimination, & stereotypes, 2014). I list three activities, each more sophisticated than the previous, to show that the teacher must start with the basics.

Lesson Plan Notes

The following is based from a Sample Lesson Six-Step Plan **format** (Matsumoto-Grah, 2002) for First Graders who are learning high frequency words, also called Dolch Sight Words (Dolch, 2021). The words increase in difficulty, from Pre-Primer (PP), then Primer (P), First, Second, then Third Grade words. **I created and used this chapter's actual Lesson Plan previously, when I taught elementary school students, so it passed the 'reality' test!** I share it with you readers, now.

In addition to learning these high frequency sight words, the teacher asks students to think of two favorite ethnic dishes or foods prepared at home, as an incentive to learn all new vocabulary words. Two words (from each student in the class) based on these two dishes or foods will be added to everyone's sight word list. The teacher asks each student to talk about the dish or food and explain to the class why it is the student's favorite.

The teacher plans to show these new words as part of the student progress report in Reading to parents at the next parent-teacher conference, scheduled in about six weeks. The lesson plan is as follows:

Six – Step Lesson Plan, a Sample

Teacher (T) says: Today, we will review our Dolch Word List and our special words we added to our list, based on your favorite ethnic food or dish which your aunty or uncle, mother or father, grandmother or grandfather prepares or brings to your house.

T continues: Many people eat different kinds of food. Bill, last week, you said that your favorite food was deer meat that we call venison.

Bill yells aloud: What's wrong with deer meat? My uncle gets it from Maui.

T responds: Nothing is wrong. That is just the point. One person likes to eat mangoes with red peppers while another person loves to eat deer meat; someone else likes to eat the crispy baked skin of a roasted pig but others prefer to eat pigs' feet soaked in vinegar.

T: Next month, students, we will talk about our individual differences and similarities. So, if Bill likes to eat deer meat that is fine. And that is normal!

T: Raise your hand if you were born here in Hawai'i. If you are not sure, then tonight, go home and ask your mom or dad, or grandparents. Next month, we will learn about how important it is to accept differences among people. **Raise your hand now**: Anyone with brown eyes? Anyone with green or blue eyes? Who is right-handed? Who is left-handed? The most important thing to remember is that we need to accept, indeed, rejoice in all our differences. Good work class! (If they do not know if they are right-handed, ask them to stand still, feet together. Tell them to take 2 steps forward. Ask them: did you walk with your right foot first? If so, you are right-handed.)

Relate the Lesson to Previous Learning or Knowledge

Teacher continues the next day.

T: I prepared the list of Dolch Sight Words, as well as the special list of food words for all of you to practice. I even have all the special words on these flash cards. (**T** shows students the large flash cards.) You can also see the words on the **printed word lists, and on posters** all around the room. Remember that we have parent-teacher conferences in about six weeks and our Dolch Sight Words and these 50 special words will be listed. Your mom or dad (or someone from your family) will meet with me, and I will show that person the words you have learned.

State the Purpose of the Lesson

The teacher needs to teach the Dolch Sight Words to the First Graders, while preparing them for the next unit on diversity. The learning of sight words actually begins in Kindergarten with the PP and P words, followed by introducing them to the First Grade List. Some of the students will already know these words, while others will not. Students will be able to read the material in the Diversity Unit better, once they learn the Dolch Words.

Sight Words (High Frequency Words or Dolch Words)

Educator Dr. Edward William Dolch in the 1930s-1940s created the Dolch Word Lists; **they are the most frequently written words in popular children's books.** The master list of **220 'service words'** (such as who, what, why, when, and, the, to, it, is) in addition to some **95 most high frequency nouns** if learned (such as she, they, I, father, sister, school) means that 80% of the words written in typical children's literature and nearly 50% of words identified in adult books would allow children to advance in reading abilities at a rather spectacular pace.

First Grade Notes

In First Grade, **the teacher is wise to begin with the easier lists (PP and P)** so that students will know some of the words already, and not feel frustrated. The teacher believes that by introducing ethnic food names with the lists, this could have a lead-in to the next unit, on **diversity**.

Objective

Students will learn the basic sight words and many of the 50 special food words, as discussed in class, by the students. Then, students will have an introduction into the up-coming unit on ethnic diversity (Diversity Learning, 2020). **At the end of the lesson,** the teacher will be able to measure/observe that the learning has taken place either through pre-post testing, class discussion, work sheet completion, poster-making, role playing, and other such techniques, depending on the grade level and educational skills of the students.

All the Dolch words should be on word lists, separated by level. The teacher should place columns next to the words, so that parents helping their children at home can enter dates tested (at the top of columns) as to when their child attempted to correctly say the word. The teacher will need to see that the student read the word aloud correctly at least 5 times over a period of several days, to be assured that the child can read the word correctly and without hesitation.

There is another page for the 50 special food words. The teacher later may test each student individually. This testing takes about 5-15 minutes per student, and thus must be spread over a one-week period. The teacher repeats testing after six weeks right before the parent-teacher conferences are scheduled. The pre and posttest results will show everyone how many words each student has learned.

Teacher Instruction

Provide information by demonstration, explanation, modeling, and guided inquiry.

Teacher continues:

T: Class, I will hold up extra-large flash cards to that all of you can see the words. Remember that last week, we met in groups – the Robins, the Jays, the Blue Birds, and the Parrots. Well, now all of you together can see the flash card, say the word, then find it on your list, and check it off. I will demonstrate for you:

Teacher holds up the flash card, with the word 'It.'

T: (Aloud): 'It.'

Class says aloud: 'It.' Each student has been given a master list of all words, by level, in alphabetical order, on four sheets of paper. If the student can read the card at the 90% level of correctness they can proceed to the next higher level. (Notice that a capital upper-case letter begins each of the words. Or, the words might be all be in lower-case. But **do not** use all upper-case letters because that makes reading and learning these words much more difficult. Children need to see the 'tall' letters like t, l, f, b, the 'long' letters like g, p, q, and the 'regular' letters like e, n, o, to assist them in remembering these sight words.

T: Good, now find the word 'It' on your PP word list. Do you see the word? Oh, Betty has her finger on it, and Matt does too. Good. Okay, now put an X next to the word 'It' to show that you can find the word 'It.' Everyone – say the word 'It again.'

Class responds: 'It' (aloud). (**Notice the number of times the students see, hear, and say the word because it takes this repetition to learn the word. Then they recognize the word from the list.**

T: Excellent. I will now show you a flashcard with a special food word. It is from Bill.

Teacher holds up the card that says 'Deer.'

Bill smiles broadly. Students say aloud, 'Deer.' Class responds in unison, 'Deer.' (Students will locate the word 'Deer' on their list and mark it accordingly.) The teacher must be aware of homophones, in this case, Deer vs. Dear. It would be wise to have some basic discussion about homophones - words that sound the same, but spelled differently, and mean different things.

T: Note - The teacher must check for understanding and provide additional guidance, when and if needed. Students appear enthusiastic about learning their high frequency words as well as their special food words. They are now curious about the new "unit" on differences among groups of people, and individuals, which will follow soon.

Guided Practice

Allow opportunities for students to demonstrate their learning and knowledge, while the teacher carefully monitors the progress of each student – providing positive, prompt feedback. The teacher will need to use the flash cards appropriately, by ensuring that everyone can see the words, and helping those who do not yet know the words. **There should be no penalty for not knowing the words, just praise and rewards for learning any of them**.

Children generally need to see, say, hear, and write Dolch Sight Words at least 10 times or more, before really knowing them. The teacher can ask students to use their new word in a sentence both orally and in writing. By the teacher incorporating the special food words, students will feel good about their new words (because each student contributed to this special food list) and the teacher will recognize each student, when the teacher first introduces the new special words.

Additional Techniques

In about three days, students will have a chance to manipulate their own deck of sight word cards so that in a group of six or seven, they will work with each other, or a teacher's assistant if available, and read the words aloud, again practicing saying the words correctly. Also, the teacher may use special crossword puzzles or special work sheets using only Dolch words (sold online or in teacher-specialty shops) to reinforce the learning.

The teacher can place extra copies of the word lists on class bulletin boards, and provide them to parents at next month's parent-teacher conference. (Place each list in a colorful folder, which the students will be able to decorate and individualize: they can write their names with colored markers and draw a picture, too. Prepare the Dolch words (by level) on **color-coded 3" x 5" index cards:** for example, use blue for Pre-Primer level words, red for Primer level words, and green for First Grade words. (Education stores often carry these sight word cards.) Although there are Second and Third Grade Dolch sight words, and 1000 Dolch Words which are somewhat advanced,

students need to begin with the basic level.

The teacher can prepare the lists (using colored paper to assist in identifying the levels) into packets, give each student their own with some extra copies for a colorful bulletin board display and also to give parents at next month's parent-teacher conference.

Closure

Teach, review, recap, restate, re-teach, and reinforce the lesson to determine if each student has met the objective(s) of the lesson.

After six weeks and prior to the parent-teacher conference, the teacher will re-test the students individually, on all the PP – Third Grade Dolch Sight words, as well as the 50 special food words, and present the student scores at the conference. The teacher will continuously give students higher-level sight words to learn, with **the food words used as an introduction to the Diversity Unit**. Each student will advance, **individually,** so no one will be 'held back' from learning higher, more difficult sight words.

The teacher ends the class sessions by referring to the word lists. The teacher will ensure that those students who master the First Grade-level list take home the Second Grade-list. In all instances, students should first hear the word, understand the meaning, say it aloud and then use the word in a sentence verbally and in writing. Learning to read with fluency improves self- confidence and promotes positive self-image.

Independent Practice:

Teachers will encourage students to practice using the word lists at home. Parents are to ignore mistakes, and simply tell the child the correct answer. **Sight words are not to be 'sounded out.'** Remember that some students will learn words at a different pace than others. This is normal. And if they laugh at saying "PP" for a list, name it something else. Teachers can call it Lists A, B, C, or even Lists 1, 2, 3, 4, etc. The point is that students need to learn the words on the first (easier) list, prior to proceeding to the next, more difficult list. Reading is so gravely important, and a good First Grade teacher is essential to students, for them to progress, enjoy, indeed love reading!

Strategies

Please note that there is an interesting article, 'Diversity in the Classroom: A Checklist,' appeared recently (Diversity Learning, 2020; Matsumoto-Grah, 2002) and **included the following categories for teachers to use** as a review when determining if their classrooms, curriculum materials, teaching methodologies, and instructor – pupil behaviors were in accordance with accepted multicultural educational practice.

Introduction to the Diversity Unit

There is a short unit on acceptance of those students who look different (i.e., in **appearance**) from other students: skin color, eye and hair color, general physical characteristics, and gender. A month or so later, the follow-on unit explores specific instances of student differences (not immediately noticeable) such as handedness (left vs. right hand preference), skills and abilities, athleticism, national heritage, citizenship status, etc. This is to prevent any students from teasing or bullying one another (in or outside of class) while they develop a good self-image of themselves. Finally, all need to understand and accept each other.

T: Just as the foods are different in color, size, and taste, people are different in handedness, skin, hair and eye color, physical height, artistic, or sports abilities, to name just a few characteristics. The teacher should remind students that the "outside" of a person (like a book cover) does not necessarily show what the 'inside' is like.

The teacher could post photos of different children from different ethnic groups around the room in preparation for this lesson plan and also ask students to draw a picture of themselves, to place up on the classroom wall. Later, at the parent-teacher conferences, the teacher will ask students' parents to send in a recent photograph their children, for the classroom wall, as well.

Evidence of Diversity

Evidence of diversity instruction will include positive comments children make about their own ethnic heritage and other ethnic groups, in addition to comments made in class discussion. Moreover, stories about people of various cultures should be available from children's literature. The list of stories may be from the school librarian, the teacher's own peers, or self (Wellein, 1976). Once the teacher reads the selected story involving multicultural diversity aloud, the teacher should verbally ask the class stimulating questions.

I have used this lesson plan to teach sight words when teaching those in grades first – third. Students love adding their special 'food' words to the mix. One year, students illustrated their special 'food words' and I posted them on the classroom wall writing the name of the food or dish clearly below the drawing on 3" x 5" index cards. **It was a natural transition, then, to the unit on diversity,** because students loved to talk about their favorite foods, combined with their favorite storybook, music, movie, camping trip, and summer fun experience.

CH 22 Multicultural Education Impact

on Social Class

My Pearl of Wisdom: Types of Schools DO

Make a Difference

Education is simply the soul of a society as it passes

from one generation to another.

G.K. Chesterton

WHAT IS THE IMPACT of social class on the development and implementation of a school curriculum designed to mitigate prejudice and diverse immigrant isolationism? Can such mitigation be realistically achieved, why and how (Creating a multicultural environment, 2020; Yeros, 2021)?

World class social scientist Jean Anyon (2014), in *Radical possibilities*, discusses schools, and groups them into four categories: working-class, middle-class, affluent professional, and executive elite, and **based not only economic levels but on the kinds of work the parents do.** Most importantly, Anyon believes that all groups of schools allow students to be transformative. She explains her work as follows:

First Type

Teachers at Working Class schools fail to teach students their own backgrounds, their history of disagreement with the status quo, and attempts to gain economic parity with others. Students learn little about social information of their own situations. Teachers stress curriculum and the mechanics of behavior, rather than a true understanding of society. They do **not teach cultural information**, only skills and knowledge involving historical knowledge.

Second Type

Teachers at Middle Class schools do not instruct students on their history or historical disagreements. Students lack understanding on how many so-called middle-class career positions are changing and becoming more mechanical and structured. However, **students learn a great deal of facts and generalizations**. The problem is that students who work hard in school may not necessarily end up doing well in the job market. However, those who attend college may be exposed to alternate views of society.

Third Type

Teachers at Professionals Schools instruct students on **their own history** (the upper slice of society) and emphasize science, mathematics, and language arts. Teachers stress the active using of student ideas and concepts, so that they would be the **planners, organizers, and doers, while the working and middle-class students would be the followers.** Dr. Jean Anyon (2014) explains that students from professional schools learn about the inequities in society, the sources of conflicts, and later in college, take physical action by joining demonstrations, awareness sessions, and other kinds of social/conscious raising groups.

These young leaders become doctors, engineers, lawyers, teachers, politicians, and writers, which lead to power and economic freedom; they experience creative endeavors, and personal exploration. Anyon (2014) believes that many of these students learn class-consciousness, the importance of intellectual/academic achievement, and success.

Fourth Type

Teachers at Executive Elite schools teach concepts including social class, economic conflict, societal problems, and social irrationalities, according to Anyon (2014).

One distinguishing concept students learn in these particular schools (Executive Elite) is that it is extremely important to maintain privilege and economic power in order to enjoy the 'fruits' of striving: financial wealth, excellent schooling, luxuries, travel, i.e., the good life.

The **second distinguishing concept students learn** in this fourth type of schools is that to be 'on top,' to enjoy wealth and power, others must be 'below' them (Anyon, 2014).

> By tracing the root causes of the financial crisis, Anyon effectively demonstrates the concrete effects of economic decision-making on the education sector, revealing in particular the disastrous impacts of these policies on black and Latino communities. (p. 1)

> Expanding on her paradigm for combating educational injustice, Anyon discusses the Occupy Wall Street movement as a recent example of popular resistance. (p. 2)

Action for All Types of Schools

To develop and implement multicultural education within all types or groups of schools (to reduce prejudice and immigrant isolationism), **educators** will need to do as a beginning, the following:

1. Ask themselves in **what type of schools they teach**? Is it the First Type i.e., Working Class Schools, or the Second Type, i.e., Middle Class Schools? Perhaps they will discover that they are involved in the Third Type i.e., Professional Schools. (Perhaps the neighborhood is middle or upper class in terms of socio-economic status, that the school emphasizes language arts and mathematics, and that students are highly motivated to do well in their studies.) And finally, they might be educators at the Fourth Type, i.e., Executive Elite Schools serving the top 2% of the nation's students.

2. Determine **what types of students, teachers, and curriculum** exist in these schools. This will take time, because it is a process. Educators will need to meet, discuss, conduct assessments, and investigate, to find valid statistical information.

3. **Prepare a matrix (a separate one** for students, teachers, administrators, and

support personnel) to fully understand their school composition. For example, the following Table 1 is a sample; it includes identifying race/ethnicity, gender, racial backgrounds (Lynch, 2015, Yeros, 2021).

Table 1

Student Population by Grade, Gender, and Race

	Chinese	Japanese	Korean	Latino	White	Black	Total#
Gender	M / F	M / F	M / F	M / F	M / F	M / F	
Grade K	1 / 0	4 / 1	0 / 0	3 / 4	9 / 4	1 / 0	27
Grade 1	0 / 3	2 / 3	1 / 0	4 / 4	6 / 6	1 / 1	31
Total (Race)	4	10	1	15	25	3	58

Total Number of Students: 58
Gender, all grades: 32 males and 26 females
Table Concept: Noel (2000); Data (Wellein) are only examples and do not represent actual statistics.

Purpose

Teachers: you would do this sort of matrix to get **a realistic idea of the gender and race in your various grades in your school population.** Then, match the results of the matrix of students with the other groups (teachers, and then administrators.) Notice if there are any **out of sync (discrepancies)** shown on the matrix.

For example, if 18% of your students in grades K-3 are Japanese, and 70% of the teachers are Japanese, this is a discrepancy. For another **example,** if 10% of your teachers in grades K-3 are male, but the student population is 65% male, then this should be noted. For a third **example,** if 75% of your teachers are middle or upper class, and the majority of your students in grades K-3 are living below the poverty line, this is an important economic-cultural discrepancy.

Teachers - Questions to Ask

- Is the prejudice in your school **overt** (graffiti, gangs, fights, racial slurs common in school conversations, memorandums from administration to parents about bullying incidents, etc.)?

- Is the prejudice in your school **covert** (small groups of students or cliques of students who separate themselves through economic class, language including specific phrases, private messages on social media, etc. that are invisible or unknown thereby excluding those who they deem outsiders.?

- Can you define the economic, social, linguistic, and other types of groups in the community, as well as in the school, to include the parents, students, aides, teachers, and administrators?

- Can you hold several brainstorming sessions in all-teacher or all staff meeting, to discuss ideas on how to reduce prejudice and marginalized feelings among students and staff, as well as the parents and community?

Administrators may bring in specialized educators and speakers to assist the teachers and others in implementing some worthwhile ideas to use in the classrooms if you want to reduce prejudice and bias, and encourage multiculturalism to flourish.

Finally, Lynch (2015) discusses other interesting aspects of multicultural education, to include "content integrations, prejudice reduction, empowering school culture and social culture" p. 1). The subject of this chapter, *Multicultural education impact on social class* is massive, and ongoing (Yeros, 2021) and merely a glimpse, a peak into this subject area. Why not try a similar matrix for your school, today?

You can create this type of matrix in any organization. If you are in the military, you can better understand your unit knowing the 'composition' of the soldiers and leaders. If you are a business corporation, you can determine if your employees are culturally similar to the supervisors. Why not try this today!

CH 23 Campus Culture: University of Hawai'i at Mānoa, a Look Back

My Pearl of Wisdom: Time is Everything

You are a marvel. You are unique. In all the years that have passed,

there has never been another child like you.

Your legs, your arms, your clever fingers, the way you move.

You may become a Shakespeare, a Michelangelo, a Beethoven.

You have the capacity for anything.

Henry David Thoreau

THE UNIVERSITY COLLEGE culture, at the University of Hawai'i at Mānoa (UHM) campus was significantly diverse when I attended full-time from 1962-1966. U.S. Congress had just mandated statehood for Hawai'i in 1959, three years prior to my initial attendance. The territorial government of Hawai'i was taking its last gulps of air. The tentacles of statehood grew cautiously at first, then reached out, exploding with tremendous abandonment.

One must understand that this land grant public university reflected the islands' diverse cultures. Hawai'i then, and now, has no majority group, race, religion, color, ethnic heritage, or identity. Following is a description, by category, of what the university was like to me, in the early1960s, when the entire state had a population under 700,00 and UHM had slightly less than 9,000 students (1960 U.S. Census, 1961) who were part of the UHM system. Life at UHM was not a 'melting pot' to me but rather a vast, distinct mixture of cultures, ethnicities, and colors, each adding its own flavor to the total mix.

Rituals

The state (which included all public agencies such as the department of health, public schools and the university system) celebrated all federal and local holidays. This included May 1st (Lei Day in Hawai'i); King *Kamehameha* Day (in June, to honor the Hawaiian king who united all the Hawaiian Islands); Statehood Day in August (when Hawai'i became a state), and several other local holidays. I am proud that my mother, Trude Michelson Akau was elected to serve on the 1950 Hawai'i State Constitution and was one of the five main writers of that historic document used to obtain statehood in 1959!

If school remained in session during a special holiday, there would always be a one to two-hour event celebrating that occasion, with hula dancing, speeches from local dignitaries, lots of fresh-flower lei, and all students and faculty in attendance.

Almost all UHM students commuted as very little dormitory space was available on the Mānoa campus in comparison to 3,700 beds available decades later (University of Hawai'i at Mānoa, Catalog, 2021). Parking on campus was abundant, mostly free, with few 'assigned spaces.'

Stories

Children's books in Hawai'i were full of tales about little *menehunes*, leprechaun-like people. These mischievous, colorful creatures were usually humorous, and the star of short stories that demonstrated a saying, such as those found in 'Aesop's Tales.' There were also many Hawaiian legends, at first oral, and then written, about gods and goddesses of nature – earth, wind, fire, water, trees, volcanoes, sun, moon, and sea creatures such as sharks and turtles which were Hawai'i's favorites.

Characters from these stories (*menehunes,* performing miraculous acts of magic, and the gods and goddesses of nature) would be found replicated on elementary and secondary student file folders, pens, pencils, tablets, college posters, student services bulletin boards, t-shirts, and such. The state university (and later, its community colleges) also used similar motifs on its folders, book covers, and sold these items at the local bookstore.

Myths

UHM has as part of its logo, the rainbow. The football team for decades had been known as the 'Bows' or 'Rainbows' although in the 1970s the team became The Warriors (University of Hawai'i at Mānoa Athletics, 2021).

Personally, I like to believe that the many colors make-up a rainbow, which represent the diversity present on campus and in the state – all races, colors, ethnicities, sexual orientations, religions – people of all backgrounds, brought together on one main UHM campus, learning and working harmoniously together for a better Hawai'i. (No, I did not forget about the community colleges or the Hilo campus, but wait – I am mainly reminiscing here about UHM.)

There was a commonly known myth about the rainbow, and why there were so many colors making up this exquisite visual, which appears in the sky after a shower, or a heavy rain. This myth was referred to in the campus newspaper, in art course projects, and writing classes. "Rainbows . . . had magical powers long before football. . . . Hawaiian chiefs considered them sacred and used them as signs of a chief's presence. A rainbow hovering over a newborn child indicated that he was of a god-like rank" (University of Hawai'i at Mānoa Athletics, 2021, p. 1).

The university, located in Mānoa Valley, was a site often drenched with rain, followed by a lovely rainbow. According to legend, Hawaiians expected the warrior to display great strength, skill and a fighting spirit (p. 1). And the rainbow was a perfect symbol.

Rainbows were displayed in all sorts of drawings throughout the campus grounds. (Interestingly, years later, in the early 21st century, the rainbow became symbolic of the Lesbian-Gay-Bisexual-Transgender/Transsexual, Queer/Questioning (LGBTQ+) activist group for many people.)

Finally, the school colors of green and white represented "not only the richness of

Mānoa Valley, but also spiritual prosperity and success" (University of Hawai'i at Mānoa, Experience, 2021, p. 2) and the local *ti-* leaf plant, considered a symbol of good luck was ubiquitous all over the campus grounds.

Population

The university's Mānoa campus was rather small, with a population of some 8,650 students (1960 U.S. Census, 1961). Life moved slowly; there was no feeling of rushing anywhere, except to class. The H1 highway was non-existent. There were only one and two-lane roads leading into and out of Honolulu city.

Personal Values

The values my friends and I held clearly reflected our home and family values: honesty, friendliness, respect especially for those older, tolerance for others and their beliefs, racial harmony, and obedience. This was an era where in many areas of Honolulu, few locked the doors to their house and cars. That is why, when Vietnam War protesters held loud, raucous demonstrations on campus and in one incident, attempted to burn a ROTC building, students, faculty, and the general populace of Hawai'i were extremely shocked. I remember reading articles in the local newspapers where community leaders blamed 'outsiders' from the U.S. mainland meaning those Caucasians who came to Hawai'i, for the incident (G. Wellein, personal communication, June 3, 2005).

Heroes

Hawai'i supported Democrat presidents for many decades. (The exception is that although the state has been decidedly Democratic for decades, it elected Linda Lingle, the first Jewish female Republican and former Maui mayor as governor from December 2002-December 2010. That must have been a fluke!) President John F. Kennedy was Hawai'i's darling, winning Hawai'i and the rest of the nation in a landslide election. Therefore, it came as no surprise, that when **President Kennedy was assassinated in 1963**, he became more than an instant hero. The nation remembered those '1000 days of Kennedy,' but easily forgot the earlier heroism displayed by a Hawai'i based unit in

World War II, the most decorated unit for its size and length of service in the history of the U.S. military (Inouye, n.d.).

More than two decades previously, dozens of Hawai'i-born Japanese young men volunteered to join the 100th Battalion, 442nd Infantry Battalion (technically, the 442nd Regimental Combat Team or RCT), considered by most to be one of the most highest decorated U.S. Army units in World War II. Later, Hawai'i elected several politicians from this all-Hawai'i group (100th Infantry Battalion, 1399th Engineer Construction Battalion, Military Intelligence Service, and the 442nd RCT) known as the **Go For Broke** guys (Senator Inouye, n.d.)

Famous local heroes from that unit were U.S. Congressman **Spark M. Matsunaga** (whose name graces the Veterans Affairs building in Honolulu), and Senator **Daniel K. Inouye** (who chaired some of the most powerful committees in the U.S. Senate for decades). My two oldest sisters had the priviledge of having Maggie Inouye, Senator Inouye's first wife, as their teacher!

Other local heroes in that era were **Duke Kahanamoku** (a famous surfer and legendary competitive swimmer, a five-time Olympic medalist, whose visage is on U.S. postage stamps), and **Patsy Mink** who forced Congress to make funding of women's athletes at secondary and post-secondary schools a priority under Title IX (Stringer, 2018). Mink ran for the U.S. Congress and was the first woman of color elected. Interesting note: University of Chicago Law School (n.d.) accepted her as part of its Foreign Quota-Program, despite her Hawai'i birth!

Students

Students were diverse. My classmates in high school were full, part, or mixed local Chinese, Japanese, Hawaiian, Portuguese, Filipino, Korean, and Caucasian. They considered themselves Christian, Buddhist, Shintoists, Jewish, agnostics, or atheists, generally between the ages of 17-18, who entered colleges directly from high school. During my last college term in mid-1960s, new groups of students from Micronesia, American Samoa, Taiwan, China, and the U.S. Mainland were increasingly found on the campus. Then later, veterans aged 22-42 were more prevalent as well. **There was no majority** in terms of race, religion, or geographical centeredness at all.

Faculty

Faculty members were diverse as well. Many were local from Hawai'i, while others were from the U.S. mainland. Subsequently, some fell in love with the islands, and decided to remain here, and call Hawai'i 'home.' Again, there was no majority race, color, religion, ethnic group, or culture. (I married one of the UHM professors in 1963, a World War II veteran from Washington state – but that tale is best left for another time, as this second marriage, with two young boys, ended in divorce seven years later.)

Staff

One of the only staff members I recall is the secretary of the English Department, who 'commandeered' each sub-office, deciding who would see a particular person, when, why, how, and where. Because this middle age Japanese lady (a real gatekeeper) had the power and authority to make appointments for the department chairperson, she controlled total access to him. She also photocopied exams, answered the telephone, and did all her 'secretarial duties'!

Physical Surroundings

UHM is in Mānoa Valley, a lush, green picturesque area of the island of Oahu, where gentle island breezes and brief morning showers keep the shrubs and lawns emerald green. Because less than 9,000 students attended school in the 1960s, there was a lot of open space between buildings, and huge shower and monkey-pod trees graced the winding roads which snaked throughout the lovely campus.

East-West Center (EWC)

The EWC was brand new in 1962, and a noted architectural firm designed lovely gardens, and a large, free-forming pool, loaded with *Koi,* expensive Japanese carp. A tiny bridge, located at the middle of the pond was picture-perfect for many weddings held there, with the pond and bridge used as the centerpiece of the photographs (East-West Center, 2021). People mentioned in news articles that they felt at peace when they visited the East-West Center grounds.

> The impact of the EWC is far-reaching. More than 50,000 people have participated in EWC programs since 1960, including many who currently hold positions of leadership throughout the United States and the Asia Pacific. Alumni include heads of government, cabinet members, university and presidents, corporate and media leaders, educators and individuals prominent in the arts. (East-West Center, 2021, p. 3)

School Values

The values of the school culture were reflected in not only the special center's buildings and grounds, but in the rest of the school campus (University of Hawai'i at Mānoa, Experience, 2021). Students congregated to talk and socialize at the student center, while Thomas H. Hamilton Library and Gregg M. Sinclair Library (in honor of former UHM presidents) served as the place to study at all hours of the night and day. UHM was the fourth most diverse university in the US, according to the 2010 report of the Institutional Research Office (East-West Center, 2021). Approximate racial backgrounds of students were Caucasians, 25%, Japanese Americans, 23%, Filipino Americans, 8%, Chinese Americans, 7%, mixed race, 12%, and Pacific Islanders and others, the balance. (Some did not identify their race, so the numbers do not add up to 100.)

I dearly loved the campus; it felt safe, and secure, and like a second home. The university offered first-year and new students no formal introduction to college life; the atmosphere was basically laid-back and relaxed. There was no dominant race, religion, culture, color, belief-system, or any other group identification common to more than a small group of students – each group was a minority. In Hawaiian, a*loha* means hello and goodbye, and signifies a feeling of family, or *ohana*. That is how the university felt to me, nearly 55 years ago.

Progress?

I visited UHM campus recently and it was an overwhelming experience. Nearly 20,000 students, faculty, and staff, visit the grounds daily, and with only 5,000 parking stalls, only a small number of students, faculty, and staff can actually park on the campus. I never located a parking space the day of my visit, so that 'adventure' was not productive. However, my memories of UHM will always remain with me as some of the happiest times of my life.

CH 24 Role of Religion in Public School:

Guidelines

My Pearl of Wisdom: To Each, His (Her) Own

It is the mark of an educated mind to be able to entertain

a thought without accepting it.

Andre Gide

MY GUIDELINES as an educator, for including religion in any **public educational organization, school, curriculum, or activity** are to be absolutely certain that there should be **none at all**. This means that there should be no reference to any religion of any kind in public school, except for the **academic investigation of that religion**, for knowledge or academic sake. Indeed, there should be probably a section in a social studies course in high school to examine the major religions of the world. But no one religion should be singled out and shown preference. **I believe totally in the separation of church and state for the following three reasons:**
Legal, Practical, and Privacy Issues

First, legally, there is no one religion accepted by people in the United States. Our democratic government was founded on the premise (First Amendment to the U.S. Constitution adopted in 1791), that its **people would be free from religion and any sort of governmental directed or sponsored religious affiliation, entity – no matter how popular**. This means Americans have the right to believe in anything they want, such as a well-known religion (i.e., Catholicism or Episcopalian, ad nauseam) or decide not believe in anything at all (atheism). Or they be not sure about a particular belief i.e., agnosticism (not sure if there is a God). Or they might wish to believe in multiple gods and goddesses. Or they may be deists, who believe in God but also believe that while God created the universe, natural laws (based on science) determined what happens after that. And by law, Americans have the right to doubt or accept any religious tenant or spiritual belief. . .ad nauseum. Many people experience different feelings about religion, perhaps depending on how there were raised, or due to special events in their life (such as praying for help and then receiving it).

The local, state, and federal governments must remain totally separate from any religion. This means that for any public agency to support religion or any particular type of religion would be illegal and unethical. Note that the laws stipulate freedom **of** religion and freedom **from** religion. Teaching about religion is different from advocating a religion. I believe that **all major religions should be studied as an academic subject.** One may learn about the principles of or Buddhism, for example, but in an academic manner.

The Anti-Defamation League's article, *Religion in the public schools* (ADL, 2021) stated clearly, "the classroom will not purposely be used to advance religious views that may conflict with the private beliefs of the student and his or her family" (p. 1). The **U.S. Supreme Court** cases of *Edwards v. Aguillard* (1987), *Engel v. Vitale* (1962), *Santa Fe Independent School Dist. V. Doe* (2000), *Lemon v. Kurtzman* (1971), and *Lee v. Weisman* (1992) all support this viewpoint.

Secondly, regardless of practicality or popularity, even if there was a public school located in a geographical area of America where the populace seemed outwardly to support one particular religion, the laws of the land still must be obeyed. Local, township, city, and state laws (for all public agencies) as well as all federal policies and mandates. must remain **separate from all religions, no matter how popular the religion.**

The public agency (in this case, a school) cannot advocate a particular religion, and must in all instances, keep religion completely outside of school. Any issue as to whether to say a prayer before a school event, for example, would be moot. **(Perhaps the event's moderator could ask for a minute of silence instead of saying a prayer.)** School districts could list all religious holidays each school year for all religions and **allow all students to be absent on three holidays of their choosing**. (For example, perhaps a student who is Catholic might choose Good Friday, as one of the three special days.) This separation of church and state teaches a valuable lesson for students and teachers as well as community members.

Finally, religious preference is private and should remain so. While education must instill in its citizens the ability to compare, analyze, and evaluate religious beliefs, the right to be an agnostic, atheist or join a church, temple, or synagogue still remains strictly a matter between the parents and their minor children. And just for the sake of argument, if religion was allowed in a public school through a school prayer at the start of a graduation ceremony for example, **which religion would be used in that prayer?** Would the parents at a local school decide on that school's religious reference or would community members simply vote?

If the majority of students wanted to bring their own brand of religion into the school to use at a graduation ceremony, for example, would the minority group then just have to allow or accept this situation? What would this acceptance of only one religion (to use when celebrating holidays and special events) teach students, teachers, community members, and others, about the rights of majority vs. minority members of society?

In summary, church and state must remain separate for legal, practical, and privacy reasons.

Personal Notes

My personal experience is that religion played a mixed role in my elementary, secondary, and postsecondary experiences for **three reasons**.

First, I grew up in Honolulu, a city completely devoid of one major religion. There were Buddhists, Shintoists, Taoists, Mormons, Jews, Catholics, Protestants,

Episcopalians, Lutherans, Quakers, and Hindus, for example, although I do not recall any Muslims at that time. The various ethnic groups were all minorities, including Japanese and Caucasians. Many of the local population were racially mixed, with intermarriage quite common among the islanders, to include Caucasians who moved to Hawai'i as well as military personnel stationed here.

My mother, Trude Michelson Akau, for example, was a Russian Jew of Lithuanian origin who married a staunch Catholic of Hawaiian-Chinese-Portuguese descent. My mother's parents escaped the ferocious Pogroms in Eastern Europe, landing in New York with jewels sewn into the hems of their coats; he was a plumber and she, a *hausfrau.*

Trude, the youngest of five, grew up in a family where education was all-important, but **only** for the male children. She earned her own money waiting on tables to put herself through the Mary Wigman School in Dresden, East Germany, Sargent College, Boston University, and Harvard University Summer Schools.

I was four when my mother earned her masters from University of Hawai'i at Mānoa (UHM). I would sit outside the building she was taking classes in on a *lauhala* mat, complete with my picture books, cheese sandwiches, slices of apples in a waxed paper bag, a thermos of ice-cold water, and amuse myself while waiting for her to finish classes for the day.

Each afternoon, someone would cautiously approach me, inquiring, "Little girl, where is your mommy or daddy?" "In class," I would reply. "Are you afraid to be alone?" "Oh no," I said. "I have my books to read and lots to eat." I still have a newspaper clipping and photograph, showing me at age four, sitting there, happy as can be.

My father's mother immigrated from Portugal to the Big Island of Hawai'i as a 'picture bride,' and married my grandfather, of Hawaiian-Chinese descent sight unseen as was the custom in those days. My father was quite an intelligent boy, even as a youngster, so his parents sent him at a tender age to St. Louis School in Kaimuki, Oahu, a private Roman-Catholic all-boys college preparatory institution known for its rigor and discipline.

In the mid to late 1930s my mother and father met at UHM and the rest (complete with eight children) is history. I was the youngest of six surviving children. The first pregnancy resulted in twins, one of which was stillborn; after three successful pregnancies, the fourth died and then came my sweet sister. This was in the 1930s – 1940s when modern medicine was at its infancy and penicillin discovered yet unavailable in Hawaii.) My father got his Bachelors and Masters in Chemistry; my mother got her Master's in Education – all at UHM.

I will save the rest of the story for another time, except to tell you that when I was an infant, my father, a staunch Catholic surreptitiously had his Parrish priest baptize me a Catholic. My mother and I never knew this until I reached adulthood! Then as an older adult, I participated in my own Lutheran church confirmation.

I never saw a Black i.e., African-American person until I was 11 years old, although I saw hundreds of very dark Hawaiians, Filipinos, and Micronesians at a very young age. My father was Hawaiian, and obviously brown. I did not know about Latinos or Europeans until I was in high school. I was 12 when I watched my first television show and ate a restaurant meal for the first time. We grew up drinking powdered milk and eating powdered eggs packaged for World War II, and I never tasted the 'real McCoy' until I was a teenager!

I later attended religious youth groups – Catholic, Protestant, Lutheran, Jewish – wait for it – because **I moved to the group with the cutest boys!** I took classes in Hebrew (I think I learned more Yiddish) but I gained not an iota of Hebrew – I was a *chutzpah* (shamelessly bold), and when the Paul Newman student look-a-like called me a *yutz* (cluelessly annoying and foolish) I politely informed the Rabbi that my busy high school schedule did not permit any further language classes. Those were the days! **Statehood in 1959 Changed Everything.**

The second reason that religion played a mixed role in my early life was that

I attended the UHM Elementary and High Schools (Laboratory), part of the College of Education, and UHM later. These 'public' schools really changed around 2001-2003 (Essoyan, 2003). But in the 1950s, I distinctly recall studying Hawai'i's major religions academically in fifth grade, and later, took an Introduction to Religion course in college. (Thank you, Dr. Mitsuo Aoki – deceased in 2010, a revered theologian, minister, professor, and founder of the UHM Religion Department!) I found that course to be a fascinating adventure.

Dr. Aoki asked us to compare the major tenants of each religion, with reference to death, life, sin, freedom of will, God or other potent beings, and so forth. We never began or ended any college pep rallies, assemblies, or speaker events with a prayer, unless it was a Hawaiian chant or *Oli*, because no could figure out from which religion the prayer would stem. That is the beauty of all religions in Hawai'i – they are all 'minority' religions.

This fabulous college professor (Dr. Aoki) spent several weeks on each religion in his course, taking my classmates and me to **that religion's main, and sometimes only, church or temple on Oahu**, and examining its history. We learned about the religion statistically (how many members lived in Hawai'i compared to the rest of the world, how many new members could be expected to join each year), and how they addressed their God. We found out who were the important saints or persons associated with that God and religion, what the followers believed in, which holidays were celebrated and why, what was their view of the afterlife, how they treat sin, redemption and so forth.

I remember visiting a Shinto Shrine, Buddhist Temple, Mormon, Catholic, and Protestant churches, a new Jewish synagogue, and finally, a special Hawaiian house where a Hawaiian *kahuna* lived (a term for local priest or priestesses although some mainlanders referred to them as witch-doctors, a terribly derogatory term). It was a wonderful learning experience, and one that stressed understanding and tolerance.

My K-12th Grade School Experiences

Every morning from kindergarten through senior year of high school, we said the

Pledge of Allegiance by putting our right hand over our heart, stood at our desks, faced the American flag attached to a long pole in the corner of the classroom, and recited it, first without the 'under God' words – then later when these words were added in 1954. No one objected to the additional words at all. We students considered leading the recitation an honor. It never occurred to me that anyone would say a prayer, because students at the school represented so many religious beliefs that it would have been impossible to select one belief over another. Our Hawaiian flag flew a bit under our American one in each classroom. Many times in class, we sang our state song, '*Hawai'i Ponoi*' in Hawaiian, following our Pledge of Allegiance and 'The Star Spangled Banner.'

In eighth or ninth grade social studies, we once again studied Hawai'i's religions, but this time, it included all major ones such as the Muslim faith. The unit, Exploring Hawai'i's Heritage or something similar was wonderful; we learned the history of Hawai'i, including what happened when the Caucasian explorers in 1778 arrived, that is, Captain Cook and his crew. Cook died in February 14, 1779 (Villiers, 2021) but not before he and his shipmates brought measles, chicken pox, whooping cough, colds, flu, venereal disease, and other illness to the islands and succeeded in decimating over 30% of the population within just a few short years.

Final Reason

The third reason religion played such a mixed role in my young life was that whenever we had a school assembly, we began or ended the event singing our state song, '*Hawai'i Ponoi*' in English and Hawaiian. **Thus, the school did not practice prayer at all**. For major events (think of the opening night of a special fair, the completion of the construction of a new wing to the school, a new principal introduced on parent-teacher conference night), a Hawaiian *Kahuna* or priest would come to bless the event, new building or principal, by chanting in Hawaiian (an *oli*), sprinkling Hawaiian rock salt around, and bringing fragrant *maile* (sacred) lei to the event. Sometimes, a Protestant minister or Catholic priest would follow, but that was not too often.

I asked my mother once, as a young, very curious teenager, to what religion we 'belonged.' She told me that when I became an adult (at age 18), I could decide for myself. But she did not feel that she or my father should make that decision for any of us six youngsters.

Unbelievably, when my mother lay dying at Kaiser Hospital of lung cancer in the late 1970s our family called upon a *Kahuna* to pray for her, followed by a **Rabbi** and later a **Catholic Priest,** and the medical staff was simply astounded. We reassured them saying that we wanted to cover all the bases! Please realize that the ancient Hawaiians held beliefs like those held by the ancient Greeks when it came to their Gods and Goddesses, and how they viewed the gods and demi-gods of fire, water, earth, sun, stars, wind, volcano, and so forth.

Today in 2021 and for the past many years, the city and county of the various islands (Maui, Oahu, the Big Island, Kauai, etc.) will have a 'ribbon cutting ceremony' to signal the start of various civic and sporting events, projects, and other important occasions. This usually requires fragrant *Maile* lei (flown in from the Big Island or even Cooke Islands) to be presented to all officials present, and untying or cutting several strands of *Maile* lei by a minister or priest who says a prayer first, to spread good luck to all. As to what sort of religion this is – I have no idea. Many believe you can be spiritual, moral, honest, kind, virtuous, loving, sincere, respectful, and good, without identifying with a particular religion, or if you want to, without praying in a particular house of God. Others believe that there is only one true God and one true religion. And that is fine, too. And people may change their minds and attitudes about organized religion (or any belief) anytime throughout their lives. In this chapter, I am simply recalling my personal experiences involving religion.

Personal Note About My Children

Later I sent my own three children to religious schools in Guam and Hawaii – (Lutheran – Our Savior Lutheran, Catholic – Father Duenas and Bishop Baumgartner, Christian non-denominational – Mid-Pacific Institute), and even one grandson to Born-Again Christian – *E' Makaala School.* Another grandson and several nephews attended

Kamehameha Schools, a wonderful private, non-denominational Protestant school for part-Hawaiian youngsters. In many schools, they attended chapel daily, read the Bible, and listened to hundreds of sermons and biblical stories. That was fine! They thrived in all schools.

So, I truly value private religious schools. Their approach to character development is superior, their school rules based on good old fashion common sense superb (there are consequences for poor choices leading to even poorer results), and exceptional academic rigor, so that there are few or no gaps in educational processes. For example, no one should learn their multiplication times table for the 6s-12s, without first learning their times tables 1-5s. No one should learn long division without thoroughly knowing short division. No one should read a fifth-grade novel without first reading lower grade level material fast, effortlessly, and joyfully.

As an experienced teacher of all levels and abilities, I can assure you that **it is these very gaps in academic knowledge that account for so many learning difficulties in children**. How can one possibly be happy learning about World War II without understanding the causes of World War I? How can a teacher assign the students in his or her class to read a newspaper article identified at an eighth grade reading level if many of the students test at below sixth grade reading level on teacher-made or standardized tests?

Clearly, public school teachers are excellent as well. In fact, many of them are simply terrific! **The difference is that private schools can choose who they want as their students whereas public schools cannot.** The government's efforts are aimed towards promotion for all, meaning that unless public-school students have terrible disciplinary problems which cannot be controlled, or students have been absent for several months, most children are promoted to the next higher grade, ready or not. Of course, some enter SPED or English as a Second Language programs, too. Public schools accommodate students of all academic levels, as well as those gifted and talented youngsters, and the mentally and physically challenged, also. This is a real blessing for many parents who are desperate for help with their children. Private schools usually cannot make those accommodations.

In addition, parents can choose to be active participants in their children's public school educational endeavors – or not. Nothing much will happen if they do not attend teacher requested parent conferences, forget to sign permission slips, or provide clean clothing for their youngsters. But I digress!

Religion – the advocating of one particular religion, has no place in the modern public education world. The American Civil Liberties Union (ACLU, 2021) in *Religion and public schools* discusses the past U.S. Supreme Court decisions. This separation of religion from 'state' is a fact that should not be in dispute, supported by numerous laws and policies on the local and state levels. Elizabeth Sciupac and Philip Schwadel (2019) wrote

> Religion in public schools has long been a controversial issue. The U.S. Supreme Court ruled in 1962 that teachers and administrators cannot lead prayers in public schools, and a decision in 2000 barred school districts from sponsoring student-led prayers at football games. At the same time, **the court has held that students retain a First Amendment right to the free exercise of religion and may voluntarily pray before, during and after school.**

> About four-in-ten teens who attend public schools say they commonly (either "often" or "sometimes") see other students praying before sporting events at school. This includes about half of teenage public schoolers who live in the South, where students are more likely than those in other regions to witness and partake in various religious expressions at school. (p. 1)

However, I feel strongly that **it is fine if you want to learn about a religion for academic reasons in all public schools in America.** But advocating one religion over another, proselytizing, or promoting a particular religion? No. A big, unqualified NO.

CH 25 Department Head Memos

on

Gender, Age, Disability, Racism, & Inclusion

My Pearl of Wisdom: Accept the Challenges

The only thing necessary for the triumph of evil

is for good men to do nothing.

Edmund Burke

FIRST SCENARIO: An Example of an English Chair Memorandum on gender and other kinds of bias at YoYo College, encouraging respectful behavior.
Memorandum to Faculty and Staff:

Recently, I have noticed a most distressing problem that may have legal implications for some of you. Therefore, I feel compelled to bring the issue to your collective attention, in an effort to be totally proactive, and nip the problem in the bud before it blossoms into something quite ugly. I want to thank you in advance for your kindest cooperation in this delicate matter. Please read carefully the following points:

1. Some of you have been faculty members for over 15 years, and have diligently worked to keep your students stimulated, learning, and excited about English issues.

2. A few of you have just recently started working here, and I know that I speak for the entire department when I say that we all welcome you with open arms, and thank you for joining us in educating our college students in the craft of English.

3. However, it has come to my attention recently that there appears to be conflict,

at times of a personal nature, between some of the tenured faculty members and the newly hired ones. The basic issue may be about **change**, which always causes a reaction in most people (Athuraliya, 2020). Nevertheless, when I hear of people being disrespectful and rude to others, I must state unequivocally that such behavior will not be permitted. Furthermore, the idea of comments that are solely **gender-biased** (or any issues dealing with color, race, age, disability, religion, national origin, sexual orientation, or ethnicity, etc.) raises the possibility of individuals filing formal grievances, or worse, lawsuits.

Let me make myself quite clear, as a leader of this English Department (ADL, Handbook, 2020). The Dean of Arts and Sciences and I will **not tolerate rude, negative behavior, or disrespectful comments in the future, by or to anyone.** Our great university has a reputation to uphold, and trust (Our View, 2020) among all parties (faculty, staff, administration, students, board of directors) must be maintained. I am positive you will all cooperate, and demonstrate this trust in your future behavior, conversations, written comments, and reports.

John M. Doe
Dean, English Department, Academic Affairs
Henry Smith,
Dean, College of Arts and Sciences

Copies Furnished:
Attorney Ray Brown, School Counsel
Emily Johnson, Provost

Insist on yourself; never imitate

Ralph Waldo Emerson

SECOND SCENARIO— **An Example of Memo of Inclusion to a Hispanic Students Group, from Director of Student Life, at Bonkers College:**

The following is **an administrator's response to a student group's petition** to establish a Mexican-Language group based on common interests (Walsh, 2020). The goal here is to not only acknowledge the signed request but to provide for an expanded, inclusive format, providing for many diverse student interests.

Memorandum to Students:

Thank you for allowing me to respond to your request for this great institution to establish a Mexican Language group on campus. I want to acknowledge your request, and stipulate the following facts and concerns:

1. Latino students are the "most segregated group in the nation's public schools . . . segregated by race and poverty . . . and [sometimes] linguistic segregation" (Schultz, 2005, p. 11). We do not wish for this to occur here.

2. We recognize that minority students make up a significant number of students at this school. **Hispanics consist of 13% of the student population.** We also have Puerto Rican students, as well as those from South and North America. In addition, there are Asians and African-Americans at this school, too.

3. Although minority students may seek assimilation, separation, acculturation, or marginality, **research shows that it is integration** that works the best, in most educational settings (Lankster, 2020).

4. Hispanics may consist of Mexicans, Puerto Ricans, Cubans, and those from Central and South America. However, there are **significant differences in the dialects among these groups** (ADL, Handbook, 2020) as well as socio-economic issues and cultural beliefs.

Considering these findings, I propose that your group may want to form a

Hispanic student social club, open **to all students of all races and cultural backgrounds** interested in Hispanic language, food, culture, and other kinds of issues (Rabinowitz et al., 2019). This school is prepared give any registered social group $500 in 'seed money' to help with costs for membership, announcements and flyers, in celebration of whatever interests the group once this Hispanic student social club is established. Such a club would thus be open to those of any religion, sexual orientation, race, national origin, color, language, interest, *ad nauseam*. We ask that you **include as many students as possible.**

Instead of establishing a social club for just one group (i.e., Mexicans only), the **Hispanic Club would be open to all individuals.** I look forward to hearing from you soon.

Harry B. Goode
Director of Student Life

Copies Furnished:
Jimmy Lee, Attorney for Bonkers College
Anna Miller, Dean, Student Life
Walden Enough, Provost

CH 26 Bilingual Education

is Important

My Pearl of Wisdom: I Hear the Silence

Words are, of course, the most powerful drug used by mankind.

Rudyard Kipling

BILINGUAL EDUCATION should remain as an option available to those students who speak little English or none at all, so that they can eventually be mainstreamed into academic classrooms (Cardoza, 2014). Initially, however, except for non-academic subjects such as art, music, physical education, home-making, wood shop, or band, most if not all students who speak little or no English desperately need assistance if they are going to understand any academic subject in school at all. Educators view Bilingual education as a program designed for students of all grades who have limited English-speaking ability who need special classes or services to do well in school.

It would be best if the Bilingual program uses the native language of the students for instruction, at least initially. Certainly, some school districts hire teachers who are bilingual in Spanish, Japanese, Chinese, or other languages, depending on the students' needs. **Unfortunately, due to many factors, a large number of school districts use only English in bilingual classrooms**. Usually, it takes students about two years for conversational English skills to develop at a minimum, and at least five years to allow students to learn academic content area subjects in English (Bilingual education, 2021).

The Hawai'i Department of Education's World Languages Program consists of instruction in 11 languages including American Sign Language, Chinese (Cantonese and

Mandarin), French, German, Hawaiian, Ilokano, Japanese, Korean, Russian, Samoan, or Spanish, at the elementary and secondary school levels (Hawai'i State Department of Education, Multilingualism, 2020).

A Brief Historical Review

A quick review of bilingual education highlights may put things in better perspective.

In 1839, the state of Ohio was the first to adopt an actual bilingual education law, allowing German-English teaching based on parental request (Goldenberg & Wagner, 2015; History of bilingual education, n.d.). Louisiana followed with an identical law allowing French and English in 1847; New Mexico passed the same law for Spanish and English in 1890. By the end of the 1800s, many laws in various states allowed for languages such as Polish, Cherokee, Italian, and Norwegian.

World War I dampened America's bilingual language efforts, but **in 1968, the Bilingual Education Act passed**, which provided federal funding to local school districts. The U.S. Supreme Court in Lau v. Nichols in the early 1970s required public schools to be proactive in the bilingual area, swiftly followed by the Equal Educational Opportunity Act of 1974 (Goldenberg & Wagner, 2015).

Limited English Proficiency (LEP) Students

Schools with students who are identified as having Limited English Proficiency **(LEP)** are required to help these particular individuals. School specialists use these identified three-steps: **research-based programs**, which experts in the field find educationally justified; **sufficient number of resources**, including personnel, training, and materials to implement a sound program; and **procedures and standards to assess the program** and modify it if it does not meet the students' needs (Arizona State University Online, 2021; Goldenberg & Wagner, 2015).

In Goldenberg and Wagner's (2015) lengthy article on Bilingual Education, and Orhan Agirdag's *The long-term effects* (2014), the 11 million students from non-English speaking homes, including students who speak at least one of 400 different languages other than English, account for nearly one in every six school-age youngsters. Approximately 3.2 million LEP students in 1994-1995 attended public schools, representing 7% of total elementary and secondary school enrollments.

Unfortunately, the majority of LEP children were **not** involved in bilingual education courses instructed by certified teacher who spoke their native language. By fall, 2017, over 10% of students in public school (all grades) were English Language Learners (NCES, 2020). Finally, growing support for bilingual education is

> evident at the state level . . . [as] nine states have approved the 'Seal of Biliteracy" which appears on the high school graduation diplomas of students who have studied and attained proficiency in two languages. Hawai'i's Department of Education established the Hawaiian Language Immersion Program in 1987, and Montana's governor recently signed into law a bill that will fund Native American language immersion programs in public school. (Goldenberg & Wagner, 2015, p. 8)

The Education Resources Information Center (**ERIC**), an online digital library of education research and information sponsored by the Institute of Education Sciences of the U.S. Department of Education Digest, presents an interesting article by well-known educator and respected author Stephen Krashen (1997) probing the question *Why bilingual education?* To summarize, the best bilingual programs allow for English as a Second Language (ESL) **instruction** with basic information in the students' native language and sheltered **subject matter** teaching, with material always in the children's native (first) language. Gradually, as children learn more English, they transition out of their native language classes. Research, explains Krashen, supports the importance of bilingual instruction.

Research in the 2010s and 2020s continue to support that premise: start young learners in their native language first, and transition them to English more each year. They need a solid base in English to learn subject matter information, such as in science, history, and government.

The problem might be economics as well as semantics. Is language immersion different from bilingual? Does the public understand that many studies support bilingual classes? Krashen (1997) **states that another problem is that there are few good textbooks in both the first and second language of the children.** These types of books are costly. Finally, Krashen ends the article by stating that LEP students usually have poor access to books in the home.

Many articles discuss how schools should educate bilingual students (Agirdag, 2014; Cardoza, 2014; Goldenberg & Wagner, 2015). I wrote this chapter on bilingual education merely as an introduction to this arena. I believe that bilingual education programs clearly continue to be extremely important to the LEP and ESL youngsters in our public schools (Arizona State University Online, 2021).

Stanford University Professor Claude Goldenberg and Kirstin Wagner (2015), in *Congress: Bilingualism is not a handicap*, discuss our nation's 11 million students who are from non-English-speaking backgrounds in

https://www.aft.org/ae/fall2015/goldenberg_wagner

> The United States has great linguistic resources we are not only failing to use— our schools are actually quashing them, if only through neglect. More than 11 million of the country's 50 million public school students speak at least one of 400 different languages other than English at home. Yet only a negligible fraction of these students are in programs that simultaneously nurture their home language while using it to help them acquire English and also to help English-speaking students acquire a second language. (p. 3)

Goldenberg and Wagner (2015) raise issues about bilingual instruction, monolingual Americans, and promoting multi-lingual students as is common in most European countries. They cite many articles, such as Umansky and Reardon (2014); Ruben Rumbaut (2014); and Orhan Agirdag (2014). Another resource on bilingualism is the *History of the Hawaiian language immersion program* (Hawai'i State Department of Education, 2020) in their exquisitely informative article.

In the *National evaluation of Title III Implementation: Report on state and local implementation* (U.S. Department of Education, 2012) the report stipulates that when we consider there are nearly 40 million elementary grade students in the United States, this means that no more than 3% of U.S. students in the elementary grades are receiving some form of bilingual education. (See also Snyder & Dillow, 2012, Table 2).

Other sources of information worth reading include Kavitha Cardoza's (2014) *Demand for dual-language programs in D.C. public schools skyrockets* https://wamu.org/story/14/ 12/12/demand_for_dual_language_programs_in_dc_public_schools_skyrockets/. Michele Silbey (2014) offers more in *World-Wise northwest parents drive demand for bilingual preschools* found on this website https://seattleglobalist.com/2014/09/02/bilingual-preschool-seattle-french-spanish-language/28747. Rob Manning (2018, December 13) also provides good information in *Oregon educators prioritize bilingual education* https://www.wallowa.com/news/oregon-educators-prioritize-bilingual-education/article_4cf3d6ff-ec8e-5aba-9a47-f37de2629d90.html. Finally, Héctor Tobar (2016, November 15) offers his perspective in *The Spanish lesson I never got in school*: https://www.nytimes.com/2016/11/15/opinion/the-spanish-lesson-i-never-got-at-school.html

Personal Note

I taught bilingual students at almost all grade levels in Guam and Hawai'i, for decades. **I believe that there is not one way to teach.** It depends on the students and their abilities to learn a new language as well as their reading, writing, and speaking abilities when they first enter an American school. An eclectic method, combining many different learning approaches might work best. The teacher must discover how the student learns best: verbally, visually, orally, aurally, tactically, kinesthetically, by writing, or by using a combination of methods.

One learning theory is that your brain learns best when several senses are stimulated simultaneously. The senses of vision, hearing, touch, smell, and taste may be combined in the learning process. For example, in a language arts class, the teacher may begin by first reading about cutting a large, ripe, yellow lemon. She then shows the students a huge yellow lemon, cuts the lemon in half, and squeezes the juice into a clear container. She shows the class and explains that she has already cut up several lemons into small pieces and each student will get one. Students are to first smell the lemon, then taste it with the tip of their tongue, think about what it feels like, what the aroma is similar to, and write about their experience using all their senses.

My mother, Trude M. Akau used this exact process listed above, to extract excellent writing in her fifth-grade students, many of them bilingual. The 'lemon exercise' was documented in her book, *Kalihi Kids Can Communicate* a compilation of several years' worth of her students' best writings.

I have witnessed students struggling in school when they do not know English at all, and their teachers know absolutely no words in their 'native' language. The classroom materials are only in English. I believe that if bilingual students had a textbook of their own language with English translation, learning English would be faster and easier. Good illustrations would also help, showing the illustration and the word meaning in both languages, similar to a 'Pictionary.' Otherwise, the bilingual student faces years of sitting in the classroom, not understanding a word the teacher says. What a waste of time and energy. What frustration!

CH 27 Song on Benefits of

Bilingual Education

My Pearl of Wisdom: Sing Softly But Strongly

It is not that I'm so smart. But I stay with the questions much longer.

Albert Einstein

(Oh, Give Me a School: To the tune of Home, Home On The Range…)
Oh, give me a school
Where the kids are no fools
Where the teach-ers love com-ing each day
Where seldom is heard
A dis-cou-ra-ging word
'Cause par-ents help stu-dents to say

(REFRAIN) OH----
Eng-lish, we will all learn
'Cause America and the world simply turns
On well spoken words
English/Spanish is heard
Our Path can be bright, so we'll earn

The high school – such growth
Some twelve hun-dred, please note
Each grade coun-selor eager to please
The VP works hard too
With the Prin-ci-pal, true
In this ur-ban town, vo-tings the key!

(REFRAIN) OH----

Eng-lish, we will all learn

'Cause America and the world simply turns

On well spoken words

English/Spanish is heard

Our Path can be bright, so we'll earn

Community support is the key

Parents, teach-ers, let's see

What the shop owners say and will do

Ath-le-tics are great

Football champs see their fate

Having scho-lar-ships and money too

(REFRAIN) OH----

Eng-lish, we will all learn

'Cause America and the world simply turns

On well spoken words

English/Spanish is heard

Our Path can be bright, so we'll earn

Po-li-ti-cians please note

If you do want our vote

Pay good mon-ey for teach-ers and schools

Keep class sizes small

We also will call

For di-gi-tal learn-ing as tools

(REFRAIN) OH----

Eng-lish, we will all learn

'Cause America and the world simply turns

On well spoken words

English/Spanish is heard

Our Path can be bright, so we'll earn

<u>Sing this song, to the tune of</u>

HOME, HOME ON THE RANGE

And think of a high school in Texas, or California, or New York, or Florida or…...

by Marsha Wellein,

on Bilingualism & Importance of Learning English

PART B: CHANGE IS THE ONLY CONSTANT

My Pearl of Wisdom: *Mea Culpa*

Here's to the crazy ones. The misfits.

The rebels. The troublemakers.

The round pegs in the square holes.

The ones who see things differently.

They're not fond of rules.

And they have no respect for the status quo.

You can quote them, disagree with them, glorify

or vilify them.

About the only thing you can't do is ignore them.

Because they change things.

They push the human race forward.

And while some may see them as the crazy ones,

we see genius.

Because the people who are crazy enough

to think they can change the world,

are the ones who do. **Apple Inc.**

CH 28 Leading and Managing Change:

Diverse Frames, 9RRC, Army Reserve, Hawai'i

My Pearl of Wisdom: Clearly, it is Time Now

The one unchangeable certainty is that nothing is unchangeable or certain.

John F. Kennedy

STRUCTURAL, HUMAN RESOURCES, political, and cultural organizational **frames explain** how the 9th Regional Readiness Command (9RRC) Education Office **(EO)** at Fort Shafter, in Honolulu, Hawai'i functioned. Most people naturally consider the Army Reserve to be a good example of an extremely structured organization. This chapter will explain the organization of the Army Reserve Education Center at 9th Regional Readiness Command (9RRC) and how it can be improved. **This and the next eight chapters are based on my time working as a civilian with the 9RRC Education Center from 2001-2012, and will explain how this military reserve organization worked during that time period,** although it could just as well have been a business or school.

The following eight chapters will examine 9RRC frames (i.e., lenses) as to how the Headquarters in St Louis and 9RRC interact with the education office, while the education office make important changes. Observers note that there are formal relationships, of course, present in all military units; the EO is no exception. As education director at 9RRC (2001 through 2012), I saw the formal and informal relationship between the 'frames,' that is, the lenses present.

Let me be clear. The Army changes when it wants to change, or it is forced to change, and changes slowly unless there is a true emergency, such as September 11, 2001

– the terrorist attack on the twin towers in New York. In 2020, the Army Reserve selected a woman, Lieutenant General Jody Daniels, as the first female to lead that service branch (Kelly, 2020). Less than 25% of admirals and generals are women in the armed services, with women comprising only 16% of active-duty soldiers in 2017. In June 2020, General Charles Brown became the first Black American Chief of Staff in the Air Force. So, change albeit slowly, is happening (Cancian, 2019). **In defense of national security of course,** the U.S. military is the deadliest force in the world, and can make changes swiftly when needed.

Education Office

The EO **(again, I am writing this information based on my employment from 2001-2012)** has established clear goals, with specialized roles for its office staff who work together as a highly productive team. Professionally printed organizational flow charts wall-mounted document the formal relationships within the command. As the education director (2001-2012) working for the Human Resource (HR) Office (one civilian and one military reserve officer) I noticed that both HR employees treated all other employees as valued members of the division. Change affects various segments of this Army Reserve organization differently, depending on several factors. However, I saw change as an opportunity to perform more effectively and efficiently.

Following is a brief review of the 15 U.S. Army Reserve Regional Readiness Commands (RRCs) in general, and 9RRC in particular, to better understand the structural, human resources, political, and cultural organizational frames (Bolman & Deal, 2003; Wellein, 2010, 2021) at the 9RRC EO in Honolulu.

Background

9RRC (later changed to 9th Mission Support Command or 9MSC in April, 2008) is one of 15 such Army Reserve commands located throughout the U.S., Puerto Rico, Asia, Pacific, and Europe. These 15 commands are responsible for hundreds of Army Reserve companies and units of enlisted soldiers, warrant and commissioned officers, according to Mr. Jaybee Obusan, Human Resource Officer for 9RRC (personal communication, June 10, 2005). As of 2020, there were approximately 199,500 Army Reserve personnel in uniform, 343,500 Army National Guard personnel, 194,800 Army civilian 'full-time equivalents,' and half a million family members and contractors (Cancian, 2020).

Specifically, these Troop Program Unit soldiers **worldwide** – commonly referred to as TPUs or Army Reserve soldiers who drill at their respective reserve centers one weekend a month – are supported by some 14,500 Active-duty Guard and Reserve (AGR). These AGRs are the fulltime military staff who basically control and manage the reserve centers, in addition to 4,660 Individually Mobilized Augmentees (IMAs) assigned special functions who take their guidance from Human Resource Command, St. Louis. These numbers fluctuate by over 10,000 during any given period (Cancian, 2019, 2020; Wellein, 2010).

An additional 113,700 Individual Ready Reserve (IRR) soldiers have already served in the Army Reserve, retired, or left the service, but the Army Reserve may recall them in time of war. (The Army maintains the legal authority to call up IRR soldiers and has done so to fight in the Iraq war.)

RRC Information

Each RRC has an Education Office (EO) that provides programs and services to the Army Reserve personnel attached to that command, following the guidelines stipulated in Army Regulation 621-5, Army Continuing Education System (ACES), (Defense Activity for Non-traditional Education Support [DANTES] External, 2006; Department of the Army, 2006, 2020; Wellein, 2021). Voluntary education and credentialing (COOL) websites for military personnel include:

http://www.militaryonesource.mil/voluntary-education;

https://www.goarmy.com/benefits/education-benefits.html

https://www.military.com/education/money-for-school/reserve-tuition-assistance.html

https://myarmybenefits.us.army.mil/Benefit-Library/Federal-Benefits/Tuition-

Assistance-(TA)?serv=125

As well as the following service specific websites:

Army: https://www.armyignited.com/app/

Marine Corps: https://www.usmcu.edu/cdet

Navy: https://www.navycollege.navy.mil

Air Force: https://www.airforce/com/education

Coast Guard: https://www.mycg.uscg.mil/Officer/Professional-Resources/

Article/245 4246/education-assistance/

Army education programs and services (Wellein, 2010, 2021) include professional academic guidance and counseling, vocational or academic undergraduate and graduate degrees, licensure, and certificate planning, Veterans Affairs educational entitlement guidance and information, military and civilian test programs. Additional services include ROTC and other scholarships, grants, and student loan information, credit recognition for military service schools, training, and experience, independent and external degree programs, and Basic Skills reading and math review courses (Department of the Army, 2019; U.S. Army Reserve, 2021).

Reserve Tuition Assistance

The largest education program, Army Reserve Tuition Assistance (TA) worldwide, cost $35 million for fiscal year 2004, a whopping 65% increase from the previous year (Ali, 2005; Wellein, 2010). Specifically, statistics for the TA program document phenomenal usage and growth of TA usage. In fiscal year 2004, the Army Reserve increased the amount of TA funding for one semester hour from $187.50 to $250 per semester hour or equivalent, to include all mandatory fees, to a maximum of $4,500 per fiscal year. This monetary increase may have helped the use of TA to explode. In FY 2005, TA cost over $39 million and by FY2010, TA cost over $174 million.

In 2020-2021, the same basic funding guidance remained in effect for Army reservists, that is, tuition covered up to $250 per semester hour (Delpech, 2021). There are no TA programs for Navy and Marine reservists in the 21st century (Absher, 2020).

TA Statistics

As more soldiers became aware of the expanding TA program, and as more education directors expanded their staff, additional soldiers began using the program. Data on degree completion may not be accurate due to frequent troop movement, especially during the Middle East Wars (in Iraq and Afghanistan).

> Initially, Army reserve funded TA program worldwide at $4.8 million but between FY 2001 and FY 2007, the Army Reserve estimates spending over $174 million for 53,806 reservists who took 434,751 academic, vocational, and technical courses during the seven year-period. (K. Brown, personal communication, December 6, 2008)

Personnel

The 2005 Army Continuing Education Services Directory (ACES) for Army Reserve commands in 2005 shows the following information:

> A. Headquarters, Department of Army, at Human Resources Command (HRC), St Louis, MO provides general oversight for the Army Reserve, including education programs, services, and funds.

> B. Ms. Jonell Calloway, Director of Army Reserve Education, is located at HRC, St. Louis, with a staff of three contractors. Her deputy, Mr. Abdul Ali, works in Atlanta, GA with the U.S. Army Reserve Command, and has a staff of two contractors. Ms. Calloway and Mr. Ali are in daily communication through e-mail, facsimile, and telephone, and many times attend the same workshops, symposiums, and meetings, so this difference in work place location does not appear to pose a problem.

15 Regional Readiness Commands (RRCs)

Each RRC with **one** Army civilian director and several contractors covers a large, geographical area **but** the Minnesota-based RRC has three DACs, while the reserve soldiers in Europe seek education services through the **active-duty Army** education center in Giessen, Germany. Note that later, Army Reserve divided commands into seven geographic and over 24 functional (Commands, n.d.), but the following information was correct at the time I worked for the Army Reserve (2001-2012):

9RRC on the island of Oahu, manages approximately **3,700** Army Reserve soldiers in Alaska, Hawai'i; Commonwealth of the Northern Marianas (Saipan, Rota, and Tinian); U.S. Territories of Guam and American Samoa; Japan, and Korea. This command covers **52%** of the world's surface.

The Army manages soldiers in other geographic areas as follows:

9th Troop Support Command (TSC), Fort Totten, NY: **2,000** troops.

63rd RRC, Los Alamitos, CA: **10,500** troops in CA, NV, and AZ. This is a very large geographical area!

65th RRC, Fort Buchanan, PR: **5,400** troops in PR, the Caribbean, and the U.S. Virgin Islands. Again, it is a very large, geographical area involving a commonwealth of the U.S. and a U.S. Territory.

70th RRC, Fort Lewis, Seattle, WA: **8,800 troops** in WA, OR, and ID.

77th RRC, Fort Belvoir, NJ: **8,200** troops.

81st RRC, Birmingham, AL: **41,000** troops in KY, TN, NC, SC, MS, AL, GA, and FL. Need I say more? This is a tremendous area, involving eight states and tens of thousands of troops.

88th RRC, Fort McCoy, MN: **25,000** troops in MN, WI, MI, IL, IN, and OH. Oh my gosh! This is the only center with three directors.

89RRC, Wichita, KS: **13,000** troops in KS, NE, IA, and MO.

90th RRC, Little Rock, AR: **17,800** troops in AR, OK, NM, TX, and LA.

94th RRC, Fort Devens, MA**: 5,800** troops in MA, CT, RI, NH, ME, and VT.

96th RRC, Salt Lake City, UT: **7,800** troops in UT, CO, WY, MT, ND, and SD.

99RRC, Oakdale, PA: **21,400** troops in PA, WV, DE, VA, MD, and DC. Look at these numbers!

Headquarters U.S. Army Special Operations Command, Fort Bragg, NC: **10,000** Army Reserve special operations soldiers **located in 27 states**. Really? 27 states?

7th Army Command, Germany, Giessen, Germany: **1,300** troops spread throughout the **various European countries.**

Army Reserve Readiness Training Command (ARRTC-Active-Duty) split between Fort McCoy, GA, and Milwaukee, WI: **12,000** Chaplain Candidates, Nurses, Individual Mobilization Augmentees, and other specially designated personnel.

In comparison, **active-duty** Army education offices are located throughout

America and in many foreign countries. For example, in Hawai'i, Fort Shafter Education Office has about 3,000 soldiers with one director, two clerical staff, and two counselors. Schofield Barracks also in Hawai'i with 16,000 troops has one director, one assistant director, and seven or more guidance counselors, three test examiners, one librarian, five clerical people, and a Basic Skills Instructor. Clearly, Army Reserve education offices are severely undermanned (by federal employees); contract workers do not fill in 'the gaps' in knowledge, experience, and historical memory.

Table 2

Army Reserve Soldiers' Education Levels in 2005 (Worldwide)

Education level	Number reporting	Percentage
Less than a high school diploma	1,741	
High school graduate	112,366	
1-60 semester hours of college	7,153	
Associate degree	9,690	
Baccalaureate degree	12,780	
Professional Nursing Diploma	894	
Graduate (Masters) degree	2,265	
Reported levels	156,070	74.5%
Unreported levels	48,930	35.5%

(Ali, 2005, p. 8)

Summary

The large number of reserve soldiers in the category of 'unknown' education levels might be the result of the **many recent unit mobilizations** (over 140,000 soldiers) to Iraq and elsewhere, because unit administrators and sometimes soldiers themselves may be slow in updating their records. In any case, dealing with this large number of soldiers who have unidentified education levels causes problems when professional educators need to develop voluntary, appropriate adult education programs and may not have sufficient funds to do so.

The following eight chapters explain exactly how the reserve education office

made important changes at 9RRC in Hawai'i (2001-2012), even while it operated within a strict military structure. I saw this structure while working as an education officer with the active- duty Army from 1983-2000; however, this organizational framework is also evident in many schools, colleges, nonprofit, and for-profit agencies.

CH 29 Changes: Structural Frame, 9RRC, Army Reserve

My Pearl of Wisdom: Understand This!

First, have a definite, clear practical ideal; a goal, an objective.

Second, have the necessary means to achieve your ends;

wisdom, money, materials, and methods.

Third, adjust all your means to that end.

Aristotle

THE STRUCTURAL FRAMES (Bolman & Deal, 2003) evident at the 9RRC Education Office (EO) (Department of the Army, 2006; Wellein, 2021) had the following characteristics when I worked there (2001-2012): **the Army specifies specific goals, office personnel have specialized roles, and formal relationships are present.** An examination of each feature provides for better understanding of the external structures present. Any changes made must happen within the confines of these structures. I have written these next few chapters because I want the reader to understand how each school, military unit, business entity, private nonprofit, and for-profit agencies operates at its most fundamental level.

9RRC Education Office and Staff - Goals

The Army stipulates the goals of the education office in writing – to provide educational programs, services, assistance, and funding for 9RRC Army Reserve soldiers and Active-Duty Army Soldiers (Department of the Army, 2006; U.S. Army Reserve, 2021; Wellein, 2010). Approximately 50% of the 9RRC's soldiers lived and drilled on

Oahu, with the remainder located on various islands throughout the Pacific and Asia. Therefore, the education office personnel made excellent use of e-mail, facsimile and digital sender, scanner equipment, and telephone service, to provide soldiers with the latest information, although Oahu-based soldiers and family members visited the education office whenever they wished.

Office Personnel's Roles

The education personnel have specialized roles. **Education Technician I** spent the majority of the time processing Tuition Assistance (TA) requests. Processing includes checking and correcting tuition and fee costs, course titles, and number of credit hours.

Education Technician II processed college and university invoices received from about 75 different institutions located throughout the Pacific and Asia, including many of the western states. Also, universities often had extended campuses such as University of Maryland in Korea and Japan, and offer online courses worldwide (DANTES, External, 2006; Wellein, 2010). Wayland Baptist University with headquarters in Texas, for example, offered degree programs in Aiea, Hawai'i and Anchorage, Alaska, while University of Oklahoma had extended campuses in Japan, Korea, Hawai'i, Guam, and Europe. Tuition and fees may change yearly. The Education Technician II also solved TA problems that the Education Technician I could not handle.

The **Education Specialist** was the overall office manager and distributed work projects to the other two contractors, as well as to herself (Judy Champaco). The Education Specialist must not only understand how to do all the required administrative tasks but also train the other contractors on their own duties as well. She then reviewed all work assigned and served as the Education Officer's assistant. Mrs. Champaco was superbly efficient and professional!

The Education Specialist usually scheduled unit and special briefings which the Education Officer delivered (on and off island), prepared the preliminary travel reservations to include air, hotel, and car rental, boxed up dozens of flyers, pamphlets, and brochures for use at these important briefings, and was the main point of contact for problems which the Education Technician I and II could not solve. The Education Specialist also helped the Education Officer order information flyers, pamphlets, and brochures about various educational subjects and then sent them to soldiers and their family members throughout the command.

Educational Regional Directors

The Director of Education, Human Resource Command (HRC), in St. Louis changed all the Education Officers' job titles to **Army Reserve Regional Director of Education** (ARRDOE). This title change reflected and emphasized the fact that each RRC was now responsible to manage and direct educational programs and services for an entire region of the United States or an overseas area (Ali, 2005). These regional directors of education served as visionary leaders as well as financially accountable officers.

Education Director, 9RRC in Particular

At 9RRC, as the ARRDOE (and I preferred the title of Regional Director), I managed almost $1 million in funding (Department of Army, 2006). In addition, I provided all professional counseling, prepared budget requests for each current fiscal year and five-years-in-the-future (for TA and program operations), designed efficient needs assessments (formal and informal), prepared and gave unit briefings, interviewed, selected, and trained Basic Skills instructors for those courses on Oahu and in American Samoa. (This Basic Skills program in mathematics and reading was **the only one offered in any U.S. Army Reserve** command.)

More Tasks

I also marketed, interviewed, and recommended participants for the **Veterans Affairs (VA) Work Study Program**, a special VA entitlement/benefit for those Army reservists who were using their VA GI Bill while attending school at the three-quarter level or more. VA paid the entire cost for such reservists to do clerical work at a VA hospital, VA center, or even a military education office. I requested and received approval for this VA Work Study Program at 9RRC and **this was the only reserve command to have it.**

At 9RRC, I established and maintained a loan library at all nine reserve centers, publicized the reserve college scholarship program (to include convening the ROTC Scholarship Review and Selection Board to numerically rank all packets submitted), reviewed and signed all TA requests (an average of $600,000+ worth a year). I also planned/participated in education and job fairs with the Army retention office personnel and other armed service branches' education directors in our region of the world throughout the year, attended professional conferences and symposiums several times a year (and sometimes spoke there), and advised the command on all matters relating to education. This was in addition to providing individual professional counseling to military personnel and their family members.

Cooperation – Share Responsibilities

It is important to note that despite the duties and responsibilities listed for each education staff member, all worked together as a team, so that when one person was absent, another assumed some of the absent person's duties. Many of these duties I undertook were an expansion and extension of the Army Regulation (Department of the Army, 2006) requirements.

If I could not brief a unit on very rare occasions, the Education Specialist prepared and delivered the talk instead. If the Education Technician I could not process all the TA requests one week because of a sudden increase in requests, then anyone on the staff was able to help. If a soldier or family member needed assistance, all staff members were available. There were, of course exceptions: contractors could not provide professional counseling, obligate government funds for travel, supplies, or equipment, sign TA forms, or use the government credit card. Nevertheless, the education office members worked cooperatively together as a high-performing team in all other areas.

Formal Relationships Present

In addition to the education office establishing specific goals and personnel holding specialized roles, **there were formal relationships present** (Bolman & Deal, 2003; Wellein, 2021). Contractors worked under non-personal services contracts after submitting bids in response to solicitations posted on the Army Civilian Personnel Office website by the Contracting Office, Fort Shafter, Hawai'i. This process began with the 9RRC Education Officer writing a Statement of Work for each contract, specifying duties and responsibilities, deadlines to meet, etc. (Wellein, 2010). **The other education offices in the Army Reserve worldwide only used the centralized contract.**

Contracts

During my employment, I was the only education officer to **write my own contracts for my office** because under the Centralized Contract, the private company hiring **contractors paid wages too low for Hawai'i** and despite many requests, would not increase their rate of pay. Contractors had to document 60 or more hours of college credit on the job application. Hawai'i's extraordinary high cost of living made it unrealistic to expect proficient, skilled contractors to work for such devastatingly low wages; **at least** $20-$22 an hour might be sufficient to start, but the private contractor would not pay above $10 per hour.

Working in coordination with the Contracting Office, I wrote the job requirements, reviewed the bids that applicants submitted with their accompanying resumes, and selected the best contractors. I was lucky. All three I hired were professional and one (Judy Champaco, the education specialist) remained with our office indefinitely. I accomplished many projects because Mrs. Champaco, a most capable individual, first worked with me at the Fort Shafter Army Education Center, and then transferred over to again be a contractor with me while I was at 9RRC. (She remained until I retired 31 December, 2012; she is still a contractor at 9RRC in 2021.) However, several contractors were reservists, later activated and thus left.

These wonderful contractors made the difference in making our education office responsive to the various needs of the soldiers. AR 621-5 establishes formal authority for all education offices, worldwide for all reserve and active-duty soldiers. However, without some common sense used in hiring office staff under the right contract, the constant turnover of personnel would have been disastrous for all.

CH 30 Changes: Human Resources Frame, 9RRC, Army Reserve

My Pearl of Wisdom: Checks & Balances are Best

If you know the enemy and know yourself

you need not fear the results of a hundred battles.

Sun Tzu

THE HUMAN RESOURCE OFFICE (HRO) was one of eight 9RRC headquarters divisions, including Logistics, Information Management, Budget and Finance, Security, Engineering, Training, and Intelligence when I worked there from 2001 through 2012. All division chiefs have their own staff. The deputy director of the command group rates all division chiefs with the one-star commanding general serving as their senior rater.

Organizational Control:

The 9RRC operates under an enormous number of federal regulations, policies, standard operating procedures, and letters of instruction (Department of the Army, 2006) that stipulate responsibilities and duties, as is commonly found in any massive bureaucracy. Strict adherence to these rules and regulations as well as those instituted by the command is expected (Cancian, 2019).

Funding

However, HRC Headquarters in St. Louis, MO., almost **totally funded all education offices, including the 9RRC** (Ali, 2005). This meant that HRC provided specific program policies and procedures and control of the education program funding was outside all RRCs' grasp. The program was thus regulated by HRC, but implemented at the local RRC level. The importance of this financial tight rope cannot be over stressed. The local command was accustomed to having stringent command and control over all its programs. **However, fully 100% of the funds for each Education Office (EO) worldwide (like much of the funds for Drug and Alcohol, and Family Readiness programs) could not be controlled, absorbed, directed, or redirected by the local command.** This was an actual **check and balance system.**

Thus, during my employment, I managed, directed, and controlled the 9RRC command's education program supervised generally by the 9RRC's Human Resource Officer (referred to as G -1) who rated me annually. Reserve education personnel felt great stress unfortunately, when we were given an extremely short deadline or suspense for requested information that always originated from higher headquarters – either 9RRC or HRC, in St. Louis. But we tried to always work as a team, to benefit soldiers and the family members.

Issue

This duet of sorts – with the education office allocation such as Operating Funds for travel, equipment, supplies, training, contract costs, and Tuition Assistance (TA) safe from encroachment by 9RRC division chiefs – was not without **problems,** of course. On the one hand, the 9RRC Human Resource Officer understood that the education funds were sacrosanct and outside the long reach of the command. On the other hand, a few of the 9RRC division chiefs at times tended to forget this fact, especially when funding became an issue, particularly at the **end** of the fiscal year. HRC in St. Louis was not required to provide the 9RRC EO a specific amount yearly for operations and TA; thus the amount of funding changed from year to year.

Human Resources Frame

The Human Resource frame mentioned in *Reframing Organizations* (Bolman & Deal, 2003) was also present within the Army Reserve military organization. However, the Hawai'i command emphasized the feeling of *ohana*, 'family' in Hawaiian. Individual employees were people with their own needs and feelings, prejudices, skills, and limitations, and managers needed to find a method to 'get the job done' while simultaneously ensuring that the workers felt good about what they are doing. This feeling was especially true within HRO, at 9RRC.

Best Practices

So, while the Army organizational structure most definitely provided a clear framework for the 9RRC EO (Wellein, 2021), the HRO full-time civilian manager, a command sergeant major reservist one weekend a month (together with his military colonel counterpart who was also a drilling reservist) tried to keep each individual worker satisfied. How did they manage to accomplish this? G1 Jaybee Obusan and Colonel Marcia Andrews were an extraordinary team. In the past, they held a monthly potluck luncheon celebrating all those who had birthdays that month (and there were always a few out of 40+ workers on Oahu).

Unfortunately, both Mr. Obusan and Colonel Andrews became severely overburdened with the constant mobilization of hundreds of Army Reserve soldiers, together with seven key staff members who rotated out of the HR Office and departed from Hawai'i. Thus, regular potluck lunches ended.

More

Nevertheless, Jaybee Obusan and Marcia Andrews still held welcome and farewell luncheons for those on their staff arriving or departing. They also publicly recognized high achieving employees through certificates or awards. However, most importantly, both recognized (and told us in fact) that their program managers i.e., Drug and Alcohol – Joanne Shimasaki, Family Readiness – Kim Goffer, and Education (yours truly) – were all highly competent professionals who knew their duties and responsibilities and consistently demonstrated high performance. I loved working for these two!

Mr. Obusan and his colonel (Andrews) graciously allowed these three program managers to do their job rather than micromanage them as so many other division chiefs tended to do (with their own staff). They did not feel threatened because these program managers were assertive and competent in specialized fields; indeed, both directors of the HRO division (civilian and his military officer counterpart) seemed to welcome these traits! They refrained from criticizing unduly, and instead, showed joint support for innovative programs and plans. They questioned, sought further clarification and details, and most importantly, defended these program managers when others questioned their abilities, ideas, or endeavors.

Although both G1 Obusan and Colonel Andrews reminded everyone in the division about certain rules and policies, they remained open to new ideas, suggestions to improve procedures, and innovative methods of getting difficult jobs done. Both remained cheerful, positive, reacting quickly to difficult situations needing immediate responses; both could quote the applicable Army regulations by number and section accurately, from memory, even under duress.

It was directly due to the unending support, indeed protection of these two individuals (Obusan and Andrews) who fostered the phenomenal growth of the TA, Basic Skills, and many other education programs, with Jonell Calloway providing generous funding from HRC in St. Louis. This is truly leadership at its best!

CH 31 Changes: Political Frame,

9RRC, Army Reserve

My Pearl of Wisdom: Know Your History

The two most important days in your life are the day you are born

and the day you find out why.

Mark Twain

THIS EDUCATION OFFICE (EO), during my employment from 2001-2012, also dealt with the ever-present political aspects of the Army Reserve. These political aspects include the "Realistic process of making decisions and allocating resources in a context of scarcity and divergent interests. This view puts politics at the heart of decision making" (Bolman & Deal, 2003, p. 185). 9RRC appears to have all the key elements of a political 'animal' even though it is part of the Department of Defense. Features include "setting of agendas, sorting through the political tension, networking, building coalitions or groups, and negotiating" (Bolman & Deal, 2003, p. 182).

The Army Reserve in the Pacific and Asia is an organization of diverse individuals and interest groups, a political entity with unique values, beliefs, information, and interests (Wellein, 2021).

Conflicts

The differences begin with the purpose and the number of people in each division, identifying their goals and objectives, and how they will arrive at consensus, or make decisions. Differences continue when reviewing the various divisions' budgets, how many years each of the division heads has been the leader, and how much power these division heads can acquire. Although a one-star brigadier general commanded the 9RRC, each division chief constantly jockeyed for power, which can stem from any of the following eight areas (Bolman & Deal, 2003):

1. Formal titles, grades, positions, sometimes referred to as positional or legitimate power.

2. Information and expertise sources of power; those who have the data and know desirable information; some may not have a formal title or rank but are experts.

3. Control of rewards, for example the ability to deliver money or jobs.

4. Coercive power, the ability to interfere, punish, block actions or constrain.

5. Networks or alliances as a source of power; groups or associates with which one seems to be affiliated.

6. Control and access to certain agendas; not just meeting but program agendas, or future plans.

7. Control of certain meanings and symbols (to include the acceptance of myths, beliefs, values).

8. Personal power i.e., charismatic personality, energy, demonstrated speaking skills, etc. (p. 194)

9RRC Information

At the 9RRC EO, my supervisor/rater was the HRO G-1 Director, Mr. Jaybee Obusan, a reserve command sergeant major one weekend a month, together with Colonel Marcia Andrews, the reserve officer, also one weekend a month. However, Mr. Obusan received communication about me from Ms. Jonell Calloway, Director of Army Reserve Education (worldwide) in St. Louis. This Missouri-based Human Resource Command (HRC) then distributed education program funds to all reserve command budget offices, including 9RRC. So, Mr. Obusan did not operate in a vacuum. (I learned that this type of arrangement was not uncommon. The supervisor rates an employee even though much of the job's directions and guidance were from higher headquarters.)

I was most grateful to Director of Army Reserve Education, Jonell Calloway for her continuous support, for if she had not intervened on many occasions, this story would have turned out quite differently. I am positive that if she were not a lady of great persistence, the Basic Skills program, VA Work Study Program, the common area computer initiative, and the rapidly expanding TA program would have languished (Wellein, 2010, 2021).

Education Program Growth, 9RRC

Specifically, the following education office "timeline" illustrates program growth, made possible with Ms. Calloway's determination, grit, and appropriate financial allocations:

2001 – Two contractors were present at 9RRC in July 2001 when HRO (Mr. Obusan) first hired me. Army Reserve in St Louis budgeted **TA** at 9RRC for **under $110** thousand with an **operating budget of $40 thousand** for supplies, furniture, equipment, and travel. There was no actual (physical) education office except for a single desk placed together with ten or more others (i.e., other employees working on programs unrelated to education) in a large open room. There were no file cabinets or bookcases for education materials, and the entire group shared a solitary printer. I held the rank of GS11, a lower rank than that held by the 9RRC Director of Drug and Alcohol, as well as the Director of Family Readiness programs.

2002 – Three contractors were present; one was the test examiner (TE). I authorized $450 thousand for TA, with an operating budget of about $55 thousand. Mr. Obusan had plans to move the education section to another building and agreed to promote me to GS12 (as requested by Ms. Calloway, in MO) equal in rank to the two other female program managers under G1.

2003 – The tremendously successful testing program, due to lack of physical space (i.e., a dedicated room), unfortunately ended. I authorized almost $780 thousand for TA, with an operating budget of $60 thousand, which was the key in program development and expansion.

G-1 moved Education to another building. I purchased new office furniture, such as, desks, file cabinets, top-to-the-line automation equipment, heavy-duty printers, and shredders. HRC (Jonell Calloway) in St. Louis recognized me as the best Army Reserve

Education Services Officer of the Year (2003); the Commanding General of 9RRC publicly presented me the award at a ceremony attended by many 9RRC full-time staff and soldiers. Ms. Calloway poured huge amounts of money into education programs at 15 reserve centers around the world and 9RRC greatly benefited from these funds. (Anyone who says money does not count does not understand reality!)

2004 – Three contractors, (two now on **special non-personal service contracts which I wrote)** worked on TA, totaling almost $675 thousand even though the Army mobilized over 30% of the reserve soldiers; we enjoyed an operating budget of $75 thousand.

2005 – All three contractors, now **on non-personal service contracts** (which I wrote), worked on TA, which totaled over $770 thousand even though the Army mobilized over 35% of the reserve soldiers; we enjoyed an operating budget of $217 thousand, almost three times the previous year's amount. The increased funding for all reserve centers, worldwide, led to greater program expansion that provided **enormous increases in program visibility** at all Reserve Centers (Army Reserve, 2019). Increased funding had a tremendous impact on recruitment of new soldiers, retention of those already in reserve units, and readiness of the force. Formal and informal survey results demonstrated these facts (A. Ali, personal communication, February 3, 2005).

From 2005-2012, the education program at 9RRC and indeed, at all RRCs, continued to expand and flourish due to increased funding and greater publicity. The Navy and Marine reservists were not offered tuition assistance (Cancian, 2020), so the Army Reserve and Army National Guard authorities were delighted to attract recruits (away from those service branches) and welcome them into their inviting arms.

Summary

Young men and women continued to enlist in the Army Reserve across America – mainly to obtain funds for vocational, technical, or academic school (J. Calloway, personal communication, February 3, 2005). HRC in St. Louis sent ever-increasing funds to 9RRC, which helped increase the visibility of the program (U.S. Army Reserve, 2021;

Wellein, 2010, 2021). Thus, politically, the Education Office became a recognized entity due to the marked increase in funding, staff, and program services. **Fully 15% of all 9RRC Reserve Soldiers were involved in school, either working on a degree or a certificate. Regional readiness commands usually had 10% or less of its troops attend school** (Ali, 2005).

I provided excellent marketing and publicity through newspaper articles, flyers, and appearing regularly on a Honolulu radio talk show (1080 AM, Community Bulletin Board). Our office received acknowledgment for good program management from Ms. Calloway, in St. Louis, and the 9RRC commanding general subsequently awarded me a plaque and certificate in recognition. (I cannot emphasize enough that these accomplishments were a result of teamwork within the education office.) **Politically**, the 9RRC education program, initially ignored by a few of the division chiefs, was on sound footing by 2005. It was indeed a win for all.

CH 32 Changes: Cultural Frame, 9RRC,

Army Reserve

My Pearl of Wisdom: *C'est La Vie*

The day the soldiers stop bringing you their problems

is the day you stopped leading them.

They have either lost confidence that you can help them or

concluded that you do not care.

Either case is a failure of leadership.

Colin Powell

THE CULTURAL FRAME or lens is the fourth aspect of investigation involving 'Change.' 9RRC has some exacting, specific attributes, which follow this cultural definition: Culture is an expression of the "interwoven pattern of beliefs, values, practices, and artifacts that defines for members who they are and how they are to do things" (Bolman & Deal, 2003, p. 243). **Culture, it seems, is both a process and a product;** one can commonly refer to Culture (Merriam-Webster, n.d.) as the way things are accomplished (at that agency or organization). The following chapter discusses my perspective on military culture from the years I was employed with the Army Reserve from 2001-2012.

Note on the Military Culture Frame

All military institutions have their own culture. For example, 9RRC has two symbols, which they recreated using specially ordered mosaic tiles and placed them on

186

the tiled floors at the two major entrances to its headquarters building. (The tiles plus labor are rumored to cost over $10 thousand.) Visitors can see these two logos as they enter or depart this building; these same logos are on almost all power point presentations, special letterhead paper, and all marketing posters.

Military culture forbids rudeness; it will not tolerate someone raising his or her voice in anger, especially to a superior. Military culture dictates that one physically rises when a senior officer (a Major and above) enters the office (gender and age are **not** relevant) Any important e-mails sent to those outside of the command's chain of authority must always have a copy sent to one's supervisor, too.

The military expects everyone to be punctual, always; if anyone is late for a meeting, that individual is expected to telephone the chairperson immediately (prior to the start time of that meeting) with a valid explanation.

More on Military Culture

Military culture also requires that **information flows downward, based on rank**, i.e. following the chain of command (Cherry, 2020). For example, if a colonel requests a report from a major, then the major will often assign a captain to do it. The captain would then complete the requested report and send it back to the major. The major, after approving it, would then send it to his colonel with a copy provided electronically to the lieutenant colonel (Cherry, 2020).

Sometimes, information moves upward, but again, **only through the chain of command**, which means that the lower-ranked individual contacts the next higher-ranked individual, without jumping over anyone. If a captain, for example, wants to let the battalion commander, usually a lieutenant colonel, know about a project, plan, or event, that captain would first notify the major, who would contact the lieutenant colonel, who would then in turn, contact the colonel. (Now what does this chain of command process tell you about lack of flexibility in the Army?)

Individuals should photocopy every important document, and later save these papers using a special Army file system. Company clerks maintain these files for a minimum of two years. (Civilians may be shocked to learn that the number of years files must be maintained is actually specified in the regulations dealing with that particular agency.) For example, test results must be maintained for a minimum of five years (Wellein, 2010, 2021) as per Army Regulation 621-5, Army Continuing Education System (ACES).

The military codifies all procedures in Standard Operating Procedures (SOPs) for any function, for example, the Military Test Program, Civilian Test program, TA Requests and Authorization, and so forth. The command requires that historical reports be filed yearly (Department of the Army, 2006).

9RRC places huge importance on accurate, regular reports, and this is part of the military culture. So are myths, vision, values, importance of reputation, hard work, rituals, and ceremony. (However, there is insufficient time to examine all these other areas of culture in this particular chapter. Stay tuned!)

CH 33 Changes: Command Group

9RRC, Army Reserve

My Pearl of Wisdom: Changes are Difficult to Accept

With guns you can kill terrorists, with education you can kill terrorism.

Malala Yousafzai

EMPLOYEES VIEW CHANGE differently at 9RRC, depending on their position assignment (Bolman & Deal, 2003). Again, I write this chapter based on my work there from 2001-2012. **The first group facing change consists of command group members** (mainly the deputy commander, military attorney, and commanding general) who truly understand that change is constant. Special staff members who advise the commanding general, such as the inspector general, surgeon, chaplain, public affairs officer, command sergeant major, and chief of staff are also command advisors.

The **war in Iraq** has changed the Reserve, worldwide. **The question facing all reserve soldiers is not if they must go to war but when** (J. Obusan, personal communication, June 15, 2005). In August 2021, President Joe Biden pulled all American troops out of Afghanistan. However, there remains many 'hot spots' all over the world: North Korea, China, Ukraine, Horn of Africa – indeed over a dozen. So, U.S. military units constantly face deployment overseas.

Nearly 40% of all reserve soldiers at 9RRC have deployed, or are returning from, or preparing for a deployment in the Middle East, Mr. Obusan explained. **Clearly, the pace or tempo of these deployments is increasing, causing a greater number of complex and costly changes.** The command group is doing its best to cope with these unexpected changes. However, with specific reference to the education office (EO), the

9RRC command, it appears, did not **initially** understand the features and impact of a professional planned, fully developed education program, and how such a program could help with military enlistment, retention, and readiness (Department of the Army 2006, 2019; Wellein, 2010).

More Details – Education

From 1998 to mid-2000, the 9RRC command asked an Army Comptroller (a major) to manage civilian education as a **collateral duty** explained Jaybee Obusan, Human Resource Officer (HRO), G-1 (personal communication, June 14, 2005). The major was to devote perhaps three hours weekly to a fledgling education program, authorizing TA at about the $50 thousand per year level. After 9RRC hired me, a seasoned, full- time professional civilian education director in mid- July 2001, the education program expanded immediately.

Expansion

From July 16 to September 30, 2001, **(10 weeks),** 9RRC soldiers used over $107 thousand in TA (Ali, 2005), more than twice what they used from the entire period of October 1, 2000-July 15, 2001 and began to contact a professional education counselor (Department of the Army, 2006; Wellein, 2021).

Two contractors initially hired by the Army Comptroller had so few telephone calls prior to mid-July 2001 that they listened with earphones to the radio much of the day as they casually processed TA requests on their computer workstations. After July 16, 2001, they had to discard their earphones as the telephone calls about schools and tuition came in fast and furiously.

The changes in the education program were enormous: As the newly hired education director, I asked for, and was granted, a third contractor, and requested additional operating and TA funds, so that the program funds for TA grew from $207,117 in fiscal year 2001 to $739,079 in fiscal year 2003 (Ali, 2005). Despite steady military deployments, 9RRC soldiers used $655,691 for TA in fiscal year 2004 and by July 2005, had used almost $550,000. The operating funds (for computers, printers, webcams, microphones, Internet providers, shredders, furniture, travel, training) grew also, from $40,000 in FY 2001, to $217,000 in FY 2005 according to the Army Continuing Education System (ACES) in 2005.

The EO gained a separate and dedicated facsimile machine, digital senders, and several color printers used for creating intriguing flyers and bright information sheets (Ali, 2005). In record numbers soldiers and family members enrolled in Basic Skills reading and math courses on Oahu and in American Samoa (Wellein, 2010, 2021). We never cancelled any courses, because we had a tremendously high number of student enrollments! In addition, we offered military personnel all the education services mentioned in earlier chapters.

New Test Program

I also served as the test control officer, instituting a military and civilian testing program in November 2002, using the 9RRC headquarters' break room for testing from 2-9 p.m., Monday through Friday and most Saturdays, 8 a.m.-noon. The Test Examiner (TE) administered military tests including 45 foreign language examinations, a flight aptitude examination, military entrance examination retests, and other Army aptitude instruments.

Civilian tests included 34 College Level Examination Program (CLEP) tests, 33 Defense Activities for Non-Traditional Education Support (DANTES) tests, the American College Test, the Scholastic Aptitude Test, and other standardized tests for reading and mathematics (DANTES External, 2006; Department of the Army, 2006, Wellein, 2010, 2021). Almost all examinations were free to the military and many were also free to Army Reserve family members.

Other service personnel from Navy, Marines, Coast Guard, Air Force, Army National Guard, as well as family members and DOD civilians began flocking to the test program, as the word spread that testing was available in the late afternoon hours and evening periods and sometimes on Saturdays (the only such military test program on Oahu with this schedule).

Bad News

Unfortunately, the command could not identify a permanent, dedicated test room (as required by the DOD test regulations) and so in June 2003, HRC in St. Louis closed our immensely successful testing program. At the same time, our TE, a young, attractive (but apparently, keenly insecure) reserve lieutenant told Mr. Obusan, Colonel Marcia Andrews, and me, "I have a problem being alone in the test room with any male testing" – this extraordinary complaint coming from a soon-to-be reserve unit commander! So, when we closed the test program, we did so with a mixed sigh of relief.

Note: In July 2021, DANTES stopped paying for GED, ACT, SAT, GRE, GMAT, and Praxis teacher examinations for the military due to 'DOD budget constraints'. How very sad.

New Quarters

In addition, whereas previously, each education worker had a small desk in a shared hallway-office, the program's tremendous expansion demanded a larger work area. By the summer of 2003, Mr. Obuson, G-1 **astutely moved the education office to another building (1550), with three connecting offices designated solely for education.** (It was formerly a printing press office so Mr. Obusan arranged for it to be thoroughly cleaned, painted, and repurposed!) This move was extremely **controversial** because various division chiefs and command group members had discussed the move (sometimes, heatedly) and possible education office locations for months earlier. (Why would they be so concerned as to the location of the new education office and what was there to discuss?)

Indeed, overall, HRO increased its staffing to such a large extent that the Drug and Alcohol program also moved into building (1550), while Family Readiness, Identification Card, Funerals, and Awards office sections moved to other, redesigned offices also in the same building; nearby Retention personnel regrouped in another section of the same building.

In summary, the 9RRC command was not prepared for the impact that education programs and services had on its troop population. **The reserve soldiers' increasing use of TA dollars proved to be a valuable revelation** to the command and demonstrated quite clearly that education remains one of the top three reasons people enlist in the service (Wellein, 2010). Some of the command group's staff, division chiefs, and commanders, despite seemingly endless one-on-one protests, lengthy meetings, e-mails and such, finally gave up their objections to the expansion of education services, bringing 9RRC into the 21st century.

CH 34 Changes: Division Chiefs, 9RRC,

Army Reserve

My Pearl of Wisdom: Technology is King

Failing is a crucial part of success. Every time you fail and get back up.

You practice perseverance, which is the key to life.

Your strength comes in your ability to recover.

Michelle Obama

ANOTHER GROUP facing change in addition to command group officers (due to an expanding education office and the war in the Middle East) consisted of the division chiefs, such as those directing Information Management, Security, Training, Logistics, and Military Intelligence. Many of them appeared to remain neutral to such innovations as the education loan library, the Basic Skills courses (Department of the Army, 2006; U.S. Army Reserve, 2021), or the 92-pocket heavy-duty revolving display racks chock full of educational materials located in all 9RRC Army Reserve Centers throughout the Pacific. I observed this when I was the director of education at 9RRC from 2001-2012.

Special Computers, Printers, Webcams, Microphones Project

When I began implementing an important computer project (aptly named Retention, Education, and Family Readiness or REF) to purchase desktops computers, printers, digital senders, microphones and webcams, to place in common areas of nine reserve centers located in several geographically dispersed areas, I ran into unexpected opposition. I wanted to purchase this equipment so that troops and their family members would gain access to computers, printers, and the Internet. Some of the division chiefs stated their objections at a series of meetings about this REF computer project.

Background

The Army and the 9RRC command leadership always demanded that all soldiers obtain special Army e-mail accounts, go online and enroll in various military training courses, update their security clearances, and respond to Army initiated requests for specific information. Soldiers needed to obtain accurate, timely information to perform better at their military jobs, and regularly check their government e-mail messages, **but many troops did not have easy access to computers,** especially those located in **American Samoa, Saipan, and Guam.** However, when the Army Reserve activated a large number of 9RRC troops and deployed them to Iraq and Afghanistan, the stark reality of the situation became rapidly apparent.

Here were Pacific-based military personnel, fighting in a war ten thousand miles away from their loved ones, without any method of contacting them. (The U.S. military command did not permit soldiers to use cellular telephones when deployed because the enemy could use the phones' electronic signals as a homing device and aim missiles towards these electronic impulse sources.) When the Family Readiness program manager offered her agency's computers for the education office's computer (REF) initiative coupled with the Retention colonel's offer of 15 more computers, the project really gained momentum.

Problems of Acceptance

Finally, in 2004, the local command agreed to assist in the purchase of automation equipment, adding to funds sent from the St. Louis HR Office to the Education Office (EO). A few of the division heads (all males) were reluctant at first to see computers made available to family members. Previously, division heads had only seen family members use one Army Family Readiness-owned computer per reserve center. Now, this new REF project called for purchasing multiple computer workstations, printers, digital senders (scanners), microphones, webcams for visualization and making them available to family members as well as military personnel in an open 'bay' accessible to all.

Specific Objections

Some division chiefs felt that **they would not be able to control family members using Army-owned equipment.** One actually said at a meeting in mid-2004, words to the effect that placing those computers in the open area of a reserve center **could turn that area into a baby-sitting room.** Part of this initial reluctance to support this common area computer project might be attributed to the fact that **some have held the position of division chief for many years, and were in the 'good ole boys' network.** (One division chief retired and his departure aided the implementation of the computer initiative.)

Another reason for division chiefs' reluctance to support this computer initiative was that some of them had apparently never visited the other reserve centers recently, **especially centers in American Samoa, Guam, and Saipan** <u>for the express purpose</u> of **checking to see if every reservist had computer and printer access** and to inspect the technology equipment.

At a fall 2004 meeting, when I explained that American Samoan soldiers need computer access at the American Samoa Reserve Center, one division chief stated that soldiers should simply use their own home computers **not** even realizing that soldiers living in that U.S. territory **were so impoverished that a majority of them did not own a computer and would likely never be able to purchase such equipment, let alone pay the monthly Internet service charges. (Local wages at the fish cannery there were barely $3.17 per hour.)**

Another division chief remarked at that same meeting that he did not understand why the troops could not simply go to the public library and use the computers there. **In fact, libraries in American Samoa, Guam, and other Pacific islands do not have computers; now, wait for it – wait — three American Samoa high schools <u>were trying to get running water</u> that year! (Yikes!)**

A third reason for the 9RRC division chiefs' initial reluctance to support the computer initiative is that the HR Officer is the only division chief with three female program managers who manage non-9RRC funded programs. No one openly mentioned this, but it **was the elephant** in the room! **Division chiefs cannot request excess funds from these three special programs** (Drug and Alcohol, Family Readiness, and Education) to flow into other 9RRC – funded pet projects, as may be occasionally desired. As far as I know, no 'fund diversion' every happened. (Yes, thank you for holding your ground, Mr. Obusan and Colonel Andrews!)

Support from the Supervisors

Please understand a little about the two directors (civilian and military) of HRC, G-1 9RRC. Colonel M. Andrews, who served as the Human Resource Officer (military) during each monthly weekend drill is a Filipina female, barely 5 feet tall and about 90 pounds 'dripping wet.' Mr. Jaybee Obusan, the regular full-time civilian director of HRO and a reserve command sergeant major one weekend a month, is also of Filipino ancestry. Both are tremendously professional and extremely competent.

Also, both appeared to be the only division chiefs of Filipino ethnicity at 9RRC at this time and this fact placed them solidly in the minority category. **Together, they commanded an entire human resource division and politically, had great power and importance.** (It was reported that some of the other division chiefs appear to be jealous of this power at times.)

At 9RRC, both these G1 directors (military and civilian) established and directed military and civilian promotion and scholarship boards, made the final determinations on awards, funerals, identification card issues, provided oversight for military health and dental plans, ranked order promotion packets, recommended procedures to follow when dignitaries visited, and of course served as the direct supervisor and senior evaluator for the three females who directed the Drug and Alcohol, Family Readiness, and Education Services Offices. **And both Obusan and Andrew soundly supported these three offices, allowing for the education office to expand 150%.**

Change - Levels

It is interesting to note that in *Management of Organizational Behavior* (Hersey, Blanchard, & Johnson, 2001) the authors discuss common levels of change. The levels these authors cite are **knowledge, attitudinal, individual, and group behavioral changes.** At 9RRC, the computer initiative (REF) required all four of these levels of change, and some of these still continue (Athuraliya, 2020). Kotter and Cohen (2002) state that urgency assists in making changes, that when the issue is important and compelling with great immediacy, some people will be able to change more rapidly. This was precisely the case at 9RRC.

Knowledge Level

The Army Reserve decided to activate, mobilize, and deploy 411th Engineer Battalion units with **over 600 troops** (from Hilo, Maui, Guam, Saipan, Alaska, Hawai'i, and American Samoa) to the Middle East in 2004.

Attitudinal Level

Family members from all locations wanted to contact their loved ones through e-mail, and many did **not** have computer access.

Individual, and Group Behavioral Levels

The combination of hundreds of soldiers in various units across the Pacific Ocean mobilizing for war, and family members desperate to maintain contact with them caused an immediate change. There was no time for complacency, no time for 'doing a study,' no time – except to act.

Urgency

The computer initiative suddenly became extremely urgent and the subsequent activation and deployment of over 700 troops in 100th Battalion, 442nd Infantry units located throughout the Pacific in spring, 2005 brought the issue of computer access by family members and troops into immediate focus. **The 9RRC command requested that the education office send computer equipment** including webcams (allowing family members to see their loved ones overseas) to all 9RRC reserve center sites (using air transport) and that reserve facility managers should sign contracts immediately with commercial internet service providers, and bill the Education Services Office. That was a win-win for all.

Note

By **2020-2021,** reservists on Guam (and perhaps elsewhere) utilized their own personal mobile devices with unlimited data plans to access the Internet. But previously of course, that was not possible. Ah, the Age of Technology finally reached Guam and beyond!

CH 35 Changes: Soldiers, 9RRC, Army Reserve

My Pearl of Wisdom: Right, Left, Right, Then Repeat

A man must be big enough to admit his mistakes, smart enough to profit

from them, and strong enough to correct them.

John C. Maxwell

THE THIRD GROUP facing change was the **soldiers.** As the Tuition Assistance (TA) program expanded during 2001-2012 when I was employed as the education officer, directions for soldiers to follow when requesting college funding grew more complicated. Soldiers faced new, detailed procedures online, to obtain military funding.
Soldier Changes

Previously, soldiers only faxed, e-mailed, or brought in their TA paperwork to the education office for processing (J. Calloway, personal communication, October 2, 2004). However, in fiscal year 2005 (beginning October 1, 2004), the Director of Education at Human Resources Command, St. Louis (HRC-STL) Jonell Calloway, stated that soldiers in **all** RRCs should request TA online, through the Internet (Ali, 2005). But, some **soldiers in 9RRC at many locations (Guam, Saipan, American Samoa, Maui, Hilo, parts of Alaska) did not have computers, others had no Army-required e-mail accounts, and many more lacked fax, Internet service, computer and printer access or such access was difficult and expensive, at best.**

Many hundreds of soldiers were preparing to mobilize (updating their shot records, wills and powers of attorney, recertifying on their weapons) while others were already fighting a war in Iraq or Afghanistan. Still others were returning (demobilizing) from the war and reintegrating once more into their communities with much needed family support. **9RRC troops were experiencing great turmoil personally, with**

employment, family, school, relationship issues and military requirements.

To those not familiar with the military, it might seem obvious that reserve soldiers train once a month at 'drill assemblies' and if **activated**, go 'off to war.' Once they have served their 12-18 months of duty, they turn in their weapons, and return to civilian life. Unfortunately, in reality, mobilization takes months of training to prepare for any armed conflict. This training may occur at their 'home station' or elsewhere, for example, on an Army base such at Fort Benning, GA.

Activation takes another 4-8 weeks of soldiers completing paperwork/forms, taking care of their dental and medical needs, vaccinations and physical exams, providing activation orders to their supervisor at work, to colleges if soldiers are enrolled in courses, landlords or property owners, banks, gyms, and many others businesses and agencies. Some employers hold the soon-to-be-vacant position for those deployed under certain circumstances (type of job, number of employees, length of activation, etc.) while others will not.

Finally, after activation is complete, that is, upon completing their tour of duty in Iraq or Afghanistan, the Horn of Africa or wherever the Army sends soldiers, these military warriors must be **demobilized**. This process of 2-6 weeks includes soldiers taking physical and dental examinations as required, turning in gear, equipment, and supplies, special weapons, ammunition, and such, and filling in seemingly endless forms including making appointments at the Veterans (Benefits) Affairs Office, civilian medical centers, filing claims for disabilities, home loans, etc. Those suffering from any type of injury or illness (e.g., medical care due to explosions, bad sprains, stress disorder, tinnitus, anti-Malaria pill side effects) must receive special care and follow-up for physical therapy, too.

Surprisingly, many reservists who the Army had not yet activated decided to return to school classrooms or to continue their educational endeavors online, and their TA usage reflected this groundswell (Wellein, 2021). 9RRC soldiers desperately needed computers, printers, webcams, and Internet access to communicate with their family members at home. Several chapters in this book discuss what the command did to meet these challenges. But changes and reactions to these changes were inevitable.

CH 36 Changes: Education Staff,

9RRC, Army Respective

My Pearl of Wisdom: Reform Continues

With More Change

When someone is nasty or treats you poorly, don't take it personally.

It says nothing about you, but a lot about them.

Michael Josephson

THE FOURTH GROUP facing change was the 9RRC Education Office personnel (DANTES External, 2006; Department of the Army, 2006; Wellein, 2010, 2021). The culture of course was military with some minor deviation.

Staff

As the education director at 9RRC from 2001-2012, I worked together with three contractors, listened to their suggestions, and implemented many, when applicable. Then too, clients' care was extremely important, because they and their family members always came first. We maintained our office hours 7 a.m. to 4 p.m. and open during lunch (except on rare occasions when the office closed for an emergency non-scheduled staff meeting), and the office even opened **during the weekend** upon a unit commander's request.

Education Contractors

Fortunately, contractors and the education director remained flexible yet focused. When 411th troops returned to their own Pacific islands, for example, I made travel plans to visit them at their home island, (together with other 9RRC program managers) and provided information about new GI Bill entitlements, TA, and an assortment of other programs and services. When I discovered that 15 Retention computers could not be used for the computer initiative, I set aside funds from the education budget to purchase additional equipment (A. Ali, personal communication, September 15, 2004).

When all three contractors inquired about flexible work hours (i.e., work four days a week, 10 hours a day) as they would be continuing their education (one, a few credits short of an associate's degree, another six courses shy of a baccalaureate, while the third one half-way through a masters), I agreed to include the four-days a week suggestion on the next staff meeting's agenda. (Unfortunately, the contract they worked under did not provide for this schedule, but I asked.)

A High Performing Team - 6 Characteristics

Bolman and Deal (2003) discuss team structure and six major characteristics of a high-performing team. Let us review these following characteristics and then see how the education office personnel relates to them.

a. The **first feature** is responding to higher management, by remaining flexible and shaping purpose to unexpected demands. The HR Officer in St. Louis together with the HR education director (Jonell Calloway) gave all RRC education directors clear authority to manage their command's education programs and services (Department of the Army, 2006; Wellein, 2010). At 9RRC, my staff and I used creative, effective, highly professional means to do so (Wellein, 2010) with Mr. Obusan and Colonel Andrews having final approval.

b. A **second feature** is demonstrating specific and measurable goals. The education staff not only followed AR 621-5 (Department of Army, 2006), in writing, but also clearly communicated and demonstrated goal attainment (Wellein, 2021). I submitted regular reports about TA usage and other programs, documenting goal attainment.

c. The **third feature** is that teams must be of manageable size; our education staff numbered four.

d. The **fourth feature** is that a team must have the right mix of expertise. The education staff had an exceptionally good mix of personalities and strengths based on reviewing the results of the Myers Briggs Type Inventory (Myers, 1998). This particular type of personality inventory identifies individuals by introversion vs. extroversion, sensing vs. intuition, thinking vs. feeling, and judging vs. perceiving and is usually considered 90% accurate. Naturally, team members must have had a sound academic base, with a minimum of 60 semester hours of college documented on a valid transcript. Many had much more, including work towards a master's degree.

e. A **fifth feature** is that members must understand the importance of a sound, working relationship. Team members at this office explored who was best skilled to perform a certain task, within the confines of their contracts, and then they did it.

f. The **sixth and final feature** of a high-performing team is that they feel collectively responsible to get the task done. Members of the education staff had continuously demonstrated this feature. Earlier, when one person was supposed to prepare two boxes of briefing materials but became ill, the other members stayed late to take over the task. When a Basic Skills instructor was stuck in a severe traffic jam one evening, I taught the course for the first hour. When HRC in St. Louis suddenly required a detailed statistical report, the Education Specialist (Judy Champaco) worked together with the Education Technician II on a Saturday morning to prepare it because I was not on-island.

Education staff members saw change as constant, inevitable, welcomed, and then as an opportunity to do their job more effectively and efficiently.

My Work Philosophy

All office members assisted one another when several clients visited the office at once, and staff made suggestions to me for adding agenda items for meetings held weekly. If a contractor was late or absent, another contractor took over the duties of the missing worker for a while. If I was late or absent, one of the contractors (usually the Education Specialist) rescheduled staff meetings or changed deadlines as needed. The spirit of cooperation was plainly evident in the office. **My philosophy is that everyone**

who does anything worthwhile will make a mistake. Expect mistakes. A person who never makes any mistakes usually is not doing anything. The goal is not to make the same mistake, repeatedly.

Ask for a Volunteer First

Managers need to find **what workers are good at doing, and then let them do it**. For example, if three people are available to work on a bulletin board, but one of them takes artistic delight in doing this type of project, a good manager will assign that job to the one who loves it. Better yet, the manager should ask for a volunteer (if the task is within the contract scope or work specifications). If there are two contractors who can research the newly released cost of tuition and fees at local universities, then the manager should ask again for a volunteer or ask one who loves to do that kind of work.

If training opportunities are available, the manager should ensure that such opportunities are rotated, so that all workers have a chance to participate. However, contractors are rarely given the opportunity for advanced, Army-sponsored training.

Special Note

During my time as the education director, I ensured that all staff personnel had their individual computer workstations, **ergonomically correct** foot stools and office chairs, wrist and mouse gel pads, air purifiers, wall-mounted thermometers to check on whether the central air conditioning system was performing well, easy access to digital scanners, color printers, shredders, photocopiers, and wall clocks. Staff personnel also had their own bulletin boards, calendar desk pads, and special telephone carbonless message pads. Telephone calls could be transferred to the appropriate individual, or recorded for attention later.

I purchased two new 18 cubic foot **refrigerators** (for everyone in the 3-story building to use), a 2.2 cubic foot **microwave,** toaster, hot and cold drinking **water machine** with five-gallon water-bottle deliveries weekly, **coffee machines** for regular and decaffeinated coffee, tea, and other items for all to use. I saw the work environment as a place where conditions should be comfortable and that means taking care of staff needs. (I should note that the refrigerators and bottled water purchases led to several unexpected issues later – but I will not discuss them here.)

Summary

To summarize, education staff faced change. The Army reserve education program had exceptionally clear goals, specialized roles for its staff members, and formalized relationships, all elements recognized in a highly structured organization (U.S. Army Reserve, 2021; Wellein, 2010). Human resource concerns and emphasis were obviously present as well, ensuring that contractors and employees felt valued, important, and highly regarded for their competency, professionalism, and deep concern they demonstrated daily, for the welfare of the soldiers and family members. Also, we all used common sense when we abided by the Army policies and regulations (AR 621-5) for Education Services.

Clearly, the frames or lenses at any organization are important and 9RRC was no exception. These frames are simply tools we use, to look through the 'glass,' to see how an agency functions. These lenses provide a clear perspective. 9RRC was a wonderful agency to dissect.

CH 37 What Facilitates Successful Change in Any Agency?

My Pearl of Wisdom: You CAN Make a Difference

We are taught you must blame your father, your sisters, your brothers,

the school, the teachers – but never blame yourself.

It's never your fault.

But it's always your fault, because if you wanted to change

you're the one who has got to change.

Katharine Hepburn

THERE ARE MANY WAYS society's institutions – such as businesses, schools, military, government – can implement significant changes even if such institutions have massive organizational structure, policies, procedures, regulations, personnel, facilities, budget, laboratories, research and development grants, present and future innovative projects and leadership issues in place (Vo, 2019).

Other writers cite Mark Twain's famous saying, "The only person who likes change is a baby with wet diapers!" to add a bit of humor to the situation. Reinhold Niebuhr, the well-known Protestant theologian said "Change is the Essence of Life" and Heraclitus, the Greek philosopher said, "The only thing constant in life is change." **Change is recurring, rather than a choice**. Thus, it is best to understand how to make the best of the situation by first **reviewing what a noted author (John Kotter) has to say about change.**

John Paul Kotter's, *Eight Steps for Successful Large-Scale Change*, include the following: **begin** with a sense of urgency, then **build** a cooperative team or group to guide the changes to be made, then **develop** the right strategy and vision, and **discuss** the importance of commitment or buy-in. The next four steps are to **empower** members to take action, **allow** for short-term victories which spur people forward to continue the changes, until **changes are made** and become **permanent** (Athuraliya, 2020; Kotter & Cohen, 2002; Wellein, 2021). Change is a process, a journey, rather than the project itself.

Ten Factors for Change

An examination of just a **few procedures that change agents should follow**, (when accomplishing change in the military, business or corporation large or small, non-profit/for profit group, or postsecondary institution, as an example), may prove instructive (Vo, 2019).

1. **Plan and manage implementation of changes** in a strategic manner. Budgets need attention, as do collaboration efforts among all key players, involved. Use strategic planning most deliberately in making changes. This includes a complete reality check first, deciding what is needed, looking at options, time-lines, resources, making decisions, implementing the changes, and evaluating the success of these changes.

2. **Develop implementation strategy data and action plans** to guide expected changes, focusing attention on needed decisions, actions, and responsible individuals. Plans are short-term (under one year) or long-term (over one year). Make decisions based on these specific short- and long-term goals, expected milestones, objectives, and decide how to determine when such goals have been reached. This also include deciding on action steps, basic schedules, decisions on resource needs and sources, methods of communicating changes and progress, evaluation and monitoring of these changes, and some sort of accountability process.

3. **Begin with easily introduced changes** that can be rapidly made and followed. Such changes should be: clear, show cause and effect, fit with the values and culture of the

individuals and groups involved, simple in concept, require minimal red tape, provide for a start-up period, and allow for almost immediate payoffs and rewards/recognition. Make changes by reducing large clusters into more manageable-sized ones. Introduce small chunks at a time; reward those who are successful in making changes while allowing a start-up period for those less capable or enthusiastic.

4. **Use a basic project and program management approach**, that is, allow sufficient time, provide people with sound information, identify funds, resources, and support services to ensure successful change-implementation, explains writer Eric Vo (2019). These would include resources for additional staff, orientation and training costs, technical assistance and consultants, conversion costs, evaluations and assessments, rewards and incentives, and unforeseen emergencies.

5. **Ensure that changes are successful** by allowing sufficient funds, personnel support, time, and attention. Specifically, these include such items as technical consultants, training and professional development so that changes can be better accepted, changes in personnel if needed, incentives to assist people (whether it be flexible hours, more pay, less overtime), and change-agents to help lead the way. Involve key personnel, and change-catalysts in assisting in the evaluation of these new initiatives, linking the new methods with the older ones to ensure success. Shared power is a bit of an aphrodisiac.

6. **Link new strategic initiatives with ongoing operations**, so that the institution continues to operate, classes or units run, personnel are paid, the physical plant works, various contracts continue, and students or trainees learn. Ask for assistance in developing new policies and procedures from the people actually performing the work, so that buy-in can be accomplished quickly.

7. **Work quickly** to avoid unneeded competition when new priorities are set. This means that if suddenly the economy falters, or a severe storm damages the campus and its dormitories, or new taxes are imposed on businesses or suddenly new deficits discovered, leaders would move quickly to instigate new strategies to meet these challenges. The federal government for example, will quickly move military units around in cases of

conflict, depending on national or world events.

8. **Concentrate on putting together groups** of advocates, supporters, interest groups, and others who are effective as catalysts for change; then use them. Be aware of administrative, executive, and legislative policies that will either hinder or help needed changes. Decide ahead of time how exactly disputes will be solved or disagreements be resolved, and which group, cultural, and professional norms will be enforced.

9. **Remember primarily that organizational changes mean cultural changes**, to include symbols, artifacts, values, assumptions, rituals, and core beliefs. Always remember that the culture of an agency will be affected by changes. Emphasize the learning aspect of change, because change is constant, and the organization cannot stop its daily business to deal with changing situations, new contracts, and altered policies. Key **stakeholders** will find that learning must become a habit and all must accept that strategies are hardly ever developed and implemented without modification and alterations.

10. **Stay the course**. There will be resistors, naysayers, and negative personalities, all fighting to halt the needed changes. The rewards of change however, are important to remember. Learning is life-long. Any changes made must be nurtured to ensure its survival because anything worth doing will take time, energy, effort, patience, and follow-through (Vo, 2019; Wellein, 2021)

Organizational Change

     There are many aspects of change: defining organizational development and change; identifying approaches for change; an awareness of the barriers to successful change; dealing with trust issues; responsibilities for change in communicating with professionals; linking good communication to productive, desired change, and dealing with values during the change process. The pace of change, planned development and change procedures, how one communicates change effectively within organizations, roles and responsibilities of change-agents, and how to figure out when changes have finally occurred (evaluation and assessment) are all-important.

Qualities of Change Agents

Handling change in any organization can be difficult, and in massive institutions such as large corporations, the military, corporations, or schools, tremendously challenging. Therefore, it is imperative that the individuals responsible to make changes in the organization possess specific qualities. In a recent Michigan State University article, *Qualities of effective change agents* (2019), the writer discusses important characteristics and qualities of effective change agents, summarized, below. **Change agents must show**

1. Flexibility.
2. Diversified Knowledge.
3. Priority and Results Focused
4. Ownership and Responsibility
5. Effective Listening Skills

Real Life Example – Army Reserve

Several years ago, when I served as the education director of 9th Regional Readiness Command (9RRC) in Hawai'i we had no computers and printers available for family members and soldiers to use. We also had no commercial Internet service for them. In fact, the only computers at Army Reserve Centers located throughout the Pacific were part of the Army system, and family members could not use them due to security reasons.

However, when the command notified the 9RRC education office in 2003 that soldiers who wanted to request tuition assistance (TA) funds would soon have to do so by going online (and using the Internet), I had to make a real change in procedures, to quickly meet the changing needs of the TA process. Additionally, family members needed to contact their loved ones who were participating in training activities or activated to serve in war zones.

Kotter's Steps – 9RRC Education Office

Using John P. Kotter's eight steps (also called eight stages in his **The Heart of**

Change (Kotter & Cohen, 2002), I implemented a reform initiative (Athuraliya, 2020). I used, as a roadmap, information from Dr. Kotter, a professor at Harvard Business School, known arguably worldwide as the number one authority on change and leadership. You can read more details about using Kotter's eight steps in Wellein (2021).

A quick review of Kotter's methodology and what I actually accomplished at 9RRC is as follows:

1. **Increase urgency** – People involved must recognize that a change is needed. As the 9RRC Army Reserve Regional Director of Education for Pacific and Asia, I was responsible for planning the budget beginning in 2003 and for three years following, to include appropriations for automation equipment (i.e., work stations, monitors, surge protectors, printers, and digital scanners). In writing, I notified the Director of Information and Management, the Director of Human Resources, the Command Sergeant Major, Retention Officer, Drug and Alcohol Director, and Family Readiness Director that **the new requirements for soldiers applying for TA included using the Internet.** Many of their **family members were desperate to use the Internet** (e-mail) to contact their loved ones in Iraq, Kuwait, Afghanistan, Horn of Africa, and in some areas of the Pacific, and there was no Internet service available without incurring a substantial minute or hourly price for using such equipment. Reservists and family members needed the Internet and equipment to enroll in distance education for college course work. Reserve centers needed computers, webcams, printers, Internet service – these reasons created the increased sense of urgency.

2. **Build the guiding team** – A group must be powerful enough to guide an important change, by working together. At 9RRC, I brought together, in a series of meetings, **all the division chiefs**: such as Budget, Information Management, Logistics, Human Resources, Security, Training, Retention, as well as the Public Relations Officer. I explained the problem and how I wanted to solve it: purchase sufficient automation equipment, to include micro-cameras on headsets, by asking for funding from Retention and Family Readiness, the two agencies in addition to Education, which had the most to gain from

implementing the initiative. Naturally, I requested the majority of funds from HRC Education Director (Ms. Jonell Calloway) in St Louis, MO.

3. **Get the vision right** – The guiding team members develop the appropriate vision and strategy for effecting changes needed. **Once 9RRC leadership understood the need for commercial Internet service** and computer equipment, and that initial funding of $67 thousand would stem from Education, 9RRC command provided an additional $26 thousand that first year. The Information and Management division would ensure that the purchased equipment be compatible with 9RRC's security processes, procedures, and networking-Internet capabilities, and that Logistics would ship all the equipment to the various centers: Maui, Big Island of Hawai'i, Fairbanks and Anchorage, Alaska, Saipan, Guam, and American Samoa. Oahu would have at least 10 workstations, and Japan and Korea would determine how much equipment was necessary. All locations would also receive heavy-duty printers with scanner capabilities.

4. **Communicate for buy-in** – People will begin to accept the need for change, and the change itself, and this is reflected in their behavior. **For the automation initiative to succeed, all the key leaders had to fully understand the project.** The **command staff** developed a policy on common area computer usage; the **retention director** donated a dozen formerly used computers to the project, while the **family readiness** director donated some used and new workstations and printers.

5. **Empower action** – More people feel able to act, rather than just discuss the situation. **9RRC leaders collectively 'put their money where their mouth was' and took action.** The 9RRC command allocated $26 thousand, and our education office allocated over $100 thousand (after the initial $67 thousand) during the subsequent three years, bringing the total to $193 thousand. The Director of Army Reserve in St Louis (responsible for all 15 regional commands) **fully supported the initiative by providing any additional funding.** Without computers and Internet service, soldiers would not be able to request financial assistance for postsecondary degrees, certificates, or diplomas, and most of the islands in the Pacific lacked free, easy, computer access for military personnel. Family

members would not have been able to readily contact their loved ones, or take online courses, either.

6. **Create short-term wins** – Allow and assist the momentum building, as those involved attempt to implement the new initiative while those resisting the change are fewer in number. **The arrival of the first workstations and printers on Oahu set the stage**. The 'doubters' quickly saw how useful the Internet service was for soldiers and family members and the news spread: the plan worked. Facility managers were contacting the education director asking how soon the equipment for their center, would arrive!

7. **Don't let up** – People must continue to work on all aspects of the initiative, "wave after wave of changes, until the vision is fulfilled" (Kotter & Cohen, 2002, p. 7). Once the centers received their equipment, the facility managers had to contact their local Internet service providers, develop a contract, and submit the invoices to my office for payment. By the ending of FY 2006, (September), $93 thousand has been committed for computer workstations, printers, printer tables, chairs, and other needs.

8. **Make change stick** – Kotter states that "new and winning behavior continues despite the pull of tradition, turnover of change leaders, etc." (Kotter & Cohen, 2002, p. 7). 9RRC leaders and facility managers now see the value of the common area computers and printers. Soldiers began using TA an almost unbelievable rate: in fiscal year 2001, $207 thousand, by 2003, $525 thousand, and in 2006, $1.015 million. Without computer access, this would not have been possible. Recruiters attract possible enlistees by explaining education benefits, while retention specialists use the same information to retain those already in the service. Family Readiness folks keep their families satisfied with free computer accessibility.

Final Notes

Was the initiative easy? No, it was not. Were there snags along the way? There were too many to count. Did everyone agree to the changes at first? Absolutely not. Were the major stakeholders convinced funding was possible? A big, resounding NO. Is this initiative continuing to work? The answer is most emphatically yes! Due to Education

Director Jonell Calloway's unprecedented vision coupled with her most-generous funding, the 9RRC computer/Internet project became a reality.

That is why **Dr. John Paul Kotter**, the Konosuke Matsushita Professor of Leadership, Emeritus at the Harvard Business School, co-founder of Kotter International, a leadership organization that helps Global 500 company leaders, a graduate of Massachusetts Institute of Technology (MIT) and Harvard, and best-selling author of several dozen well-respected teaching materials, journal articles, videos, and some 20 textbooks, **is my hero**!

Dr. Kotter is an internationally known respected speaker on Leadership and Change and has received dozens of national and international awards throughout his professional career.

The ideas presented here are but a brief glimpse into this world of making change – to see some of the challenges, recommendations, and research findings. Let us begin.

CH 38 Real Life Changes: A Result of Life Experiences

My Pearl of Wisdom: Change Takes Place Over a Lifetime

Change will not come if we wait for some other person or some other time.

We are the ones we've been waiting for.

We are the change that we seek.

Barack Obama

THE FOLLOWING is an excerpt from a 30+ page interview transcript with Master Sergeant (MSG) Lallier, a veteran Army sergeant, describing his personal history, life experiences, Army training, work and travel, resulting in major changes in his personal values and culture. **Additionally, his viewpoint on many subjects changed over the course of his life because of his life experiences.** The interview (modified here) is considered part of qualitative research, which usually involves case study, narrative, phenomena, interview, observation, or grounded theory (Patton, 2002; Rutakumwa, Mugisha, Bernays, Kabunga, & Tumwekwase, Mbonye, & Seeley, 2019). Such research techniques are widely accepted in the academic community though some believe such studies are not sufficient in scope, depth, and numbers to be important.

An advantage of using this qualitative research method (interview) is that by spending time with only one individual through the process of interviewing, tape recording, and then transcribing just one person's life experiences, a researcher could gain much information about this person's culture, background, and learning experiences. **The subject provided a rich, totally unstructured personal glimpse into ethnographic, qualitative research and his experience dealing with bigotry and racial prejudice.**

Introduction

MSG Stuart Lallier, Pacific Area Manager, Headquarters, Retention Office, 9th Regional Readiness Command (9RRC), Honolulu, agreed to an interview while we were on an Army business trip together on Guam. I told him that the interview was for my Ethnology Project, which involved a lengthy tape-recorded interview; he graciously agreed. **The purpose of this 90-minute tape recorded meeting** (Rutakumwa et al., 2019) **was to discover changes in an individual's life** as it relates to culture, values, ethnicity, diversity, racial intermarriage, religion, travel, second language, body size, and color discrimination, resulting in a significant change in attitude, values, cultural and personal beliefs, and emotional growth.

Background Information

MSG Lallier stands six feet tall, fair complected, is 200 pounds of what appears to be solid muscle; he continues to lead an athletic life. He has held several professional body building contest titles, including Mr. Oahu, Hawai'i-1981, Mr. Hawai'i, Hawai'i-1984, Mr. All Army, Germany-1986, All Army Europe, Germany-1987, Mr. Europe, Germany-1988, Mr. South Pacific, Hawai'i-1991, Mr. Hawaiian Islands Hawai'i-1992, Mr. Western America, California-1994, Las Vegas Body Building Champion, Las Vegas, Nevada-1995, and Heavyweight Mr. Universe, Guam-1995.

MSG Lallier's deep blue eyes sparkle when he speaks and he has a wonderful sense of humor. He wears his dark brown hair cropped short, as is the custom with military personnel, and speaks rapidly and succinctly.

At first, when I explained the interview assignment and selection criteria of the interview subject, MSG Lallier told me that he would not be a good candidate, because he and I were of the same racial background. I asked him what that was. He explained that he was a *Haole* (Hawaiian, for White or Caucasian) and that I was the same. I told him that **I was not,** that I was part Hawaiian, Chinese, Portuguese, and Caucasian (Russian). He seemed surprised, and then smiled and chuckled a bit. I had previously seen him with his wife, a lovely woman of Filipino descent. I chose MSG Lallier because he was White, from the Continental U.S., married to a native-born Catholic Filipina from the Philippines, and together, they had one son, **a true multi-racial or biracial family**.

Furthermore, MSG Lallier was from a Catholic, middle-class working family with one brother and one sister, whose grandparents partially raised him; he spoke French with them and understood spoken Italian with his friends as a youngster.

Interview

W (Wellein) and **L** (Lallier)

Lallier is age 44 and 100% French, born in the U.S.; both parents and grandparents are French from Canada and France, respectively.

W: Tell me a bit about your parents.

L: My dad spent 30 years in the Air Force Reserve; he repaired cash registers working for both IBM and NCR corporation for his full-time job. My mom was a computer entry technician and then later became an administrator at Bryant College, a business college in Rhode Island; she never got a degree.

Lallier explained that he talks to his parents every few months but he is not as close as he should be. He telephones his brother on a regular basis, once or twice monthly, but he does not talk to his sister regularly, because "She has her own family. She's gotten married so I don't speak to her that often."

Elementary School Years

W: Okay, now, let's talk a little about your elementary school experiences.

L: The first part of my life, up to age 10 when I lived in the city, I grew up in a neighborhood that was 99% Italian. So, (chuckle) I had to basically learn to be kind of a tough kid right off the bat. But everyone I knew was Italian and Catholic.

W: So why was there anything to fight about?

L: It's just that if you live on a different street, Italians fight based on who lives on what street, who your uncle is, and if your uncles don't like one another; if you cut through someone's yard, they shoot BB guns at you. (**L** and **W** chuckle.)

Lallier subsequently moved into the suburbs, about 10 miles away from the city, where most neighbors were White. **He did not speak Italian, but understood it**, because he grew up with Italian friends. He said he never saw many Black Americans in Rhode Island; he didn't go to school or play sports with any of them. He attended Catholic school run by nuns.

L: I got smacked with rulers. I still have nightmares when I go into an Office Depot today.

W: You mean the rulers might attack you? (Both chuckle.)

L: I went to LaSalle Academy, a **private school** run by the Christian Brothers and then graduated from a public school. Everyone was Irish, French, or Italian White. I never had any Asian instructors. I did, however, have an assistant principal, who later turned out to be one of my best friends. We called him Chief because he was a Cherokee Indian, huge, about 310, and if you saw him today, you would think he was Samoan.

High School and Beyond

Lallier said that after his high school graduation, he planned to enter college, but ended up joining the Army. His parents had encouraged him to go to college.

L: At that time, I was very, very thin; I only weighed about 145 pounds. I was allowed to play hockey with some colleges in Rhode Island but that summer they told me that I was too small to ever play in college or to become a pro. And because they discouraged me and said I would never grow bigger than 150 pounds, I wanted to just leave all that behind. The Army offered me an opportunity to live in Hawai'i (as my duty station).

Lallier explained that he was a lifeguard in high school, loved the beach, the sun, and warm weather. He did not want to play hockey anymore, as he could never be a professional. "I felt that my dream had been taken from me and so I just decided to go somewhere that they didn't play any hockey at all."

Army Background

W: Let's talk about Basic Training, Army Boot Camp. Where did you go?

L: I went to Fort Dix, New Jersey, to Basic Training where the Army first introduced me to other races and cultures. I had no actual prejudices, because **growing up I really didn't have any experiences dealing with anyone of other races.** Maybe, you grow up with prejudices because you don't know they are prejudices. It's just things that you say or things that are said to you. I didn't really have any preconceived prejudices in my heart and my soul that I can remember. **I had a Spanish as well as a Black drill sergeant and they were great; they were both outstanding.**

Lallier stated that both Spanish and Black drill sergeants 'treated him well' and made him a squad leader right off the bat. He could have gone to his mom's college (where she worked) tuition free; both his brother and sister graduated from Bryant College. But instead, he joined the Army, and went to Hawai'i in 1979.

Hawai'i and the Multicultural Experience

W: What was your reaction to the multicultural experience here in Hawai'i?

L: When I first came to Hawai'i, I was stationed at Schofield Barracks, with a wide variety of people. We had Blacks, Mexicans, Spanish, Puerto Ricans, and Asians. A couple of my closest friends weren't in the Army; one was Japanese and the other, Filipino and of course they both exposed me to their cultures. **This was completely foreign to me**. But it wasn't really a problem. But after a while, I noticed that there was a problem between people who were from Hawai'i and Whites (from the U.S. mainland). And then, I started to run into problems; occasionally, I'd be called *Haole* (White*)*, but I never took it personally.

W: You're talking about *Locals (*those from Hawai'i)?

L: Right, *Locals* vs. *Haoles*. I had a few run-ins, a few times in *Wahiawa*, because I lived outside of Schofield Barracks, and I used to work out at a gym in *Wahiawa* (2 miles away*)*. So, I was motivated to physically work out so I could defend myself.

W: How so?

L: My local friends actually encouraged me, 'cause they said Stu, you know you need to pack some weight on, because if you don't, you are at risk of getting beat up quite often. So, I started working out with them and my body grew pretty easily, and I was encouraged by local people here to enter bodybuilding competitions.

W: And did you?

L: Yes, in Hawai'i and elsewhere; I won a few different bodybuilding titles, too. I stayed in Hawai'i until 1982, then I decided to get out of the Army and enter the Reserves for a while. And I stayed here in Hawai'i working at a fitness center. Then I rejoined the Army again and I went overseas, to Germany. But before I did that, I got married to a local Filipino girl.

Information About Lallier's Wife

W: Did she come to Hawai'i directly from the Philippines?

L: Yes, she and her parents are from the Philippines. **She came to Hawai'i when she was nine and didn't speak any English.** She only spoke Ilocano, which is a dialect of the Philippines.

W: And do you speak Ilocano?

L: No, but I can understand some, a few words, but I can say some things that maybe she doesn't like (chuckle). But other than that . . .

W: (Chuckle) So what happened?

L: One parent came here, and they were able to sponsor her dad and some of her other uncles, and they were able to bring their families over. They had Resident Alien Cards, Green Cards. Her dad was a construction supervisor and her mom was a housekeeper at the Hyatt Hotel. My wife has five sisters and two brothers; they all have different occupations. She's in the middle. One of her brothers was a policeman; her sisters are cooks, nurses. My wife is a branch manager for Bank of Hawai'i.

W: And does she use her language at work?

L: Yes, that's part of what has made her successful; they've kept her at branches that deal primarily with Filipinos. Because she gets along so well with the Filipino customers. What's amazing is out of her whole family **she is the only one that was able to lose her accent.** When she speaks English, she does not have any accent at all. I asked her how she did that. She said she was just motivated because she knew that to be successful, she had to learn how to speak English without an accent. She said she spent two years in school **not** understanding anything the teacher said.

W: But she still graduated?

L: Yes, she graduated from Farrington High School. Which I found completely unbelievable because I had a hard enough time in school and I could understand English!

W: (Chuckle) Okay, all right, so you met her, you married her, and then you both went to Germany. Is that correct?

Family

L: I took her to Germany. Right. And then we had a son.

Lallier summarized his experiences in Germany by explaining that initially, **he learned to speak some German** because he was competing in bodybuilding contents and his sponsors were Germans; he was also sponsored by Germany fitness centers. He used to travel all over Europe representing the Army in bodybuilding. After almost five years in Germany, the Army sent him on recruiting duty to Santa Cruz, California and later, to the Recruiting Command in Hawai'i. Subsequently, his wife and son returned to Hawai'i.

W: Did you have any problems making friends with other people in the community because obviously you were a biracial couple?

L: Actually no, I didn't run into any serious issues in Europe. **I had a German landlady who basically adopted my wife and son, and she couldn't speak any English.** My wife seems to get along with everyone, really accepted, no matter where she goes. But she did experience some prejudice when I took her home to meet my parents. We went to Rhode Island. **My dad is a very prejudiced individual and he didn't make my wife feel too welcome over there.**

Parents' Reaction

W: Even with a grandchild?

L: Right. Which kind of upset her a little bit because she just couldn't understand that. Because she has absolutely no prejudices. My dad didn't seem to accept the fact that I had married a Filipino. But my mom had no problem with that.

W: So, you're the only one in the family that married a non-White.

L: Yes. And she's very dark.

W: Okay**, she is different in skin color and race.** But she speaks English fluently.

Multicultural – Multiracial Son

W: What language do you speak to your son?

L: English.

W: And does your son speak any other language besides English?

L: He understands Ilocano but doesn't speak it. Right now, he is attends Kapiolani Community College, Hawai'i. He plans to take the first two years of the pre-Pharmacy program, transfer to the University of Hawai'i in Hilo, and then become a pharmacist.

Father and Mother

W: Okay. Now, let's talk about your father's reaction to you marrying someone who was not White. **Is it possible that your father was prejudiced but you just did not know this?** Did your father share the same values as you did previously?

L: You know, **that's what I think is the problem**. I noticed in the Filipino culture, that if you leave home at 18, the family wonders what they did wrong, why you left. The family is willing to support you, to help you to get your college education, but the family likes to stay together as a unit. Whereas, I was brought up that when you're 18, you're on your own, out of the house, and you are expected to fend for yourself. So, I just grew up thinking that's how everyone was, and I didn't know any other way.

W: And your mom?

L: She always used to tell me all the time, when you are in my house you are under my rules, but once you are 18, you can move out. You can do what you want to do.

W: You said that maybe, she encouraged your brother and sister to go to college. Did she encourage you to go to college?

L: She encouraged me to go to college but she didn't encourage me to stay at home. She wanted me to be out, from under her roof. Later, my brother said she changed her tune and she did not make them feel that they had to leave home, that she wanted them to stay. And she has basically tried to keep them close. What I did made difference for him and my sister. **I never really gave much thought to other cultures. We just assumed that that's the way it was.** That everybody was that way. But when I got to Hawai'i, and made friends, I started to look around seeing how people treat each other. **I was amazed.** I asked my friends, don't your parents hassle you to move out? No. And when I visited them at their house, **their parents actually asked me if I needed a place to stay and invited me to live with them.** And I had a Filipino family with my Filipino friends and I had a Japanese family and a Chinese family and they all made me feel like part of their family and I found that strange because my own family showed me the door.

W: Perhaps, this culture (in Hawai'i) has a different way of viewing the age of majority (18)?

Effects of Maturity

L: Yeah, and it's affected me. Because I do everything I can to let my son know that I'm there for him, and I have never told him, not one time, that when you're 18, you've got to bail. You know, I want him to complete his college. I want to make sure that he's a success before he decides to break away, if he decides (to break away), which I'm sure he will . . . **but it's going to be his choice, because I didn't appreciate being forced out.**

W: You came from a European/American/White, Anglo-centric type family, and **you have your own family, which is multicultural/multiracial. Was that something you expected?**

L: Well, I love the Asian way of thinking, **I like the Asian culture.** I have spent, I think, the majority of my years actually in the Asian culture and so **I have grown to adopt that as my own.** I have over 20 years in the Army, now; at the end of 2006, I plan on retiring.

W: Let's talk for a moment, about your family. Who does your son resemble?

L: My son has dark eyes, but he is tall like me, six feet. He has similar facial features. But he has dark skin, dark hair, dark eyes. As for prejudice, I have run into this in Atlanta, Georgia, against me when I've been by myself. But not by other Whites, only by Blacks. And I ran into prejudices here, *Locals* vs. *Haoles*.

Filipina Wife

W: Has your wife indicated there has been any prejudice she has experienced herself?

L: Well, she ran into some (prejudice) in my hometown area, when she went to Rhode

Island, but it came **from women** especially when they saw her with me. But in Europe, she never had any problems. I never ran into any problems there either.

W: What about any kind of prejudices she felt, at work in Hawai'i?

L: She said there were sometimes customers who will make racial comments if they get upset at the bank.

W: What kinds of comments?

L: She told me that once, there was a Korean guy who started cursing them [bank tellers] out, calling them all FLIPS [an ethnic slur for Filipinas], and said that he knows that Filipinos don't like Koreans and all this stuff. But it was just a guy who was irritated.

An Analysis of this Interview

In summary, I enjoyed the interview experience. MSG Lallier has a particularly interesting background. He is a Caucasian who grew up in a White, middle-class working family, in a White, middle-class working neighborhood, understanding first French, then Italian. He joined the Army, and eventually married a Filipina from the Philippines and they settled in Hawai'i. **He showed substantial emotional growth in understanding the cultural value shift he experienced as an adult. He only learned as an adult, that there really are cultural and value differences among people.**

He told me that he assumed that everyone, at age 18 with a high school diploma, was expected to leave the house to make it on their own in life. He said he was amazed to discover that in Hawai'i, teenagers and young adults lived with their families for years, even after some of them married. This "family orientation" was initially strange. **However, he has adopted this belief because his only son lives at home now**, and attends a local community college. Unfortunately, MSG Lallier's father still has trouble accepting his gracious, Filipina wife although MSG Lallier's mother completely accepts her. So, Lallier grew up not realizing that his father was a racial bigot.

Personal Note

I found the entire subject of parental support interesting, because I personally assumed that anyone from a middle-class family would support their children, of any age, providing the children were attending school.

In addition, I know of few instances personally where young adults in Hawai'i who are in college or working full or part time can live on their own, economically. The cost of living is so extraordinarily high in Hawai'i, parts of California like San Francisco, Texas (Houston, Dallas), Illinois (Chicago), New York (Manhattan), Massachusetts (Boston), and similar high-cost of living locales that young adults need the support of their families, to attend school, even if they work part-time or even full-time. Studio apartments rent for a minimum of $800 per month (in 2005), and $1,200+ per month (in 2021), but that usually does not include all utilities (Internet, cable, gas, water, and electricity), which average $375+ a month, plus parking expenses.

It is quite common for adult children to live at home in such expensive parts of America. In these high-cost areas, rental costs are high together with security deposits and last-month's rent, so, together with transportation costs (think train, subway, taxi, Uber, personal vehicle, insurance, parking) the cost for an independent life style may be even higher. If young people move out, and live independently, that usually means they have several roommates, and all are working full-time or are college students with part-time jobs. Even so, many will need financial support from their families.

Personal - More

Perhaps I could have learned more from this assignment, if I was not born and raised in Hawai'i, of a racially mixed background (Hawaiian, Chinese, Portuguese, Russian), from parents who did not share the same religion (Catholic and Jewish). I attended pre-kindergarten through undergraduate school in Hawai'i, with students and teachers diverse in all respects. Growing up in Honolulu meant that some of my peers and instructors were Buddhists, Shintoists, Catholics, Jewish, Protestants, Quakers, agnostics, from every racial and ethnic group found in these islands (many with four to six racial extractions).

All through high school, I dated a variety of young men, from all races, colors, backgrounds, religions, values, economic and social levels, and attended the University of Hawai'i at Mānoa on two scholarships. My parents were both professionals, but with six children to care for, there were little if any leftover funds to pay for college. Most of us simultaneously worked while attending college, or went to school on scholarships, or did both.

Later, I taught at Hawai'i Job Corps (1969-1971) and then lived in the U.S. Territory of Guam (1972-1980), working there as a teacher of bilingual/ trilingual students full-time. I was also a part-time English as a Second Language and a U.S. Citizenship instructor (adult night school); I taught a culturally diverse adult student population. I also wrote many federal grants.

My own children are multiracial and they married interracially – my oldest son married a Greek-Chinese-Hawaiian-Nauruan-Portuguese lady, my second son has spent some 30 years with a part-Filipino-part-Caucasian woman, and I have a daughter who married a Puerto Rican-Portuguese-Filipino-Caucasian man. My late, beloved spouse was a Guamanian (CHamoru) from Guam (whose father was Filipino and mother, CHamoru) who learned English at about the age of 13. I also worked for the Army (1983-2012) all over the world and loved the multi-national people I met and the experiences I enjoyed in many foreign countries to which I was assigned.

In summary, I enjoyed interviewing MSG Lallier. I learned that even now, in the 21st century, **prejudice is alive and well** and continues in families and thus, society (to include its institutions such as schools, businesses, organizations). Lallier's father shows bias towards Lallier's wife, for no logical reason. **But Lallier changed his own attitudes, beliefs, values, and behavior because of his own personal life experiences:** Army life, traveling, interracial marriage, a biracial son, friends, and gaining maturity in the process. Change continues for Lallier, although he could not alter his father's biased, bigoted beliefs.

The physical transcribing of the complete interview took six hours, over four Sundays. This ethnographic experience was stimulating, one which I shall always treasure.

CH 39 Ethical Issues and

Qualitative Research, 9RRC, Army Reserve

My Pearl of Wisdom: Volunteering, Military Style

Education is a better safeguard of liberty than a standing army.

Edward Everett

INTERVIEWING SOLDIERS at 9th Regional Readiness Command (9RRC) about their use of Army Reserve Tuition Assistance (TA) involves several ethical issues (Army Reserve, 2021). Interviewing soldiers (including a carefully worded written survey) was part of my doctoral dissertation, as I planned to test several hypotheses **such as working full-time, little or no access to the Internet and computers, and that lack of information about Army reserve TA results in soldiers not using their educational benefits** (Absher, 2020, 2021; Department of the Army, 2006; U.S. Army Reserve, 2021; Wellein, 2010). A carefully worded written survey seems appropriate, when I interviewed soldiers.

Volunteering, Military Style

In addition to first getting written authorization for the interview and survey from the commanding general of 9RRC (via my own supervisor, who had to go up the chain of command himself) I used concepts on ethical considerations taken from several sources (American Educational Research Association, 2021; Patton, 2002) and from the class lectures at Argosy University as well.

Five Ethical Issues

One ethical issue involves the fact that volunteer soldiers may stop the interview prior to and during the interview at any time. I must explain to soldiers that they may change their mind (about participating) without negative consequences. Researchers not familiar with the military should note that usually the term 'volunteer' does not mean that soldiers actually have the option to say no. **There is almost no such thing as a true volunteer in the military**. In fact, the military is well known for using the term 'volunteer' to mean that the senior ranking soldier will select lower ranking soldiers who he or she desires to do the chore, move the equipment, run an errand, paint the wall, etc.

Those selected are then designated as having volunteered. Therefore, it is quite important that the researcher fully explain to the soldiers that they indeed have an **actual choice** in participating in the interview-survey project, and that absolutely nothing will happen to them if they decline. (They will **not** be made to do 20 sit-ups, 30 push-ups, 40 jumping jacks, or run a mile under 'X' minutes with a 30-pound backpack if they refuse to volunteer.)

A second ethical issue involves the concept of providing soldiers with information about the purpose, procedures, and method of interviewing and completing the survey. Soldiers also need to know how the information gleaned will be used. They also must be protected from risk and harm, to include even the perception of harm. The Army also strives to attract young men and women into the service, and thus, must avoid any negative perceptions.

A third ethical issue is that the informed consent should be clear to the soldiers. In the military, anything of importance is written, with the soldier signing and dating the document to show that the soldier indeed understands what he or she is doing. Thus, informed consent must be able to withstand direct scrutiny and inspection by the U.S. Army Inspector General, Army lawyer, or any other official who reviews procedures if soldiers complain about them. Thus, documents should avoid almost all abbreviations, symbols, acronyms, technical, and complex terms.

A fourth ethical issue is that of the right to privacy and confidentiality. Soldiers must understand that the interviewer would never identify any soldier by name, rank or unit, but rather use only ranges of ranks. For example, enlisted junior soldiers hold the rank of private through specialist, and senior enlisted soldiers hold the rank of sergeant through command sergeant major. Although the researcher would never individually identify the particular senior soldiers, there still cannot be a 100% certainty of anonymity. That is because some units have very few senior enlisted soldiers.

If I interviewed two senior soldiers (E-8) from Unit A for instance, it might be possible to identify these two E-8 soldiers because there were no other senior enlisted available from their unit, unless the researcher takes great care in protecting their personal characteristics. An additional part of this privacy and confidentiality issue is that a researcher must be careful to secure and store transcript survey materials and interview data, and to restrict unauthorized access to them as well.

A fifth ethical issue deals with ensuring that those involved in the research have the capability, capacity, and comprehension abilities to fully understand what it is that they are doing. Army reservists must pass a standardized military entrance examination that emphasizes reading and math (at the 10th grade level). Then, they must endure months of physical training and tests (running, chin-ups, road marches), withstand all types of stress (e.g., separation from family and loved one, emotional turmoil), as well as learning skills of a specific occupation such as military police officer, nurse, radio dispatcher, dental hygienist, medical technician, water desalinizer, and helicopter repair mechanic. The military assumes that soldiers have a certain amount of the big C's: **capability, capacity, and comprehension.**

Anyone who does not mold to fit Army standards is evaluated by a psychologist or psychiatrist and then might be terminated from service usually during the initial training period, which may last for a year or longer, depending on the job the soldier must learn. Soldiers seriously depressed or emotionally ill are released from their military contracts immediately.

Summary

To summarize important ethical issues when performing qualitative research such as surveying and interviewing Army reserve soldiers, the researchers must remember to allow soldiers to volunteer or withdraw from the project at any time without any negative consequences. The researcher must also give full disclosure as to the purpose and procedures of the meeting while protecting soldiers from any perceived or actual risk, provide informed consent, ensure privacy and confidentiality for those who participate, and lastly, remember that capability, capacity, and comprehension by military subjects are a must.

Volunteering for military service is totally separate, of course, from volunteering to participate in research. Ethical issues must be identified whenever soldiers are involved in research, always in the interest of the soldiers.

CH 40 Innovative Credit Card Usage:

9 RRC, Army Reserve

My Pearl of Wisdom: Money Talks

Learning is not compulsory. Neither is survival.

Dr. W. Edwards Deming

THIS CHAPTER IS ABOUT MY WORK at Army Reserve, HI, from 2001 through 2012. Beginning in 2000, the United States Army Reserve authorized Tuition Assistance (TA) for soldiers to attend schools to obtain their diplomas, certificates, associates, bachelors, and masters degrees (Absher, 2020, 2021; Wellein, 2021). This chapter discusses a new TA process – what, why, when, where, problems, recommendations, and what Jonell Calloway, the Director of Army Reserve worldwide in St Louis actually did. Subsequently, the process was refined, soldiers faced fewer restrictions and by then, the pattern for success was obvious: keep it simple so that everyone wins at the end – the soldier, the colleges, and the Army.

My work at the 9RRC from 2001 through 2012 forms the basis of this discussion. I included information about using the government credit card to show how important it is to first recognize a significant problem, identify possible causes, and then implement workable solutions.

What is TA

TA covers all postsecondary tuition and mandatory fees, up to $250 per semester hour, not to exceed $4,500 per fiscal year (Wellein, 2010, 2021). In the beginning of FY 2007, the Director of Education, GS14 Jonell Calloway, Human Resource Command (HRC) St. Louis, Missouri, mandated that all 15 Army Reserve Regional Readiness

Command (RRC**) education offices pay college invoices/bills using a particular government credit card.**

Unfortunately, only three RRCs complied. Previously, college business officials submitted bills to the RRC education office most geographically nearby which verified the information, then the reserve office sent the documents to the RRC Budget/Finances office, and this office sent the bills forward to the main **Army's Defense Finance and Accounting System (DFAS) in Rome, NY for payment.** Talk about a circuitous route!

Major Problems

DFAS would take from three to seven months to pay schools, while a few schools would inadvertently not receive any payment at all. Schools sometimes disenrolled soldiers already in classes, or refused to send transcripts to them citing lack of payment from the Army as the reason. In mid-2007, 9RRC in Hawai'i decided to use the government credit card to immediately pay college invoices, which proved most successful, once we worked out all the many kinks.

Executive Summary

9RRC located at Fort Shafter Flats, HI supports Army Reserve Soldiers throughout Pacific and Asia. Geographically, this includes approximately 3600 soldiers located in Fairbanks and Anchorage Alaska, Maui, the Big Island of Hawai'i, Oahu, Commonwealth of the Northern Mariana Islands (Saipan), United States Territories of Guam and American Samoa, as well as Japan and Korea (Commands, n.d.).

The TA program at 9RRC is quite popular with 15% of the reserve soldiers using it; the worldwide average for Army Reserve soldiers at other Regional Readiness Commands (RRCs) is only 8.9% (Ali, 2005; Department of the Army, 2019).

From 2000-2006, colleges and universities enrolling 9RRC soldiers received TA forms from 9RRC, billed the 9RRC Education Office (which sent all invoices to 9RRC Budget Office), and then waited months for their payments, with some of these bills accruing substantial interest. Unfortunately, some schools penalized student-soldiers when payments were late by **dropping them from courses, preventing them from**

graduating or receiving official transcripts. What a dreadful mess!

DFAS in NY was supposed to pay the school's bills within 30 days because after that**, interest would accrue**. Unfortunately, DFAS would take many months to pay schools, while a few schools would inadvertently not receive any payment at all. DFAS also charged interest on late payments or unpaid bills. Additionally, at times, DFAS would claim not to have received the invoices and TA forms, despite the documentation sheet from the faxing process, proving that DFAS actually did indeed receive the invoices

The problems with DFAS would result in G8 budget personnel again re-faxing documents a **second and third time** to DFAS.

Credit Card Usage Change

In early 2007, the Director of Army Reserve in Human Resources Command, St. Louis (HRC-STL) sent a memo to all regional directors of education, including me, mandating that each RRC education office would pay all school bills for TA promptly by government credit card. However, we education directors did not receive any specific, written procedures from the headquarters **budget officer.** Based on command structure, the Army Reserve education director in Missouri had no way of dictating specific procedures to the budget offices (a different agency) at 15 RRCs located inside and outside of the continental United States.

Thus, I contacted all the other 14 RRC education directors asking if they were indeed, using a government credit card to pay the schools directly, and if so, for some information including memorandums, process methods, and a list of **who did what** in terms of budget and education personnel at their command. Two RRCs immediately responded (88RRC in Wisconsin and 96RRC in Utah), each with totally different credit card payment processes. After reviewing those RRC e-mails and attached documents, reviewing the procedures with Director Calloway in Missouri and noting that each RRC did it "their own way," I decided to implement my own simplified plan, using elements from both RRCs combined with my own.

9RRC Plan to Use a Credit Card

The 9RRC's plan consisted of first discussing possible methods and procedures with my office staff, supervisor, and then informally with the G8 Budget personnel involved. **I then prepared a memo** stipulating which individual was responsible for each particular task, under what circumstances, exactly when and how, and sent the memo to the resource manager at G8 through my supervisor, for discussion prior to implementation. G8 responded immediately. The budget officer wanted to meet to discuss the contents of the memo, specifically to address the G8's role in paying schools by government credit card.

After a lengthy meeting with G8 staff members to include two budget analysts and the resource manager, it became clear to all that **the credit card process would involve the education staff almost entirely,** with the resource manager (in concert with the G4 credit card manager) mainly involved in the 'loading 'of the credit card with TA funds. Moreover, the education technician would be responsible to document the disbursement of TA funds to the various schools weekly using a specially created Excel spreadsheet.

Finally, I then revised my memo, sending it to the 9RRC resource manager through her supervisor and to Jonell Calloway for final editing and approval. The new plan to pay school invoices by government credit card officially began at 9RRC in mid-August, 2007. (Subsequently, all RRCs followed suit, using the identical procedures, finalized by Director Calloway.)

Findings

Four major findings became significant because these new TA processing procedures affected soldiers nationally and internationally. Army reserve soldiers attached to 9RRC were also living in California, Oregon, and elsewhere, as they live and can drill (referred to as a battlefield assembly) monthly with a nearby geographically close unit or a distant one and still maintain their affiliation with 9RRC. This is true for all reservists in the 15 reserve commands; they can live in one state, but drill in another location.

The first finding is that schools fully embraced the new credit card process. They could be paid within one week from the invoice submission date. What a change!

The second finding is that the time it took to process TA payments was reduced from an average of twelve weeks to one week. Again, wonderful!

The third finding is that schools no longer asked student-soldiers to withdraw from school, miss graduation ceremonies, or pay tuition costs up-front, while schools waited for government payment. Finally, soldiers were protected!

Finally, the fourth finding is that the Army stopped paying tens of thousands of dollars in interest to schools for late payments, and the schools returned tens of thousands of dollars in prompt-payment rebates to the Army. It was a win-win situation for all.

In making recommendations for HRC in St Louis, to improve the new credit card processes, Director Calloway did the following:

1. Encourage and later direct that all Regional Readiness Commands (RRCs) participate in the credit card payment process, by sending all education managers and budget managers clearly written processes and procedures.

2. Request that all postsecondary institutions participate in the credit card process by sending all their business office managers a memo explaining procedures, showing how schools may be paid promptly through this new method of payment.

3. Explain in a memo to the Budget Director of U.S. Army Reserve Command (USARC) in Atlanta, Georgia, (with a copy sent to all 15 RRC budget managers) tips on to how to use the government credit card to pay for school invoices.

4. Stipulate that rebates from Bank of America, the company that owns the credit card, are to be actually **credited back to the 15 RRC TA accounts monthly, rather than be diverted** into the general 'U.S. Treasury fund.' This matter may be best handled by the Chief Budget Director, USARC, in Atlanta, Georgia.

A monthly report prepared by each RRC's budget office should include the date, dollar amount of the rebate, how long this transfer takes, name of institution, with a fund receipt confirmation and sent to Jonell Calloway at HRC-STL. One G4 Logistics Card

Holder Manger at a mid-west RRC headquarters office implementing this new credit card payment plan stated that she personally had never seen any rebate previously returned to the TA account. So, this is an extremely serious issue: rebates could be well over fifteen to thirty thousand dollars from just one small college, for one term.

9RRC was dealing with over 65 colleges usually offering 4+ terms per year (regular and summer programs). Many other RRCs were handling invoices from dozens of colleges each term, in various states, so money saved in rebates was significant!

Background Information

The 9RRC in Honolulu is one of 15 such commands located across the United States, Puerto Rico, Europe, Pacific, and Asia, to provide Army Reserve soldiers a home post, where they can attend monthly drills (called battle drill assemblies) one weekend a month. Each soldier has an essential job to perform at these drills (such as computer technician, truck driver or mechanic, medical assistant, etc.) and later, if activated, mobilized, and deployed, to serve in the war zones in the Middle East or elsewhere. Beginning in 2001, the Army leadership ordered approximately half of the reservists worldwide to active-duty due to fight in the continuing war in Afghanistan and Iraq (J. Obusan, personal communication, March 4, 2007).

One of the three main reasons young men and women enter the military reserve is due to educational benefits (Ali, 2005; Wellein, 2010). A major educational benefit is TA. Each soldier may work towards **one each** of a diploma, certificate, associate, bachelor, and master's or first professional degree with TA funds going directly to the postsecondary institution (not the individual soldier).

There are other educational programs and services offered to military personnel, such as the Veterans Affairs' GI Bill, the External Degree Program (DANTES External, 2006), lucrative Reserve Officer Training Corps (ROTC) Scholarships and many more (U.S. Army Reserve, 2021). But TA usage is number one for many reservists.

Organization Description/History

The HRC-STL in Missouri provides command and control over the 15 regional readiness commands. Sometimes, there appears to be a political struggle for power between HRC-STL and the United States Army Recruiting Command (USARC) located in Atlanta, Georgia according to the Director of Army Reserve, HRC-STL (J. Calloway, personal communication, July 2, 2007). Ms. Calloway provides many millions of dollars for funding the TA program, as well as for operations (supplies, equipment, travel, etc.) for the 17 RRC education services specialists and contract services (approximately 70 contractors who staff the education services offices).

Before 2000, the Army only offered **regular TA** to active-duty soldiers, and not reservists. The 9RRC was one of the first commands to do so, on a reimbursable basis. The TA program proved so popular with soldiers that they identified it as an especially important program, which Ms. Calloway in St. Louis noted, when she implemented the new, standardized TA program to all reservists the following year in 2001. Ms. Calloway asked the Chief of Army Reserve for funding, and obtained **$4.8 million for TA**, and additional funds for operation and contract costs. **The TA program grew exponentially,** so that in fiscal year 2006, HRC-STL spent over $44 million just for TA, alone.

Service Description:

By directing all education offices to pay schools using a government credit card and by-passing the DFAS office in Rome, NY, everyone seemed satisfied: the soldiers, colleges, DFAS, 15 RRC budget and education offices, Mrs. Calloway, and her supervisors. The 9RRC Budget Office's responsibilities would only include tracking the payments of invoices to colleges using their own proprietary software program for accountability. The army could thus save huge sums of money.

Glorious, Remarkable Technologies

Each Army Reserve education office uses a specially developed proprietary software program, Web-Enabled Education Benefit System (WEBS) which Jonell Calloway, Director of Education contracted American Telephone & Telegraph to develop over a three-year period beginning in 2003. She allocated AT&T the funds, assisted by her very capable Deputy Director Abdul Ali, and provided the company with specifications. Training and evaluation by users (including all the other regional directors of education) improved WEBS yearly.

WEBS is an exceptionally fine tuition tracking system; it allows the education office personal to pull up soldier-requests for courses from some 5000+ colleges and universities, enter grades earned, views funds obligated and disbursed, and perform some 50 or more activities related to TA usage and funding. These include fund-denials, degree plans, counselor-comments, which schools are owed money, which Army units used specific amounts of tuition funds, names of soldiers (enlisted vs. officers, or both, alphabetically or in any other order desired) who were denied (or obtained) TA funding. Mrs. Calloway continues to refine WEBS, so that the features are more user friendly. Again, the WEBS discussion here was during my tenure a Fort Shafter, 2001-2012.

Staffing at 9RRC

9RRC education services office consists **of one Department of Army civilian (DAC)** who serves as the Army Reserve Regional Director of Education for Pacific and Asia holding the rank of GS12 (equivalent to a Lieutenant Colonel), and **three contractors.** I wrote these three Army contracts, myself as I explained earlier.

Other RRCs have completely different numbers of education contractors, depending on their size and locations. If one RRC provides services to 25,000 soldiers located in six states, it will need many more contractors than perhaps another RRC with only 10,000 soldiers located in three states. So, using the government credit card to pay college invoices was a stroke of genius.

Additionally**,** I requested and received authorization in 2003 **to establish a Veterans Affairs (VA) Work Study Program site,** and thus three to seven program participants work part-time in the education office throughout the year, although they constantly change from one semester to the next. **9RRC was the only reserve center to request a VA program**. VA pays the student workers directly (minimum wage but without tax charged) and these student-workers provide excellent office assistance: they maintain paper supplies for printers and facsimile machines, photocopy thousands of flyers and informational papers and brochures, reproduce materials for the Basic Skills courses the education office offers and manages each year, etc.

G8 Budget staff's involvement in the payment of TA was substantially reduced to that of obligating the funds, which they do for all Army programs. Therefore, **the budget officer could reduce the amount of work** of one budget specialist for this tuition-payment process from 50% of a work year to perhaps **5% or less** of a work year.

Overall Evaluation of Goals and Limitations:

I designed and administered a survey via e-mail to 25 school business officials (out of 65 schools we dealt with), to obtain feedback about the new TA/invoice process. Seven officials responded, indicating that they really liked the new credit card payment system and why. We used an internal evaluator; it would have been interesting to have an external one as well. When I left 9RRC in December 2012, the credit card process and WEBS was working well.

Chapter Summary

The Director of Education at HRC-STL directed all 15 RRCs to use the credit card process to pay school invoices in December 2006. However, only 9RRC and three other RRCs initially complied. Additionally, there was no opportunity to determine how much money DFAS was spending on interest to colleges due to late bill payments (and conversely, how much money DFAS was saving due to prompt bill payment.)

Many colleges across America increase their tuition and fee rates yearly, if not bi-annually and postsecondary institutions in Hawai'i and the Pacific are no exception. If researchers were able to make accurate predictions about such increases, perhaps the Army would provide sufficient funding at the beginning of each fiscal year (in October) rather than the Army Reserve and other branches of the service always requesting additional funding mid-year or later.

Paying schools by credit card will help speed up this "prediction of tuition and fees process" because the Army Reserve can now pay at least 90% of the schools' invoices by the end of the fiscal year (in September). Previously, under the DFAS payment method, the Army Reserve was paying about 50% of the schools **late, after** the current fiscal year ended.

Recommendations by HRC-STL:

A. Continue the credit card process at 9RRC, expanding the procedures used to other RRCs. HRC-STL will encourage all RRCs to quickly transition to this new credit card payment system by establishing set procedures, and then sending these procedures-list to all RRCs with a copy to their budget offices. In the meantime, Ms. Calloway asked education directors at all RRCs using the credit card method to send their ideas and procedures-sheet to her office, where she **can finalize just one procedural list, and then send them out to all the RRCs.**

B. Encourage the Chief Budget Officer for United States Army Reserve (USAR) to send out a detailed message to all budget officers in all RRCs to help education offices with this transition from former DFAS involvement to the new credit card procedures. Also ask these RRC budget gurus to use the sizeable rebates given to each RRC from Bank of America, for "prompt payment" action to fund even more TA dollars.

C. Stipulate that all RRC's education offices conduct a monthly review on this new process of paying college invoices, to ensure that procedures go smoothly.

Testimonials, Comments Made by Stakeholders

Many school business office personnel have expressed their approval of the new credit card process in telephone conversations and e-mails. The Resource Manager, G8, in Hawai'i stated on more than one occasion that the new method of paying schools will save enormous time and energy. Education Office personnel concur. **The taxpayers will of course, win** because DFAS will not have to pay any interest to schools for making late payments (over 30 days), and will gain funds from colleges through prompt payment. Soldiers will no longer be forced to drop courses due to non-payment of tuition, and they will not have to pay colleges upfront, hoping that the Army will reimburse them. Thus, important stakeholders – soldiers, college officials, education officers and staff, and the Army, will be satisfied. A hearty thanks to Jonell Calloway, folks! She is a true visionary.

PART C: ADULT AND HIGHER EDUCATION: LIFE'S CHALLENGES

My Pearl of Wisdom: Gotcha Now!

There are those that look at things the way they are, and ask why?

I dream of things that never were, and ask why not?

Robert Francis Kennedy

Change is the law of life. And those who look only to the past or present are certain to miss the future.

John Fitzgerald Kennedy

CH 41 The Adult Learner - Many Factors:

Adults Learn What They Want,

When They See a Need!

My Pearl of Wisdom: Rainbows Follow Rain

When people talk, listen completely.

Most people never listen.

Ernest Hemingway

EDUCATOR STEPHEN LIEB (1991) discusses barriers adults have against participating in the postsecondary learning experience. He mentions childcare, transportation, scheduling problems as well as insufficient funds, low confidence, little interest, not enough time, and general lack of information. Many other factors include expensive access to Internet services, lack of computer/printer equipment, and working full-time (Walsh, 2020; Wellein, 2010). However, Lieb mainly focuses on what he calls lack of motivation by adults. Unless adult learners have a real need for the learning experience such as requirements for a present or near-future job, or a license or certificate for promotion, adults may not see the value of the learning experience (Wellein, 2021).

Finally, Lieb concludes by stating that adult educators need to determine why their students are in class, so that they can figure out how to best enhance the learners' motivational base. One of the principles of good teaching is that it can never be reduced to simply technique. Adult learners must always see the value and importance of what they are learning, which involves the motivation factor (Doctoral Journey, 2018).

Pedagogical vs. Andragogical Models

Dr. Malcolm S. Knowles, considered the father of andragogy by many adult educators, discusses the basic difference between **teaching children (the pedagogical model)** vs. the **teaching adults (the andragogical model)** in his famous, seminal textbook, *The Adult Learner* (Knowles, Holton, & Swanson, 2005). The military, elementary, middle, and high schools, most colleges, churches, and many other institutions (Wellein, 2021) **use the pedagogical method (i.e., for children), based on four (false) assumptions** (Knowles et al., 2005):

First, the instructor considers the learner to be a dependent individual. This means that such learners are passive and only follow directions given by the instructor.

Secondly, the instructor believes that the learner has little if any experience that can be useful in the learning process. Only the instructor has the experience needed; this requires a one-way communication method of learning, from instructor to learner.

Third, the learner is told that he/she must understand specific information, to get the next promotion, advance to the next grade, or pass a particular barrier (such as school admissions).

Finally, the learner only learns when external forces from employers, parents, partners, trainers, and teachers demand that he/she understands, or suffer the consequences of poor grades, no certificates, no promotions or acceptance in schools.

Dr. Knowles (2005) contrasts the above pedagogical model learning model (children) with that of his contemporary andragogical learning model (adults), which has the following characteristics:

- The adult learner directs the learner's own life. This includes deciding on what and when to learn.

- The adult learner brings to the learning experience a wealth of **experience**.

- The adult is **not** a blank palette. This [life] experience provides a valuable resource to other learners as well as to the instructor.

- The adult learner is prepared to learn when he or she perceives the **need to know** something, i.e., is ready to learn for a reason; the pressure to learn is internalized.

- The adult learner must experience an actual need to learn . . . learning needs to be **problem-focused or task-centered**. Adults want to apply what they have learned as quickly as possible (Knowles et al., 2005 p. 295).

Pedagogy, literally 'leading children,' on the other hand is based on the following premises:

- The learner is dependent on the teacher because this individual decides all learning activities, i.e., what, how, when, where and for how long; the **teacher decides everything**.

- Only the teacher explains and evaluates the learning experiences.

- The teacher follows **only** standardized curriculum.

- External motivation is the rule. Learning is not self-directed.

- Learning styles such as reality based, holistic, etc. are not encouraged.

- Students' own personal experiences are **not** often included in the learning process. (Knowles et al., 2005 p. 295)

To summarize **Dr. Knowles (2005), pedagogical (learning by children) orientation is concerned with content while andragogical (learning by adults) orientation is mainly concerned with process.**

Teachers of Adults Should Remember (Peterson, 2019; Walsh, 2020) **to**:

1. Enjoy the experiences adults bring with them into the classroom and use such experiences as resources for both teachers and students. **Learners can be an excellent resource for instructors.**

2. Accept that adult learners have already **established** lifestyles, opinions, beliefs, and values. Be sure to respect these different cultural attributes even though they may be totally different from those held by the rest of the students and teachers. Learners must be ready to learn. They bring a great deal of life experiences into the classroom, sometimes more than the instructors. They can share these life lessons with others.

3. Use **eclectic teaching methods** with adult learners. One teaching style will not fit all. Explore the tactile, kinesthetic, visual, auditory, participatory, small-group

discussions, and combinations of such teaching styles, to reach adults – all adults. Merely using the lecture method generally proves to be difficult for adults, as it is for those of any age. Learning speed and reaction time may be slower for adults than younger learners, but age does not slow down adults' ability to learn the subject matter.

4. Understand that **adults learn** by relating new information to that already (previously) learned; adults prefer learning single concepts and understanding how that concept applies to practical, real-life requirements. They want to know how that new information applies to them, that is, what is the reason for learning the new skill or information? Why now? If they have no experience with the subject presented, they might find learning of that subject difficult. Learners are self-directed and must decide that the information is important, rather than the instructor just telling them it is. The learners' self-concepts are important, and autonomous.

5. Plan breaks throughout the day, if adults are taking daylong classes or sessions, but at least regular hourly breaks. Students should be comfortable in appropriate chairs designed for adults, as well.

6. Support the development of **self-esteem and ego**. Respect all students' questions and comments and **never say** "I just covered that area" or "You are old enough to know." (Yes, readers, I have actually heard that in many classrooms over the years! Haven't you?)

7. Avoid the transmission of mere knowledge for knowledge's sake when teaching. Adult learners enjoy a problem-centered approach to learning. **Use examples in real life,** and discuss real case studies. Ask adult learners to apply the new information they learned immediately to real problems and situations. Learners are highly motivated to identify and solve issues that affect them. They are also self-motivated as they are internally driven rather than externally driven to learn.

Some investigators (Knowles et al., 2005; Peterson, 2019; Walsh, 2020) believe that there are **three broad categories of knowledge** about how adults learn, to include **motivation factors common to adult learners, curriculum design factors, and**

important information factors to teachers of adults using direct instruction in the classroom.

Three Broad Categories of Knowledge – a Review

Motivation to learn is the first vital factor. Adults seek knowledge to deal with specific events in their life and the greater number of life-changing events, the more likely these adults will search for new learning opportunities. Then too, adults must perceive a relationship between the life-event and new knowledge offered. Third, adults will seek out the new skill to deal with the life event if they believe that learning is a way to solve their problem. Finally, adults like to increase their self-esteem or at least maintain whatever they have already.

Curriculum design is another broad category, and covers over a dozen areas of concern. First, adults tend to like single-theory, single-concept application courses, rather than general survey courses. Most adults need to connect the new ideas gained with what they already know to understand and make use of the new ideas. They reevaluate the new ideas slowly if they experience any conflict with the older ideas, or if the ideas are too abstract.

Additionally, some adults discover taking fast-paced courses with unusual or unique learning tasks initially difficult. Adults tend to enjoy reinforcement, practice, complex tasks divided into easy learning segments, followed by additional reinforcement. Then too, adults tend to be more accurate when using trial and error methods with practical applications available.

Many adults are not risk-takers and wish to use previously approved solutions to problem solving. **Some take errors personally**, and this tends to affect their self-confidence levels. Educators must understand that adults have their own values and belief systems, hold various viewpoints at different life stages, with life experiences considered more important than mere theories. Adults like self-designed/self-directed learning projects, rather than large group projects to control the learning pace and time limits. Teachers must remember that many adults can accept how-to-do-it facts more readily than abstract information. And teachers, trainers, and supervisors: praise liberally and often!

Important Information Factors

Educators believe that adults risk their self-confidence and egos when encountering foreign or culturally different ideas, and **some have had negative experiences when attending school at an earlier time in their lives**. Then too, adults come to class with a variety of life experiences that teachers should expect and use as resource material. Finally, adults welcome open-ended questions, but at times, must be reminded to remain civil during heated discussions (Klein-Collins, 2018). Combining new skills and information takes time, but when teachers use eclectic teaching methods, adult learners tend to retain information easier than just listening to lectures.

Issues/Concerns

Two important concerns which educators discuss in various literature are that **some older adults may lack readiness skills** to use new technologically advanced equipment and materials, and/or programs, **and also may not be oriented appropriately to the learning process** as they have been out of the classroom in many cases, for decades. Teachers should address these two issues (readiness to learn technical skills and learning processes development after lengthy school absences) early on, to ensure that the classroom experiences for adult learners are positive and rewarding.

Learning Variables – A Discussion Summary

The first learning variable is motivation of adult learners. Instructors set a positive feeling or tone of the class session, and establish an appropriate level of difficulty of material. Adult learners should receive regular, specific, helpful feedback and acknowledgement from the instructor that they have mastered the material, or specifics as to how to do better. Adults must be interested in the subject for real learning to occur in an easy manner; they need a valid reason for learning the materials, skills, or gaining information for such learning to be effective.

For example, prior to taking the pre-law school admissions test to enter law school, most adults certainly want to prepare well for that examination. The **motivation** for scoring high is obvious. These adults may attend a two-day workshop learning about the Law School Admission Test (LSAT) in preparation for the exam, following a rigorous month of self-study using a LSAT study guide. Another example is an adult who needs to pass the GED test to apply for a job, or enter the armed services. Motivation to study and do well on the test is extremely high!

The second learning variable is reinforcement, the act of encouraging or strengthening a belief or behavior (Merriam-Webster, n.d.). Usually, teachers can provide positive reinforcement when teaching new skills, to strengthen them. (Unfortunately, some instructors tend to use mainly negative reinforcement when teaching.) In the example cited above, if an adult took the LSAT prep class, but then scored poorly on the LSAT, this student might need to work on specifics, i.e., learning how to reread test questions prior to choosing an answer, for example. Reinforcement involves skill building, sound academic preparation, always working toward mastery of the subject.

The **third learning variable,** in addition to motivation and reinforcement, is **retention**, the ability to remember new or previously learned material. Retention for adults is directly affected by understanding how they can use and apply the new information. If adult learners do not connect a meaning or purpose for the new skill or information, they will have difficulty in remembering and retaining the information learned. Practice by learners will directly affect their level of retention.

The **fourth and final learning variable is transference**, the skill of adult learners to utilize the new skill or information learned, either positively or negatively to another task. Usually, transference happens when the adult learners can directly associate new information or skill with some aspect of what they already know. If they can revisit a familiar pattern or skill, if they see similarity with the old vs. new information, **or finally**, if they learn critical information which is helpful to them for real-life jobs or school, these adult learners will transfer newly gained knowledge to what they already know.

Summary

The best motivational factors for adult learners are **high interest (in the subject matter) coupled with selfish benefits**. If learners understand how the new skill will help them in a practical manner, they will usually learn faster, retain a greater amount of information for a longer period and participate fully in the learning experience.

As a side note, my husband who worked at Waiawa Correctional Facility took Sign Language I, II, and III at the nearby adult night school, sponsored by the Department of Education. Why? **Because three of the inmates were deaf.** They could not communicate their needs with the staff, including the nurse. An interpreter could visit, on a specific time and date, to allow these disabled men to discuss court appearances or family issues. But for **everyday needs**, no.

So, Daniel as an adult learner, saw the need for learning Sign Language and did so, to communicate with the deaf inmates. This is a perfect example showing that the adult leaner will learn when he is motivated, ready, and knows he will use the information immediately.

Basic Skills Courses, Army Style – a Perfect Example

Personally, adult learners who take the 9th Regional Readiness Command's (9RRC) Basic Skills course at Fort Shafter Flats (Army Reserve) in Honolulu, and demonstrate good attendance (show up for class 75% of the time or are in class 45 of the 60 hours of instruction) are precisely the types of adults discussed in this chapter. These students are highly motivated, and take the reading and mathematics review course for a specific purpose as follows:

- To take the military entrance exam to enter active-duty or reserve service; they are civilians.

- To prepare for college placement examinations; they are applying to colleges.

- To retake the military entrance exam to re-enlist, change military jobs, enter specialized fields such as warrant officer corps or become a commissioned officer; they are already in the military.

- For other reasons, such as wanting to prepare to enter the civilian job market, or help children with their homework. Learners in this category usually drop out of the Basic Skills course by the fourth-class session or as soon as they feel they have learned enough material to meet their needs; they can be military or civilian.

Adult learners are highly motivated, receive appropriate reinforcement, retain their new skills, and are then able to transfer this new skill or information to real life.

I have seen this happen with new students in the **Basic Skills courses** (Department of the Army, 2006, Wellein, 2010, 2021) at Fort Shafter, Honolulu; Schofield Barracks, Hawai'i; as well as Larson Barracks, Germany; North and South Camp, Sinai, Egypt; Soto Cano Air Base, Honduras; Fort Kobbe, Panama; Camp Zama, Japan; Comp Howze, South Korea; Fort Buchanan, Puerto Rico; Army Reserve Center, American Samoa; and a few other locations where I directed the Basic Skills program. Military family members (or those without military affiliation) ages 16 and above could join active-duty and reserve personnel whenever there was space available.

In a recent article by Jaclyn Walsh (2020) she writes about how adults can prepare themselves prior to returning to school. Her suggestions include using the school's career counseling offices if available, taking basic review courses (math, computer and English skills) at adult education centers or 'night school,' and reminding themselves that 'I am not alone.'

Other articles and books on adult learning mention that many adult education programs address life changes or life-span issues, such as marriage, divorce, finances, retirement, parenting, health, spiritual growth, job seeking, and citizenship,

Finally, another earlier article, *Introduction to adult learning* (Conner, n.d.) discusses an overview of adult learning theory, lists important books about andragogy, provides links to other related websites, and finally discusses other key adult learning resources. Maria Conner mentions that in many western societies, people believe that aged adult learners demonstrate diminished capacity to learn new ideas, data, and skills. However, Conner (n.d.) states that the premise that older adults have impaired learning abilities is **not** supported by most writers.

Finally, Conner mentions such notables as Malcolm S. Knowles, John D. Bransford, John Dewey, Stephen D. Brookfield, Patricia Cross, and Sharan B. Merriam who agree with her ideas.

Adult Education in Hawai'i – My Personal Story

Personally, I taught adults for many years, in adult evening school programs both in Hawai'i and Guam, as well as undergraduate and graduate level courses at the University of Guam and Leeward Community College, University of Hawai'i. The greatest joy I ever experienced when teaching adults occurred while teaching highly motivated adult women from the Philippines, Thailand, and Taiwan, who were preparing for the U.S. Citizenship test in Honolulu.

Students took the U.S. Citizen course at night, specifically to prepare for American citizenship testing. They were highly motivated, came to class regularly, and participated fully each class session. Their goals were totally transparent: they wanted to prepare for and pass the Citizenship Test, and embrace American society.

U.S. Citizenship Preparation Course Highlights

This particular evening course (U.S. Citizenship Preparation) was eight weeks long, two hours a session, two times a week offered by the state's adult education program at *Leilehua* High School in *Wahiawa,* Oahu. These twelve women came early to class, stayed late, brought their local foods to class for snacks and shared with everyone; we enjoyed a tremendous learning experience. We not only covered the rather slim textbook, but we played games like Jeopardy, using only questions dealing with citizenship issues. They wrote the questions and answers, so that they created reusable Jeopardy cards in class when working with a partner, such as 'What do the colors of the American flag represent?' or 'Name three of the privileges guaranteed in the Bill of Rights'.

I also asked them to stand in front of class, and talk about themselves and their lives, including what brought them to Hawai'i, and why they wanted to become

American citizens. Some of the stories were heart-wrenching!

Midway through the course, I invited a representative from the Immigration and Naturalization Division (responsible for U.S. Citizenship testing and processing in Honolulu) to class, to discuss test preparation, documents required for citizenship, and specific procedures to follow. Our students invited their family members and school administrators, too; we added extra chairs to accommodate everyone.

On the last day of class, we discussed the various foods class members baked or cooked, invited the administration school staff to the get-together, and had a wonderful time. Students presented me with a special crocheted lei (which I still possess), several real flower lei, and a photograph of the class members with me in the middle. Everyone had a copy of that photo, taken earlier! What a fabulous teaching experience and that course took place more than three decades ago.

Later, I attended their swearing-in citizenship ceremony at a packed Honolulu courthouse. There was hardly a dry eye! I met all my students' husbands or significant others, children and in some cases, grandchildren. These women had a goal – to become U.S. citizens. They may have waited for years, but finally accomplished this goal. They serve as a great example of Dr. Knowles' principles of the adult learner.

Job Corps Teacher – Another Real Adult Learner Tale

A significant life experience occurred when I taught young adults at the Hawai'i Job Corps Center (1969-1971). The situation was that my hours of work were 7:45 a.m. to 4:45 p.m. with an hour for lunch. I was newly divorced, and had two little boys. Their nursery school opened at 7 a.m. and closed at 5 p.m.; it was located about a 30-minue drive from my workplace. I felt that I had little control over my life at the time. I was new to the job, desperate for money to support my sons and myself, and could not afford to be late in picking them up from school as there was a significant monetary penalty for any lateness. I had a diminished sense of self.

I am including this story here, because I confronted real life problems, analyzed them, thought through options and consequences, and then decided on the most appropriate solution – a true adult learning experience. **Here are more details.**

My Family Support System

My family support consisted of my mother, a teacher, who would meet me every Saturday morning at *Ala Moana* Park, near Waikiki, and take her grandchildren swimming, enjoy a picnic lunch, and then drive them home to me, about one hour away in Hawai'i *Kai*. My loving mother caring for the boys for a few hours on Saturdays allowed me time to shop, clean the house, sandwich in a medical or dental appointment, and run errands. An older sister sometimes came to spend the weekend with me, perhaps every three or four weeks. That was always a welcome relief.

I was working on my **teaching certificate** at the time, so I would drive to the University of Hawai'i at Mānoa (UHM) a minimum of twice weekly in the evenings, leaving my sons in the care of a teenage babysitter (who lived thankfully, next door). To say I led a hectic life was an understatement.

My Problem – Analyzed

My strategies to deal with the problem of driving my sons to their nursery school and still work eight hours (teaching) were two-fold. First, I met with the director of the Job Corps Center, James Bacon, and explained that I needed to amend my hours slightly. By **reducing** my lunch period from 60 minutes to 30 minutes, and coming to work earlier **and** leaving earlier (just 15 minutes each way), I could then take care of my children's needs as well, and continue working at the center as a teacher. I also discussed the fact that with my teaching certificate (I had taken over 20 semester hours of graduate classes by then), I would be the first teacher that the center employed who was fully credentialed. That would make the center look quite progressive. The director who held a master's degree in social work was impressed with my plan, and agreed to amend my hours.

Solution - Aha

This simple act of slightly altering my work hours (which never interfered with any of the students' classes) allowed me to keep my job, maintain the children in an excellent nursery school, and created great loyalty on my part, to the Job Corps Center in general, and to Director James Bacon, specifically. Please remember that this was more than 50 years ago, when a woman new to the job rarely if ever asked for any type of job-change (hours or duties). I had a real-life problem and solved it the best way possible.

Common Misconceptions

Many authors have stipulated **misconceptions about adult learners**, and I will mention them here because **none of them are true**: adults are just too set in their ways, they cannot seem to ask for help, they only learn one way, they do not know enough about the subject to benefit from the class, they need to learn how to learn, they lack computer skills, and finally, they may resent other, younger students and feel out of place. **Again, these ideas are only myths!**

Personally

The longer I worked at the Hawai'i Job Corps Center, the better I felt about myself. Initially, my self-worth was low. I was going through a nasty divorce. My academically brilliant Ph.D. husband (who could read seven languages including old German, Latin, and Greek) was a functioning alcoholic who had moved out, but contributed almost nothing in child support. I had an eight-month-old baby and another, still in diapers, just about 26 months old. So, the two-year old went to nursery school once he was potty trained and a wonderful neighbor cared for the baby until age two, when I could take both to the nursery school.

I requested a scholarship for my older son, explaining to the nursery school director my dire situation and the nursery director granted it. (Food stamps helped me for three months while job searching, and then I finally landed a teaching job with Job Corps.) The longer I taught, the more successful I felt. That feeling of increased self-confidence allowed me to feel an increased sense of control. That was such a traumatic time in my life that some of the events that occurred remain crystal clear to me even now, several decades later.

Additional Notes

Recently, I read several excellent articles about adult learners. In *The essential characteristics of adult learners* from the Doctoral Journey (2018) of Grand Canyon University, (https://www.gcu.edu/blog/doctoral-journey/essential-characteristics-adult-learners) the school discusses its Doctor of Education programs. A multitude of schools offer a doctorate in this adult learning field. To summarize, adults prefer to learn and do, rather than just listen, are accustomed to collaboration and group discussion, have a great attention span and like to focus on narrow topics. They understand new information through their own, personal, life experiences, and often enjoy sharing with others. Grand Canyon clearly understood this appeal to doctoral-seeking students.

In Rebecca Klein-Collins' *Never too late: The adult student's guide to college* (2018), (https://www.npr.org/2018/12/23/678799694/in/never-too-late-finally-a-guide-for-adults-going-to-college), the writer offers sound advice for the perspective mature college student returning to the college campus (pp. 1-4):

- Do your own research to determine if this college is right for you.

- Check to ensure that this college understands your life style.

- Determine if it will allow prior learning assessment from previous work or military experience to be documented, and perhaps added to an assessment of your skills.

- Ask questions; never assume anything; maintain copies of everything submitted.

Finally, Jaclyn Walsh's *7 tips for adult learners returning to school* (2020) (https://www.petersons.com/blog/7-tips-for-adult-learners-returning-to-school/) includes sound advice to **older students returning to the college campus**: attend college orientation, use free career counseling sessions, take some free or nearly free basic review courses, try a hybrid class (online and direct instruction combined), and realize that other adults over the age of 30 or 40 may be in class (military or veterans). Advice continues: do not be afraid to join other adult students in study groups, visit the learning center on campus for free tutoring, and take a skills-interest inventory to help determine your college major. Often adults in school can teach their professor and fellow students much about life. Let us rejoice in their efforts to better themselves.

Summary

My Argosy University professor, a wonderfully skillful teacher, Dr. Andrew Niesiobedzki, mentions **six factors which serve as motivation sources for adult learning**: social relationships, external expectations, social welfare, personal advancement, escape/stimulation, and cognitive interest. I agree. Adults have many years of experience so teachers need to draw upon them, use adults as resources. Adults also need to be treated as adults, who have set values, beliefs, opinions, tend to be problem entered and self-directed, and demonstrate a variety of learning styles. Adults utilize knowledge based on their past and present jobs or roles in life, and want to learn specific information that they can apply to their personal situations.

As an adult educator, I certainly loved teaching adults of all ages. Most of them were quite serious about learning what they needed to, and once they obtained that information, were grateful to me and others who assisted them.

I really enjoyed Malcom S. Knowles' *The Adult Learner*, the definitive classic in adult education (Knowles et al., 2005). As I had many years of experience teaching adults as well as children, his book gave me great insight as to the specific differences involved. Dr. Knowles' thorough discussions on pedagogy vs. andragogy, use of learning contracts with learners, personal adult learning styles and inventories as well as other teaching techniques were awesome. Recent articles show that adult educators are now more aware of adult learner characteristics.

I believe that this book by Dr. Knowles et al., (2005) should be required reading for educators at all levels. If teachers, pre-kindergarten through graduate school, including professional development trainers (civilian and military) understood the difference in pedagogical vs. andragogical teaching – learning styles and methods, processes, organization, orientation, presentation of materials, motivational factors, recognition, technologies best suited by subject, grade, age, and interest levels, then the world of education would be 200% better!

CH 42 The Role of the Federal Government

in Public Education

My Pearl of Wisdom: Auntie and Uncle Sam

It is amazing what you can accomplish if

you do not care who gets the credit.

Harry S. Truman

STUDENTS, TEACHERS, parents, community members, politicians, board of education members, those in higher education (i.e., stakeholders), as well as the news media continue to pay a great deal of attention to the question of exactly what role the federal government should play in the governing of American public education. It was not just one ripple skimming across a smooth pond. Indeed, dissident voices can be heard, clamoring for attention, from all socio-economic classes, and from all perspectives.

A Quick Historical Review

To fully understand the issues involved, a review of the events leading to the monumental federal legislation, **Every Student Succeeds Act (ESSA) of 2015** (U.S. Department of Education, 2015; Wellein, 2021) which followed the No Child Left Behind [NCLB] Act in 2002 (U.S. Department of Education, 2004), is in order.

1. **Sputnik-1957**: Individual states were responsible for educating their citizens' children, until the Soviet Union launched their satellite, **Sputnik** in fall 1957 (Wellein, 2021). Suddenly, alarmed Americans – ordinary citizens, policymakers, and educators realized that they were not number one in the world of math and science.

2. **National Defense Education Act** (NDEA)-**1958**: America's public education system was suddenly under a microscope. **New federal education dollars** helped to warm the hearts of the states-rights activists to accept federal intervention in what was once a states-only issue.

3. **Teachers:** News media personnel both on paper and television covered various aspects of education, and the **problem of qualified teachers being poorly paid** was a serious issue. Life Magazine published a series on the crisis in education stating that **"teachers were wretchedly overworked, underpaid, and disregarded"** (Kimmelman, 2006, p. 6) and that teachers need more time to prepare their daily lesson plans.

4. **Elementary and Secondary Education Act (ESEA) of 1965**: U.S. President Lyndon B. Johnson included this law as part of his Great Society endeavor.

5. Throughout the **1990**s, regional and national educators asked for more standardized educational goals and objectives. Federally sponsored education conferences, symposiums, and summits united the various state departments of education and school boards/districts in understanding that the problems with educational underachievement were **state and national issues** and many dealing with federal funding could only be solved at that level.

6. The **NCLB legislation** (2002) was the result of all these endeavors, in an ongoing effort to improve the quality of American public education (Nolen & Duignan, 2021). The federal government not only **created legislation which stipulated who was to do what, when, how, why, under which circumstances,** as documented by which assessment instruments but "included serious sanctions for those states and schools that did not take educating all students to meet their standards with qualified teachers seriously" (Kimmelman, 2006, p. 24).

7. **Every Student Succeeds Act** (ESSA) in 2015, a massive work of legislation established uniform standards for all states (U.S. Department of Education, 2015).

A brief summary of the reasons for federal involvement in education below may prove informative.

Federal Government Action

Clearly, the federal government absolutely must take charge of educational reform in the U.S. because historically, the states have failed; the American Federation of Teachers (AAUP, n.d.; AFT, 2007) agreed also. The ESSA included much needed help when dealing with special education and disabled students. Only the federal government is powerful, wealthy, and persistent enough to deal nationally with identified 'challenged' students, and many other costly state education issues, according to many noted educators, and most importantly, U.S. Congress.

To understand the importance of federal oversight, it might help to simply ask which other entity, agency, public or private could force all states – rich or poor, north or south, agrarian or industrialized, racially mixed or homogeneous – to comply with national mandates and norms **if not the federal government?**

Pros and Cons

The federal government must impose federal legislation on all 50 states because historical patterns clearly demonstrate **the uneven path each state has taken** towards improving education. **Additionally,** although states have the responsibility of certifying teachers and are responsible for education within the state, states lack sufficient funding, the necessary vision, as well as the ability to impose sanctions on its own departments of education at the local and state levels. Unlike the U.S. government, nearly all states must have balanced budgets yearly (Lipsky, 2005).

However, there are many vocal **opponents** to any federal involvement in state public education. Two major arguments are as follows:

First, federal government legislative mandates should have no role in overseeing state institutions **because each state has different needs**.

What each state should do is to assess its own situation, and reduce the number of children living in poverty; minimally 27 million or nearly 40% of all children in the U.S. in 2004 do (McGarvey, 2004). At least there is widespread recognition of the correlation between child-poverty and poorly educated youth.

Second, the federal government cannot solve problems by mandating change, that is, 'throwing money' at the situation, ignoring the local needs of schools, families, social situations, and other factors by forcing states to comply with federal directives, all in the name of progress.

ESSA (U.S. Department of Education, 2015) addresses those types of issues by standardizing requirements for all 50 states, disallowing each state its individual standards.

Summary

Vociferous opponents of federal involvement in public education claim that because each state has different needs, it is impossible for the federal government to set national policy that will address the specific educational needs of each state. Critics claim that the economics of families largely determine their children's readiness to learn. So, states must address the poverty problem first, not later.

Secondly, individual state problems cannot be addressed by the federal government passing sweeping legislation on educational matters, forcing states to comply with such laws. Each state (except Hawai'i) has dozens, if not hundreds of school districts varying in size from the tiny to the massive. (If all it takes is money, then why hasn't education significantly improved over the last 50 years?)

Conclusion – Positive and Negative

The states had over 200 years to get it right in the field of education and have not done so. **The unevenness of the quality of public education is astounding**. In some school districts in America, students flourish in an educationally rich and engaging environment, attending classes in well-maintained facilities, taught by experienced, credentialed teachers who love what they are doing as much as the children love the learning experience.

In addition, test scores document the administrations' claims that students are thriving, parents are supportive, and the community members and political leaders eagerly send their own family members to those schools. The future, for these children, is bright with endless options and possibilities.

However, in many other school districts, the situation is dismal and depressing. Absenteeism rates are high both for students and teachers. Graffiti, gang members, and acts of violence are seen on school campuses and surrounding neighborhoods. Test scores reveal how poorly students are doing in the classrooms. Professional staff development is spotty at best. Teachers may need more assistance with aides in SPED classrooms. Perhaps teachers are teaching in subjects not their major or minor areas. Or maybe some teachers are not fully credentialed. There are insufficient numbers of textbooks for students to take home to study and an obvious lack of technology on campuses. Parent and community involvement in the schools is almost non-existent and middle-class families try to avoid moving into these school districts.

The state of America's children 2021: Child poverty (Children's Defense Fund, 2021), shows that 71% of children in poverty are children of color; more than 1 in 5 children live in poverty (https://www.childrensdefense.org/state-of-americas-children/soac-2021-child-poverty/)

Geography is important: no states have White child poverty rates 20% or higher. Historical, systemic racism and institutional barriers mean that children of color have been particularly vulnerable to child poverty (NCES, 2020). Black and Hispanic children experience some of the highest poverty rates in the country.

Finally, students are simply not engaged, with many of them dropping out before graduation (Wellein, 2021).

Pandemic

In March 2020, the COVID-19 pandemic hit America. The various states handled the virus onslaught differently, depending on **many factors**: if they had previously prepared for any type of major catastrophe – weather, health, or otherwise for example, and if they had enough nurses working in Intensive Care Units at local or regional hospitals. Other factors were if the hospitals and clinics had a good supply of personal protective gear, if there were sufficient numbers of doctors, lab technicians, ventilators, oxygen, ICU beds, if most of a state's population enjoyed good medical plans and coverage, if, if, if. . . . Schools shut down – some for months, others continued distance learning through summer, 2021 (Our View, 2020).

The educational system in the U.S. was jabbed a dozen, indeed, a hundred times – by this virulent virus that raged across the globe. Vaccines, of course, are a game changer! But even in late 2021, several variants of the COVID-19 virus are surfacing and unless more people are vaccinated, the prognosis not just for America but the world appears grim. America eradicated Polio by the late 1970s by federal officials mandating that everyone receive a polio vaccination beginning in the mid-1950s. Smallpox was eradicated throughout the world by the early 1970s. Thus, there is no doubt that almost 100% mandatory vaccinations for all indeed work!

Now – What to Do?

The federal government must take control of improving the education system of all children attending public schools in America. ESSA of 2015 (U.S. Department of Education, 2015) is noted for **specifying standards in several major areas**, that schools make adequate annual progress and report such progress or lack thereof, that public school children are instructed by highly qualified teachers, and children are evaluated to ascertain whether progress has been made or not, and to what degree.

Finally, the federal government will impose penalties for those institutions that fail to make the required progress, while simultaneously offering opportunities for students to transfer to other schools, accept vouchers, receive free tutoring services, attend charter schools, or learn online or by hybrid instruction.

The ESSA (U.S. Department of Education, 2015) highlights include the following:

Advances equity by upholding critical protections for America's disadvantaged and high-need students.

Requires—for the first time—that all students in America be taught to high academic standards that will prepare them to succeed in college and careers.

Ensures that vital information is provided to educators, families, students, and communities through annual statewide assessments that measure students' progress toward those high standards.

Helps to support and grow local innovations—including evidence-based and place-based interventions developed by local leaders and educators—consistent with Investing in Innovation and Promise Neighborhoods

Sustains and expands this administration's historic investments in increasing access to high-quality preschool.

Maintains an expectation that there will be accountability and action to effect positive change in lowest-performing schools, where groups of students are not making progress, and where graduation rates are low over extended periods of time. (p. 2)

Never in the history of America has such national legislation directed, indeed, mandated that public schools in each state be held strictly accountable to the federal government and to its citizens for educating its future populace and leaders (U.S. Department of Education, 2015).

The addition of the COVID -19 Pandemic is an added stressor, calling for even greater federal government intervention: COVID-19 testing, contact tracing, vaccinating (by age and occupation categories), adequate equipment, supplies, protective gear, ventilators, ICU beds, and medical personnel. Individual states cannot do all this, and many are operating budgets in the 'red.' Unlike the federal government that overspends year after year, state budgets are restricted to only spending what they actually have.

The federal government's role in taking charge of educational reform, in addition to this new challenge of controlling, confining, and defeating the COVID-19 pandemic is enormous. Vaccines can only be created and approved at the federal level with states working closely to ensure all in America 'get vaccinated,' another example of the fierce power of the federal government.

CH 43 The Most Pressing Issues in Today's Higher Education System

My Pearl of Wisdom: Challenges are Scary

The difference between genius and stupidity is that genius has its limits.

Albert Einstein

THERE ARE MANY important issues facing higher education systems in the United States today. Among these are **technology issues,** for instance, maintaining quality of online or distance learning programs; **multiculturalism,** such as, how to meet the diverse student population needs in terms of race, color, national origin, disability, sexual orientation, gender, religion, and cultural practices**; size and complexity**, that is, the dynamic expansion of colleges and programs, and the resulting increase in student population. **Finally, there is specialization and departmentalism**, for example, the increasing sophistication of undergraduate and graduate program and course offerings, the splintering of major subjects into sub-specialties, and the resulting differentiations in the departments (Walsh, 2020; Wellein, 2021).

Many other issues of course, concern postsecondary administrators, professors, students, and the community at large, to include rising tuition and dormitory costs (but sometimes with unstable enrollments), union demands (but with student loans and debts accumulating), campus safety and security (but with no consensus as to what to do), instructor-wages keeping pace with the cost of living (no argument here), and governance issues of attracting major grants, dealing with student mental health issues, and increasing graduation or degree completion rates (5 key challenges, 2018).

Additional challenges include student debt, declining state funding, lower world ranking, and lower college completion rates (5 key challenges, 2018). "The U.S. has the highest college dropout rate. We're number one in terms of the number of people who start college, but we're like number 20 in terms of the number of people who finish" (p. 4). What to do?

- Offer competency-based education.
- Offer online or distance education.
- Attract more international students.
- Align with what industry actually needs.

Perhaps no single issue is more important than the effects of the horrific pandemic of 2020-2021 as it relentlessly sweeps across America, leaving many university campuses empty, and dormitories increasingly vacant. Some parents simply took their college-age children home while others encouraged their offspring to continue their education online. Vaccines will affect these issues, if the vast majority are indeed, vaccinated.

However, in this chapter, we will examine only four major issues facing postsecondary institutions: technology, multiculturalism, size and complexity, and specialization and departmentalism. A summary of each challenge is in order.

Technology Challenges

The proliferation of online learning programs is tremendous; there are thousands of distance education programs in America. The Department of Defense (DOD) for example, has an agency which recommends particular military-friendly distance learning programs, because there are so many from which to choose (Wellein, 2010). DOD's agency, Defense Activity for Non-Traditional Education Support (DANTES, External, 2006), uses several objective criteria to determine whether to include an institution on its website. Postsecondary institutions must hold regional, national, or special vocational-technical accreditation.

Programs online must use the same textbooks and course materials as found on campus for direct instruction. Instructors who teach online must have the same credentials and use the same syllabi (approximately) as those who teach on-campus courses. The number of 'contact' hours for online courses must be the same as direct instruction courses. These are just a few of the elements colleges and universities use in maintaining high quality courses.

Naturally, course delivery systems are sophisticated, using the Internet as the base (5 key challenges, 2018), including Podcasts, YouTube videos, Google Classroom, Drop Box, special, proprietary programs purchased by particular institutions, and many dozen more. In fact, there are so many technologically sophisticated delivery systems that this topic cannot be addressed in this chapter but can be reviewed in Wellein's *Educational Essays, Book 1* (2021).

However, the pandemic of 2020-2021 really altered distance learning and its myriad of programs and technologies 100%. Even once most Americans are vaccinated, education may never return to its pre-pandemic ways. Hybrid and distance learning methods have expanded exponentially and face-to-face learning will always be impacted by these new delivery methodologies.

Multiculturalism Challenges

Multiculturalism is gaining in importance at many institutions. Some 20% of Hispanic adults, for example, have a postsecondary degree compared with 36% of all adults, and remain the largest racial group to gain in significant numbers (Multicultural and diversity guide, 2021). However, Hispanic instructors are not being hired at the same rate as the population growth. Racial problems on campus must also be addressed involving Americans of Asian descent (Au & Yonamine, 2021) who discussed this issue in *Dear educators, It is time to fight for Asian America* in the website, **rethinking schools** at https://rethinkingschools.org. Black Americans, native Americans, and Pacific Islanders are also targets of harassment.

There are issues on some campuses, when dealing with the religious right (born again Christians), or those outside the mainstream religions such as Wiccans. How will universities deal with these various issues that can polarize students and older individuals returning to campus, such as offering educational services to disabled veterans returning from the war in Iraq and Afghanistan? Some 33% of LGBTQ+ students, some considered lesbian and homosexual activists have seriously considered leaving college due to sexual harassment and other issues (Multicultural and diversity guide, 2021). Colleges also face an influx of bilingual and trilingual college students, some from foreign nations, while others are from American communities.

Growing Size and Complexity

The increasing size and complexity of colleges and universities are growing trends. In comparing sizes of postsecondary institutions historically, please note the following:

1. In **1870**, there were 563 colleges in the U.S, with a total of 5,553 instructors, and a total of 52,000 students.

2. In **1920**, there were 1,041 colleges in the U.S., with a total of 48,615 instructors, and a total of 598,000 students.

3. In **1956,** there were 1,850 colleges in the U.S., with a total of 298,910 instructors, and a total of 2,637,000 students.

4. In **2020** there were 3,982 degree-granting colleges in the U.S., with a total of 1.54 million instructors and a total of 16.6 million undergraduate and 3.1 million graduate students (Moody, 2021; NCES 2020, 2021).

Needless to say, colleges have bureaucratic layers: students, advisors/counselors, faculty members, department chairpersons, assistant deans, deans, provosts, assistant presidents, presidents, board members, *ad nauseam*. Colleges hire faculty members to teach, write grant proposals, manage research facilities, direct special projects, chair important committees, run endowment groups, and fill special 'chairs.' Some noteworthy nationally acclaimed professors, such as recognized authors and Nobel Prize winners help attract millions in special grant monies, adding prestige to the institutions while simultaneously appealing to prospective students.

Specialization and Departmentalization

Finally, postsecondary institutions tend to be highly specialized and departmentalized. For example, the University of California at Berkeley has departments called Poultry Husbandry, Romance Philology, Food Technology, and Naval Architecture; at Colorado State University (CSU, n.d.), students can earn degrees in Artificial Intelligence and Robotics, Cyber Security, Fundraising, Virtualization, and Cloud Computing. There are thousands of programs to choose from, in all American colleges and universities now.

These many challenges of technology, multiculturalism, expansion of programs, specialization, and departmentalization subsets **are just a few of the pressing issues facing today's higher education system.** Rising student debt, changes in undergraduate and graduate enrollment, meeting union demands, increasing instructor salaries and dormitory costs, attracting lucrative multi-year research grants, maintaining campus security, and meeting diverse student population needs must be addressed as well.

Finally, the threat of COVID-19 infections among campus students (who commute as well as live in campus dormitories), instructors, staff, and support personnel adds to these many postsecondary institutions' concerns. Some postsecondary institutions are now requiring those living in campus dormitories or/and taking face-to-face classes to be fully vaccinated. Once vaccinations become nearly mandatory (for most individuals) then perhaps the postsecondary community will have one less hurdle to overcome in addressing all the previously stated issues.

CH 44 Leeward Community College,

Tenure Issues

My Pearl of Wisdom: Tell Me, Oh So Sweetly

Or

Oh Me, Oh My

You will either step forward into growth, or

you will step backward into safety.

Abraham Maslow

AUTHORS HOSTETLER, Sawyer, and Pritchard (2004), spend a great deal of time in their book on college teaching discussing the many steps a newly minted doctorate student can take after graduation day has come and gone. Steps trying to land a position include exhausting time spent sending in applications, interviewing, and then waiting. Other steps referenced by Hostetler et al. (2004) involve how to survive the first few months on the job, getting along with peers, deciding how to present courses, writing for publication, writing up research, etc. Many educators have discussed these issues but obtaining tenure is a hot-button topic.

Writer and Professor Rob Jenkins (2016), from Georgia State University Perimeter College in *Community-college FAQ: How long before I get tenure* discusses what it takes to obtain tenure, and what is the typical salary to expect. Based on his research from *The Chronicle's* survey and his personal experiences at four different community colleges over more than 30 years, Dr. Jenkins discusses **continuing**

contracts as a faculty member, and that salary is usually based on rank and longevity. **Tenure** is a tantalizing golden apple, out of reach for many.

Reality Hits Home

Now, here is the reality of what happened to me, several years ago, at Leeward Community College (LCC) one of 10 schools of the University of Hawai'i system. I responded to a newspaper advertisement for a full-time Reading Instructor at Pearl City's LCC **on the island of Oahu**. With over 10 years of teaching experience in the field of reading (all levels), combined with a master's degree in reading education, I was more than a little qualified and quite excited at the job prospect. Alas – good fortune was not to be.

Situation

Time seemed to pass slowly however, when I received no telephone call or mail about my instructor application status. Just when I was going to accept another offer in a less desirable location, performing fewer desirable tasks, Elaine, the secretary of the of LCC's Language Arts Department called one evening late, inquiring if I could come in for an interview. (I thought it a bit odd that she did not inquire if I was still available, until I later discovered that there were eight part-time and ten full-time Language Arts instructors, **most of whom were desperately waiting for jobs each semester, and advancement.)** The part-timers wanted full-time positions while many of the full-timers wanted **tenure**, the legally binding 'golden' status of job permanence.

Until the college awarded tenure, none of the non-tenured instructors really knew from one term to the next if a job would be available until the very last moment. Elaine, a most astute and capable secretary, had correctly assumed that I was available to teach because it was late in the summer and most fall college teaching jobs were filled by then.

Challenges

The multiple challenges I faced and the responses I made to these challenges were sometimes farcical and often, just plain frustrating. The details are as follows:

1. **The interview** with the Language Arts Department Chairperson went

amazingly well, and Arlene Watson extended an offer to me. I found Arlene to be quite decent and very knowledgeable. (I later discovered that one of the tenured LCC instructors who I knew from my college days had put in a good word for me; I was exceedingly grateful for this act of kindness.)

2. However, instead of the full-time instructor position I had interviewed for, LCC offered me a **half-time position** with added courses paid to me per credit hour, **making it in reality teaching fulltime but for about 65% of the advertised pay.** This was **not** Arlene's doing. She apologized to me and explained that while she did the interviews and recommendations for hiring, she had nothing to do with the financial terms. **Thus, LCC got a full-time instructor (me) and saved almost $4,000 by hiring me on those terms, earning my unbelievably deep animosity in the process.** (Perhaps this 'system' is no longer used at LCC? I can only hope!)

3. I appealed my hiring status (and 'salary cut') to the dean of academics. After all, wasn't the **job notice for a full-time instructor**? And didn't the language arts department head want me to **teach five classes a week**? And wasn't teaching five classes a week **full-time**? Even though LCC posted a vacancy announcement for a full-time position, the college hired me to teach half-time but paid me only by the credit-hour for the 'rest of the courses taught,' saving LCC thousands of dollars.

4. Alas, the dean succinctly informed me that the hiring of full or part-time instructors was dependent on the student enrollment number for that college term, and nothing could be done. The fact that the dean's job was specifically to approve job announcements and pay levels did not escape my notice. LCC had deliberately waited until the last moment to hire an instructor to teach five classes (full-time) and **got me – paying me thousands less** than advertised.) Student enrollment was never an issue but most certainly pay was! **Whoever LCC hired would teach five courses – the equivalent of full-time work. The dean basically told me to 'suck it up,' feel fortunate that I had a teaching job, and 'go forward.'** I felt numb with despair.

5. Apparently, eight instructors in the Language Arts Department were operating

on a part-time basis, **some of them even moving from one community college campus to another weekly,** to teach an extra course here or there each term, and getting paid by the credit hour. I also never heard about any part-timers getting yearly contracts either.

It is quite revealing to read the 2020-2021 LCC Catalog (University of Hawai'i LCC, Catalog, 2021, also Faculty & staff, 2021), listing **Lecturers Names** because they are listed by last name order with no 'credentials' mentioned. **The Faculty and Staff** section however, listed names by last name order together with their credentials. What does this tell you? Yes, LCC did not think much about its 'lecturers.'

6. To pay my monthly bills, I was forced to supplement my LCC income by teaching part-time for two different Hawai'i Department of Education adult community schools each week, for two years following my LCC weekly classes, until one day, after rushing out of a late afternoon LCC course, **I could not remember to which adult school campus I was supposed to drive. I sat in my car in LCC's parking lot and bit my lower lip to stem the flow of hot tears.** One full-time (more or less) and two part-time jobs were a bit much to handle.

7. During the following two years working at LCC, I spent at least 25% of my time (**outside** of my normal 40-hour work week, teaching five courses, each meeting three times weekly for about an hour each session, seeing students during office hours, correcting papers and preparing my lesson plans) applying for various private, city and county, state of Hawai'i, and federal jobs.

8. Finally, during the third year of suffering from frustrated rejections and few if any telephone calls or interviews, I obtained a temporary three-month position as an academic guidance counselor at Fort Shafter, a Honolulu Army post for active-duty soldiers. I was elated!

Lessons Learned

This experience proved most fortuitous. My Chrysler Le Baron's tires were on their collective last millimeter of rubber, and I was becoming depressed after sending out over 150 job applications and interviewing with only 12 or so agencies. Three of these state agencies called me back to re-interview with a **larger** number of committee members **interviewing me again** at least three times for the **same position. One particular agency, Kapiolani Community College, did not hire me,** I think because although I am part Caucasian, Hawaiian, Chinese, I look totally White, had a *Haole* last name (although nee *Akau*), and replied when asked to state a personal like or strength, "I like to work with really competent people." (Yikes!)

Word to the wise: **racial intolerance is alive and well in dear Hawai'i *nei* and never be this totally honest with those you do not know and who do not know you!** Later, I learned that the college hired an Asian gal with much less experience and education than I had.

My Advice

Advice to new faculty facing the same situation, that is, accepting a Non-Tenure Track Appointment, as discussed by Jay W. Rojewski (Hostetler et al., 2004) includes the following: **never give up, never give up, never give up.**

I understood that LCC's position was a temporary appointment, carrying no strings or promises. Also, my department chair asked me to supervise a master's degree candidate in reading from the University of Hawai'i main campus of Mānoa (and I accepted the honor), receiving a nice letter of appreciation from the UHM provost's office. So, the school seemed to 'like' me. That was okay.

However, the horrific uncertainty of working as an LCC instructor from one school term to the next, and never knowing if the school would even offer me a position for the next semester (despite rave evaluations) was more than a bit disconcerting. Worse was the knowledge that even though I would teach five classes (which was full-time), I would be paid less i.e., by the credit hour for some. And tenure would never be possible.

Update

I also contacted the Human Resources (HR) Department at several city, county, and state agencies, asking why I did not get even a telephone call in response to my numerous job applications. "We are forced to take employees presently working for us, even if they barely meet the minimum qualifications. You cannot be considered unless there is no one available [working] in our system." The HR lady was apologetic.

So why bother placing notices in the newspaper and online for these jobs? I inquired.

"We are required by policy to do so. I am sorry. I can see you have triple, quadruple the qualifications for these positions. Again, I am so sorry," she explained.

What a waste of taxpayers' money, and applicants' time, energy, and hope, I thought.

Readers: I checked with several **HR people recently** in early 2020. The policies have not changed. They are required to advertise for open positions but must select anyone who meets the minimum qualifications **if these applicants are already in their system.** Such a waste – society gets exactly what it pays for – agencies hire the least competent applicants if they already work for the city and county, state, or federal government, providing they meet the 'minimum quals' [qualifications].

Later, when I applied for a full-time federal position and the Army unexpectedly chose me out of over three dozen applicants, the hiring official informed me that it was because I had performed so capably working as a three-month temporary counselor. **Lesson learned. Even if the position is a temporary one, never hesitate to give it 200% effort.**

I finally became a permanent Army civilian later, when a permanent guidance counselor at Schofield Barracks **died suddenly in a flaming car accident**, making that position vacant. (Permanent job status after a long probationary period is like tenure in the federal government!) So, I only got a permanent DOD job due to someone's violent death. I did not know if I should have been happy or sad because I felt both emotions; happy to obtain the new counselor position, but sad at the thought of someone dying for me to get it. How strange, how serendipitous!

CH 45 Fink's Taxonomy of Significant Learning

My Pearl of Wisdom: Metamorphosis is a Start

They cannot stop me. I will get my education, if it is in the

home, school, or anyplace.

Malala Yousafzai

A BRIEF REVIEW of the six types or levels of learning are important in understanding L. Dee Fink's taxonomy (Fink, Creating, 2013). "For learning to occur, the learner must experience change. No change, no learning. And there must be lasting change, if significant learning is important in terms of the learner's life" (p. 1).

Terry Heick (What is, n.d.) in *What is the taxonomy of significant learning* discusses Fink.

Dr. Fink's Learning Levels

Fink organizes the learning levels as follows, from low to high:

1. **Foundational knowledge**; understanding and remembering facts, and information.

2. **Application;** skills, thinking, critical, creative, and practical thinking, so that certain kinds of learning are useful.

3. **Integration;** connecting people, ideas, and intellectual power.

4. **Human dimension**; learning about others and oneself.

5. **Caring;** developing values, interests, and feelings.

6. **Learning;** how to learn. (Fink, A taxonomy, 2013)

Compare and Contrast

In contrast to Dr. Fink's theories, L. W. Anderson, and D. Krathwohl (Anderson & Krathwohl, 2001) describe the hierarchical nature of cognitive skills as follows:

- Remember: recognize, recall;

- Understand: summarize, compare, explain;

- Apply: execute, implement;

- Analyze: organize, differentiate;

- Evaluate: check, critique, judge; and finally

- Create: generate, plan, and produce. (p. 31)

According to Anderson and Krathwohl's team, the outcome-based language is preferred while still maintaining the hierarchical design; each skill builds on the prior skills learned.

Significant Learning Information

Let us be clear. Dr. Fink appears to respect Dr. Benjamin Bloom and his associates, for developing cognitive taxonomy in the mid-1950s (Heick, What is, n.d.) and sees his new taxonomy as an actual successor to Bloom's learning theories. However, Dr. Fink mentions other kinds of learning, to include how to learn, leadership and interpersonal skills, as well as ethics. Also, important communication skills, character development, tolerance, and the ability to adapt to change is important. Furthermore, Fink's ideas suggest that a broader definition and an expansion and use of the cognitive domain would be in order. These levels of learning are **not** hierarchical but are based on relationships and adaptability.

More

Finally, Dr. Fink (Heick, What is, n.d.) specifies that each type of learning activity and level is related to other kinds and levels of learning, and may enhance the learning already achieved. **This is synergistic learning**, whereby the learner builds upon the information and concepts already learned, applies this knowledge and skills, cares about the product or activity, relates what is learned to other ideas, and understands the significance of the learning experience. **Dr. Fink states he considers this learning experience to be significant** (Fink, Creating, 2013).

Fink uses such teaching methods as lecturing, then lecturing with discussion, using panels of experts, brainstorming, videotapes, class discussion, small group discussion, case studies, role playing, report-back sessions, worksheets/surveys, index card exercises, guest speakers, and value clarification exercises. Instructors find much to examine here, to make the typical classroom sessions robust and stimulating.

Another source of information about Fink's learning theories is discussed in the Journal of College Student Development (Wawrzynski, 2004) when Wawrzynski reviews Fink's book, *Creating Significant Learning Experiences*. "The author [Dr. Fink] draws on almost 30 years of teaching in higher education and two decades of faculty development to create a vision of how individual faculty and institutions can [perform]" (Wawrzynski, 2004, p. 1). Concerns about student learning quality, with integration of course design, learning activities, and classroom support are apparent.

Wawrzynski does stipulate, however, that **there are dangers and risks** associated with implementing some of Fink's concepts, for those who are without job tenure or political connections.

Personal Example

If I was to present a class activity incorporating various aspects of Dr. Fink's significant learning taxonomy, one excellent activity (which I have used several times myself), to help students (usually senior high and postsecondary levels) recall material discussed in class and in the textbook is as follows:

1. The professor (within the first two weeks of the course) assigns each student in the class a textbook chapter to read, review, and outline.

2. The professor provides the appropriate guidelines such as number of pages of the outline, and explains that **each student will develop 10 multiple choice questions** consisting of four choices for each item. Each student submits an answer key, as well as the actual test items. Then each student lists the page numbers where the answers were in the chapter as well. Finally, the professor stipulates that the test questions must not deal with minor issues, or memory-type questions, but with concepts, and major vocabulary.

3. Each student presents his or her 'chapter' to the rest of the class through a 10-12 page **PowerPoint** slide presentation, and provides a copy of the presentation and chapter outline to each student with a list of the test questions and answer key. (The professor makes class copies from the original, to distribute to class members on the day of the student's presentation.)

4. The professor explains that **this assignment is worth** 35% of the course grade: 10% for the PowerPoint and outline, 10% for the test questions, 10% for the class presentation (think of a colorful power point show), and 5% for overall assignment.

5. For each test question that the professor actually uses on the course midterm or final examination, that student **earns an extra bonus point**, to count towards his or her final grade.

Summary

One such class activity is the assignment of chapters as previously explained with the professor providing many sound examples. The students only select questions involving major ideas and concepts in that assigned chapter, and **lose a point if** they select minor, mundane ones. Each student submits his or her questions, answer key, page numbers where answers are located, and a brief outline of the material itself to the professor by the due date.

Finally

After students turn in their assignment, the professor grades the work, and produces copies for each student in the course. Robust class discussion is an important feature. Finally, the instructor explains **that half of all the test questions for all midterm or final exam will come from these chapter questions.**

The activity described above uses at least **three of Fink's cognitive learning theories: foundation knowledge, application, and then integration.** Reinforcement and retention may be involved, especially when students begin to care about their assignments, and then 'learn how to learn' (Heick, What is, n.d.). **Many teachers believe that the best way to learn any sort of material or process is to teach that material or**

process to others. I have used this technique throughout my career.

Dr. Fink provides many examples of Significant Learning activities. Terry Heick (What is, n.d.) in his article expands on these activities. **If one wants to be certain that learning has occurred, ask that individual to teach that concept or material to someone else.** In the exercise described above that is precisely what takes place, and significant learning is more than just theory, but reality.

CH 46 Relevance of Accreditation Bodies in Institutions of Higher Learning

My Pearl of Wisdom: A Lesson to the Wise

The world will not be destroyed by those who do evil,

but by those who watch them without doing anything.

Albert Einstein

ACCREDITATION OF POSTSECONDARY institutions is an extremely important and relevant issue. "The lack of the appropriate type of accreditation can literally ruin an institution, no matter how famous its reputation" (Bear & Bear, 2001, p.16). There are literally dozens of unaccredited institutions, poising as legitimate ones (U.S. Department of Education, 2009, 2020).

Dr. John Bear, a noted author, public speaker, educator, and world-famous expert highly regarded by federal law enforcement agencies asked to testify frequently in court, states "accreditation is one of the most complex and confusing issues in higher education. It is also one of the most misused concepts-both intentionally and unintentionally. Let us try to make some sense out of the situation" (Bear & Bear, 2001, p. 16). He makes the definition of accreditation a bit clearer by writing that "quite simply, it is a validation – a statement by a group of persons who are . . . impartial experts in higher education, that a given school . . . has been thoroughly investigated and found worthy of approval" (p. 16).

A graduate of University of California, Berkley, and Michigan State University, author of 35 books with major publishers (Harcourt Brace, McGraw-Hill, Time-Life, Ten Speed Press, etc.), and consultant for the FBI, General Motors, Xerox Corporation, and Encyclopaedia Britannica, Dr. Bear is the authority on diploma mills. He has been cited as an expert in over 100 newspaper and magazine articles. He lived in Hilo, Hawai'i from 1990-1999; he co-authored with Allen Ezell, the seminal book, *Degree mills: The billion-dollar industry* (Ezell & Bear, 2012).

Agencies

Recognized accrediting agencies are governed by the 2020 U.S. Department of Education (www.ed.gov) and/or the Council for Higher Education Accreditation (CHEA, 2021) (www.chea.org.). Veterans Affairs, the federal student loan programs, and U.S. military service branches will only acknowledge and utilize schools which have proper, legitimate accreditation credentials as will most religious, private, and public vocational-technical institutes, colleges and universities.

There are six regional accrediting associations representing the various geographical sections of America and its territories, several national accrediting agencies, and about 80 professional associations which accredit specific programs and departments within a school or college (Bear & Bear, 2001).

The U.S. Department of Education's Network for Education Information (U.S. Department of Education, 2008) states that while it does not evaluate foreign degrees or qualification, it strongly recommends that schools in America that wish to admit students, hire employers, or assist state and territorial licensing boards turn to legitimate credential evaluation services to judge non-U.S. qualifications and documents.

Fake university accreditation agencies might resemble legitimate ones, such as the bogus Accreditation Council for Distance Education, Council for Distance Education, Global Accreditation Bureau, or National Academy of Higher Education. Nevertheless, these illegitimate businesses are **worthless**; see https://www.geteducated.com/college-degree-mills/204-fake-agencies-for-college-accreditation/ (List of accreditation agencies, 2019).

In addition, https://www.geteducated.com/college-degree-mills/161-college-degree-or-diploma-mill/, offers readers *10 ways to spot a diploma mill* (2020). Another URL with more information is *Diploma mills* (2021) https://www.collegechoice.net/diploma-mills/ declaring that "diploma mills sell degrees without requiring true academic achievement" (p. 1), rake in over $200 million, award about 500 Ph.D. degrees monthly, offer 300 websites, showing 98 fake accreditation agencies in America.

Jamie Littlefield (2020) in *What you need to know about diploma mills*, offers more information at https://www.thoughtco.com/what-you-need-to-know-diploma-mills-1097946. Another excellent article is from Medical Assistant Career Guide (10 tips to avoid diploma mills, 2020) https://www.medicalassistantcareerguide.com/10-tips-to-avoid-diploma-mills which provides sage advice as well as important information.

Finally, in the USAcollegex.com article, *How to detect a diploma mill* the Academic Integrity Blog provides even more detailed information found on this URL (How to Detect, 2018): https://www.usacollegex.com/not-to-be-fooled-by-a-diploma-mill-part-2/ .

Consequences

The consequences of a postsecondary institution that lacks or has lost appropriate accreditation are severe.

One consequence when an institution is not accredited either regionally or nationally is that **federal funds usually cannot be authorized.** This means no Pell Grants, federally subsidized student loans, or funds from the GI Bill entitlement programs under the auspices of the Department of Veterans Affairs, and DOD military services. These massive federal agencies usually provide funds to former or present military members who attend postsecondary schools. All other federal agencies such as the Treasury, Homeland Security, Justice, Transportation, and Agriculture prohibit funding to unaccredited schools as well. This is financially devastating to any postsecondary institution.

Another consequence if students attend unaccredited schools (by self-paying), is that they cannot transfer credit earned to a legally accredited school because **accredited schools will not accept documentation of courses taken and credit earned from**

unaccredited institutions. This means that any funds spent for unaccredited quarter or semester hours are for naught. Unsuspecting students lose time, energy, self-respect, and lots of money. It can be a devastating experience (Ezell & Bear, 2012; Littlefield, 2020). On the other hand, some people will knowingly purchase bogus degrees with the expectation that they can obtain a job, or a better job, enter a new career, join the military, etc. But I shall reserve that discussion for a later time.

A third consequence of students attending unaccredited institutions is that unsuspecting consumers **expect certain services** from those who hold themselves out to be proficient, licensed, certified, or degreed, and that these expectations carry ethical, moral, and legal implications (Gibson, 2017). Imagine what it means for a young parent to discover that their child's dentist is not certified by an accredited institution, or that the automotive mechanic fixing his or her Honda Civic attended an unrecognized vocational school (Clifton, Chapman, & Cox, 2018). There are over 200 accrediting agencies as of 2004, that are "**not recognized** by CHEA or the U.S. Department of Education" (Ezell & Bear, 2012, p. 240), affecting thousands of schools.

Role of Agencies - Summary

What roles do accreditation bodies play in higher education? These legitimate and recognized accrediting agencies allow for some strong measure of safety and security to those who enroll in legitimate academic or vocational-technical schools. In addition, government funding such as Perkins Loans and Pell Grants can only be provided to accredited schools. Transcripts can be only accepted from and to legitimate institutions. This also means that students can be assured that their diplomas will be recognized as valid by governmental agencies, private businesses, as well as non-profit or for-profit agencies (Grant, 2019). Students will not have wasted time and money.

Consumers who pay for services from carpenters, doctors, or engineers or any other provider, will also be certain of 'getting what they pay for.' **Accreditation, when properly implemented, means that those who hold credentials, licenses, diplomas, and degrees have actually learned a body of knowledge, regulated by specific**

agencies to ensure that the information is current and correct.

In summary, accreditation protects the public, and provides public recognition to institutions that meet accepted standards. But the late American entertainer Phineas Taylor Barnum of Barnum & Bailey Circus was right when he famously remarked, **"There is a sucker born every minute."** Get the facts! Don't be a fool!

CH 47 Diploma Mills: Impact on

Higher Education

My Pearl of Wisdom: What's in a Name

Education is the art of making man ethical.

Georg Wilhelm Friedrich Hegel

THE PRESENCE OF DIPLOMA mills in America is offensive to all those who are honest, decent, and care about the value of higher education. Not much has been written about diploma mills in the past. However, two famous authors (Ezell & Bear, 2012) have written an iconic, influential book, *Degree Mills: The Billion-Dollar Industry That Has Sold Over a Million Fake Diplomas* in which they cite scary information and statistics.

Diploma mills, also referred to as degree mills, are a costly problem in the United States, and in many other parts of the world (U.S. Department of Education, 2020). Callahan (2014) in a dissertation, ***Exploring Characteristics of Religious Affiliated Colleges Labeled "Diploma Mills": A Multi-Case Study of U.S. Court Decisions*** states that over 600 higher education institutions have been identified as alleged diploma mills (by government authorities).

Table 3

Top 10 U.S. Locations by State for Diploma Mills and Number of Diploma Mills

CA 134	FL 57	LA 39	AZ 28
HI 94	TX 53	IL 29	
WA 87	NY 44	NV 29	

(Diploma mills, 2021, p. 4).

Personal

There is evidence of the presence of diploma mills in Hawai'i (Yamane, 2014), as well as elsewhere within the 50 states, U.S. Territories, and foreign nations (U.S. Department of Education, 2020). I have received unsolicited e-mails from such fake businesses and institutions here in Hawai'i, and from a brief literature review, there is evidence to document hundreds of such fake businesses across the United States (Buy a degree, 2020; Best fake diploma maker, 2020; College degrees for sale, 2021; Fake diploma prices, n.d.).

A few years ago, Jaybee Obusan, my supervisor at the Army Reserve office in Honolulu asked me as the Education Officer to authenticate a college transcript he obtained from a soldier. The college's name was extremely similar to a well-known one with a difference in spelling by only two letters.

Even more disturbing, the address showed the same city and state as the well-known institution, and the appearance of the transcript resembled the legitimate institution. It had a raised seal and initially appeared to be a valid transcript. After much research, I told my supervisor that it appeared to be a fake document. He told me that he would call in the reservist and inquire as to how he had obtained the transcript, as the military had used it (for points) towards a promotion for the young man. (Points are important to reserve personnel because when points reach a certain level, soldiers' monthly pay increases.)

Sources of information, provided by Havocscope can be found at Fake diploma prices (n.d.): https://www.havocscope.com/fake-diploma/. For example,

Fake Diploma – Indonesia: $648; Iraq: $1,500 - $7,000

Fake Pilot License-Philippines: $30,000 - $50,000

Fake Teaching Diploma – Vietnam: $50 - $600

Fake Bachelor and Master's Degree – Mexico: $1,555 online

Fake College Transcripts – Massage School: $10,000 - $15,000

Authorship for Research Paper in China: $1,500 - $24,850

Fake MBA Degree Online – United Arab Emirates: $5,445

Fake Harvard Degree – Russia: $40,000

Fake Yale Degree – Vietnam: $1,200 - $1,500

Bogus degrees are a big business, as many companies will charge their clients hundreds, if not thousands of dollars. Even countries, such as Nigeria, sell fraudulent degrees. I enjoyed personal e-mail correspondence with authors Ezell and Bear. In their famous book, ***Degree Mills: The Billion-Dollar Industry that has Sold Over a Million Fake Diplomas*** (2012) they name many people in public and personal life who have not actually earned the degrees they claim to have. Their book makes for good reading if you enjoy stories about clever scams, frauds, and their perpetrators.

Problems Then and Now

The U.S. Department of Education Database of Accredited Postsecondary Institutions and Programs (n.d.) (https://ope.ed.gov/dapip/#/home) is a really excellent website; see also U.S. Department of Education (2020) https://www.ed.gov/accreditation?src=m for a list of legitimate nationally accredited agencies. You can also go to the search bar, type in 'diploma mills.' Another source, the U.S. Department of Education (2019) lists national accredited agencies, www.ed.gov/sites/default/files/accreditation/accreditation-handbook.pdf. Another good website to access more information is Best Schools (2021) https://thebestschools.org/magazine/online-college-vs-deiploma-mills/.

It appears that this lack of public exposure to the dangers of diploma mills makes it easy for the operators of these fake businesses to stay in business! Confusion is rampant.

Counterfeiting degrees and diplomas represent one category of the problem. In addition, there are **four other types** of businesses, schools, and individuals who offer fake, disreputable, or questionable degrees: "schools too new or too unusual . . . schools involved in geographical issues . . . schools involved in religious issues . . . [and schools which are not really schools but] degree mills" (Ezell & Bear, 2012, pp. 59-60).

Also, **some schools are geographically separate from their 'home base'** or may have extended campuses in America as well as outside the United States. (Schools that are legitimately accredited and offer courses and degrees through distance learning are **not** degree mills!) Then, too, some schools claim **religions exemptions** from traditional recognition and accreditation on the grounds of religion. And **finally,** degree mills pretend to be legitimate institutions but **actually just sell their diplomas, certificates, or degrees to anyone with a valid credit card**. How sad!

Thousands of people in America have purchased fake degrees (Buy a degree online, 2020; see also Buy a degree online, Global scam (2021). Previously, Robert J. Cramer (2004), when testifying before a congressional subcommittee, identified roughly **2000 degree-granting schools** that fall in one or more of these four categories. This means that many people, who the public believes to hold real degrees and certificates, are in fact, fakes, and charlatans.

More Examples

Ezell and Bear (2012) cite the following examples: a Los Angeles teacher with a fake doctorate in 2004, a Florida sheriff who purchased a degree outright, a so-called physician with fake medical degrees sentenced to 14 years in prison in North Carolina, and a community college professor who committed suicide when exposed to holding two worthless diplomas. The list continues with the discovery of University of Iowa staff member with five fake degrees, including two doctorates; an Alexandria, Kentucky fire chief with a fake degree he purchased; a Quincy University president in Illinois who resigned over his fake diploma; and the Democrat candidate, David LaPere, in California who lost his election when the public discovered his fake degree from Wexford University.

Finally, Ezell and Bear (2012) state that a Toccoa Falls College president of the private Georgia Christian liberal arts college (Donald Young) resigned in disgrace over stating he had a master's degree, state representative Gloria Schermesser, from Michigan claimed to hold a degree from the fake Columbia State University, and the list goes on and on (Clifton et al., 2018; Gibson, 2017; Grant, 2019).

In addition, a Guam police captain lost his position when the degree document he submitted for his job was found to be purchased and fraudulent (N. Wellein, personnel communication, November 20, 2011).

Ezell and Bear (2012), in Appendix E of their book, list more than 200 accrediting agencies **not recognized** by either the U.S. Department of Education or by the Council of Higher Education Accreditation (CHEA).

Recently, in searching the Internet for 'diploma mills' in 2020, I located several articles on this subject of fake degrees including a massive list of unaccredited institutions **(almost 300)**, by alphabetical order. Here is a brief sample (List of unaccredited institutions, 2021):

- Alexandria University, Nevada (not to be confused with Alexandria University in Egypt)
- All-American University, Nevada (not to be confused with American University, Washington, D.C.)
- All Saints American University, Liberia
- American Andragogy University, Hawai'i, Bolivia
- Ashwood University at various locations (not to be confused with Ashford University)
- Brookside University, Barbados
- Burnell College, United Kingdom
- Burnett International University, Haiti, St. Kitts
- Cambell State University (not to be confused with Campbell University, NC)
- Central State University of New York (not to be confused with NY State U)
- Clayton University, Hong Kong, China, San Marino, Nigeria, India

More information on accredited educational institutions can be found at U.S.

Department of Education (2019)

www.ed.gov/sites/default/files/accreditation/accreditation-handbook.pdf. The Federal

Trade Commission (College degree scams, 2021) offers a 'search bar' where you can

type in the subject you want further information on at https://www.ftc.gov/faq. Or you

can check with your state's Better Business Bureau or state attorney general's office. The

Office of Personnel Management (OPM) also will assist in verifying federal applicant's

degree legitimacy. Unaccredited, fake institutions appear live and well in the 21st century.

The public can lose confidence quite easily in higher education institutions, when

consumers discover public officials, teachers, private doctors, dentists, architects, and

others in society have obtained their positions or advanced in them by purchasing

counterfeit degrees and diplomas (Cramer, 2004). What does it say about legitimate

schools that do nothing to identify and solve the problem of fake diploma mills? If

postsecondary institutions cannot solve the problem, what is preventing them from

bringing it to the attention of those in the law enforcement world?

What does it say about law enforcement agencies at the local city and county,

state, and federal levels, once notified about illegitimate schools, that continue to ignore

the problem of fake diploma mills and counterfeit documents? What does this deplorable

situation say about our lawmakers in our Western society?

CH 48 Diploma Mills: Questions, Analysis, Problems

My Pearl of Wisdom: Is Fraud Worth It?

Twenty years from now you will be more disappointed

by the things that you didn't do than by the ones you did do.

So, throw off the bowlines, sail away from safe harbor,

catch the trade winds in your sails.

Explore, Dream, Discover.

Mark Twain

DIPLOMA MILLS in America are a billion-dollar business, selling over a million fraudulent degrees (Clifton et al., 2018). Little officially appears to be known about this deplorable situation due to the ending of the **task force known as DipScam, the FBI's sting operations** in the 1980s. After **Operation DipScam**, it appeared to onlookers that the diploma-mill problems were in decline. However, with the retirement of Task Force Leader Special Agent Allen Ezell, and the FBI's subsequent interest in savings-and-loan scandals, illegal drugs entering the U.S. borders, and terrorism/security problems domestically and internationally, the issue of diploma mills took a back seat (Ezell & Bear, 2012).

State agencies seemed unwilling or at least less willing to move forward on their own to prosecute operators and managers of fake degree businesses. Finally, more ambitious white-collar criminals appeared to discover in the past decade just how lucrative it could be to sell degrees online.

Diploma Mills in Higher Education, an Introduction

The presence and growing numbers of diploma mills in the world generally, and in the U.S. specifically, represents a danger to its society and its citizens. Retired FBI agent Allen Ezell defines Diploma mills as "organizations that award degrees without requiring [their] students to meet educational standards for such degrees" (Ezell & Bear, 2012, p. 21). These authors further stipulate that diploma mills "receive fees from their so-called students on the basis of fraudulent misrepresentation and/or make it possible for the recipients of its degrees to perpetrate a fraud on the public" (p. 21).

2020 Update

Diploma mills (2021) explains how students can protect themselves in 10 ways:

1. Check if the university is accredited or not and by which accrediting body.

2. Notice if there are any classes, or interaction with professors or the school, and if any examinations are required.

3. Determine if admission to the school is based only on a valid credit card.

4. Ask if the degree is based solely on work experience and faxed resumes.

5. Note if the degree is produced within 30 days of application and money.

6. Review the costs: a typical sum is $400-$2,000 for an undergraduate degree and up to $3,000 for a graduate degree while doctorates cost many thousands more [for just buying the bogus degree].

7. See if the school has multiple complaints against it; check with the Better Business Bureau.

8. Speak with the school's online 'counselor' and if the counselor assures a caller that international online universities cannot be accredited in the U.S. by CHEA that is a big red flag. The Council for Higher Education Accreditation or CHEA is known nationally and internationally.

9. The school's website lists absolutely no faculty.

10. The school offers online degrees to U.S. citizens but it is located in a foreign country.

Furthermore, the country issues the degree. Think of Nigeria! (pp. 3-4)

Several websites in 2021 can be used to demine if a school is just a diploma mill in disguise. These online sites are as follows:

https://www2.ed.gov/about/offices/list/ous/international/usnei/us/fraud.doc

https://www2.ed.gov/students/prep/college/diplomamills/diploma-mills.html

https://www.consumer.ftc.gov/articles/college-degree-scams

https://www.chea.org/international-directory/accreditation-service-international-colleges

http://www.geteducated.com/diploma-mills-police/college-degree-mills/161-college-degree-or-diploma-mill/

Diploma Mill Dangers

Why do diploma mills pose a danger to society? Television News explains the harmful effects of diploma mills to those who purchase fake degrees as well as to the public at large, in *Fake diplomas causing real problems* (Grant, 2019) and Gibson (2017) as follows:

First, those who are unaware of the fraud committed by themselves and the actual diploma mill operators when they purchase postsecondary degrees, **can be fired** by their employer and **face legal problems** as well. If individuals use fake degrees to obtain jobs, or later, if they use their fake degrees for promotion or greater career advancement and are discovered, these agencies may prosecute them under both state and federal statutes.

These statues, according to Ezell and Bear (2012), deal with Unlawful Trade Practices Act, Mail Fraud, Consumer Protection, and U.S. Code Title 18, dealing with Aid and Abet, Conspiracy, False ID, Computer and Mail Fraud, Fraud by Wire, Forfeiture, Money Laundering, Racketeer Influenced and Corrupt Organizations (RICO), Trademark Violations, and Tax Evasion. Employers sometimes will fire workers who have used a fake degree to obtain their position, and that can be disastrous for their families and society. If those individuals become bankrupt and homeless, they may become a drain on social services, the health system, charitable agencies, and society.

Second, companies who employee workers with fake degrees have deceived the American consumers and public, and the potential for negative publicity and damages caused by those hired may be extensive (Gibson, 2017). For example, if XYZ Medical Corporation hires a physical therapist who never actually graduated from an accredited school, clients may sue the therapist and owners of the group to recover damages – either physical damages for poor care, mental suffering, or both. ABC's 20/20 television story several years ago concerned a New York accountant who purchased a medical degree and was working as an emergency room physician. The horrifying list of frauds goes on and on.

Another case discussed in that same ABC television segment was a NY high school dropout who purchased a doctorate and ran a sex-therapy clinic. Many couples divorced following their 'treatment' at the clinic. The negative publicity alone could be enormous, forcing businesses to close. Employees who purchased certificates or diplomas may be subject to prosecution, jail time, and exceedingly high fines, leading to other adverse consequences: divorce, civil law suits, depression, and suicide.

A **third** group harmed by diploma mills according to Gibson (2017) and several other writers including Clifton et al., (2018) are the **taxpayers who are paying for the salaries** of those unethical local, state, and federal government employees such as public-school teachers, school principals, support staff, as well as elected officials, and military officers, who obtained their position based on fake degrees. Agencies also pay higher salaries many times to those who acquire higher educational levels and when public employees use fake diplomas to advance themselves, the taxpayers are the losers.

Another problem is that some of the accreditation agencies used by diploma mills are as fake as the documents diploma mills sell. **Some 200 illicit accreditation agencies have been identified thus far.** The public's confusion can be readily understood. Legitimate accreditation is confused with legal **types** of accreditation (Grant, 2019). The layperson can mix up vocational-technical, regional, national, and special accrediting agencies. Even novice educators may easily find this issue of fraudulent accreditation agencies difficult to fully grasp.

Finally, diploma mills must not be confused with institutions offering students the opportunity to obtain certificates and degrees by non-traditional methods, such as taking courses online or entire degree programs through correspondence (Wellein, 2010, 2021). Tens of thousands of students each year obtain their degrees legitimately through distance education, or hybrid programs i.e., a combination of face-to-face direct instruction and online classes.

Diploma mills on the other hand, sell degrees and certificates without individuals doing actual course work. 'Students' also do not take any standardized examinations, or other types of tests, but simply pay the fake institution (usually online) and obtain their fraudulent certificates or degrees.

Millions and Billions of Dollars

In case the reader is under the impression that diploma mills are a relatively minor problem only in America, Clifton et al., (2018) stipulate after extensive research in England, that **diploma mills represent a billion-dollar industry**, which have sold over a million fake diplomas; UK nationals have bought fake degrees from multi-million-pound diploma mills in Pakistan (p. 1) and the problem is growing. Buying a fake degree, certificate, or diploma is not illegal in the UK but using one when applying for employment is fraudulent and could result in a 10-year prison term.

Websites

The American Associate of Collegiate Registrars and Admission Officers produces two publications on how to help identify fake credentials and fake schools, as seen in the website: https://www.aacrao.org Use the search bar to access their articles.

The Defense Activity for Non-Traditional Education Support (DANTES, Mission, 2006) is an agency operated by the Department of the Navy, for all branches of the service. It is a massive supplier of educational materials to American military education centers across the globe and funds counselor assistance, college level testing, and other similar programs. See its website: http://www.dantes.doded.mil .

Authors Allen Ezell and John Bear (2012) set up a special website to update the information contained in their book, **Diploma Mills,** and also to report to interested individuals relevant news and developments from schools and universities about this problem. They will respond to questions, react to responses, and exchange ideas at allen5617@msn.com. Those interested should visit the website as follows: www.degreemills.com for further information.

In July 2021, I wrote to Allen Ezell, to verify his e-mail address. He did, answering most promptly, and told me about a massive diploma scam happening in Pakistan, by a company named Axact which is pulling in millions of dollars a month! Investigative writer Ezell said to see Walsh's (2015) article:

https://www.nytimes.com/2015/05/18/world/asia/fake-diplomas-real-cash-pakistani-company-axact-reaps-millions-columbiana-barkley.html?auth=link-dismiss-google1tap .

Apparently, Chairman and CEO of Axact & BOL, Shoaib Ahmed Shaikh, has some 2,000 employees at his news channel company and an assortment of other companies (hotels, internet, media group, and entertainment corporations); primarily a vast network dealing with selling fake diplomas and certificates to anyone with money (https://www.bolnews.com/about-us/).

In *Fake diplomas, real cash: Pakistani company Axact reaps millions* an article published in the New York Times by Irish author and journalist Declan Walsh on May 17, 2015, Walsh explains that the Pakistani-based corporation AXACT is perpetrating a massive, on-going scam raking in millions of dollars from those buying diplomas or degrees, nationally and internationally. (The Pakistani government forced this reporter to leave the country in 2013.)

Summary

Diploma mills issuing fake certificates and degrees are a billion-dollar business in the U.S. and elsewhere. Diploma mills hurt the individuals purchasing the illicit documents, the public at large because people holding fake degrees are committing consumer fraud, and hurt the taxpayers who are led to believe expensive lies (Clifton et al., 2018; Gibson, 2017; Grant, 2019). In the case of medical personnel who deal with life and death decisions, engineers responsible for the design of bridges and buildings, and many other critical areas of life, fraudulent degrees may result in terrible consequences for all.

Taxes fund the salaries of employees at the city, county, state, and federal levels of government, so when employees receive raises and promotions because they have obtained these fake, sometimes higher degrees, then the taxpayers lose. In private businesses or corporation, those who hold positions of authority, respect, and lie about their credentials hurt everyone. Those involved in the purchasing of fake certificates and degrees for fraudulent purposes commit fraud and may be criminally negligent. It is the diploma mill owners and managers, of course, who rake in tens of millions of dollars by fooling the public. Do not be fooled yourself!

CH 49 Self-Assessment for Course Preparation

My Pearl of Wisdom: Ready, Set, Go!

The aim of education should be to teach us rather how to think,

than what to think — rather to improve our minds,

so as to enable us to think for ourselves,

than to load the memory with thoughts of other men.

Bill Beattie

In this chapter, I explain how I prepare for any college or graduate level course, with 150% success as my goal. Listed here is what I usually do; it serves as a guide for anyone who wants to do well in school online, using a hybrid format, or via face-to-face direct instruction. I earned a 4.0 in all my masters and doctoral coursework.

10 Actions

1. **Read all textbooks** prior to the first day of class. Read the supplementary ones, if possible.

2. **Use a color-coding system** of highlighters and colored pens, to mark all major sections of the text books, indicating main ideas, supporting theories, specialized vocabulary, specific definitions, etc. But careful, however, to not over highlight or over mark. I choose colored file folders and clearly label them also, to specify syllabus, assignments, due dates, etc.

3. **Formally outline the textbook chapters,** print the outlines and make copies for everyone in the class to be helpful.

4. **Reread major sections of the textbooks** during the course period (usually six to ten weeks), and prepare to respond to questions, state any concerns, prepare and write assignments.

5. **Turn in all assignments early**. I prepare written assignments using MS Word,

and then copy and paste onto the "posting" bulletin board for online courses or if writing papers, prepare, save, and later post. Prior to doing this, I write, edit, rewrite, and re-edit my written assignments several times. As a former language arts teacher, I learned that **it is only in the rewriting process which produces good writing**.

6. **Respond to the postings online** a minimum of two times each week (for online courses**)**, although usually, I respond much more often than that. (I always exceed the minimum mandated by the professor.) If it is an in-person, direct instruction course, I respond to assignments promptly.

7. **Reread sections of the APA Manual as I write my papers**. Each time I take a course, I learn more about the APA format. Be certain which edition to use. For example, I began my doctoral journey using APA Level 5. Just when I was completing my studies (2010), my university chair stated that all dissertations must use Level 6.

8. **Use a software program such as PERRLA, EazyPaper, Academic Writer, Scribbr, StyleEase, or something similar; there are many available,** recommended by your school, which helps greatly with the APA format when preparing papers and citations. However, any software program is still not 100% perfect. You must check, then recheck all work prior to submitting it for class credit.

9. **Give 150% effort towards what you do,** or probably, it is not worth doing at all. Striving for excellence is my motto, to the best of my ability, given present time constraints. I feel that when an instructor assigns work, I should then do it thoroughly, rather than "coast by" or pretend to have read the material or textbook. To do anything less is to only cheat yourself.

10. **I give each course my full attention**, in terms of time, energy, enthusiasm, and devotion. I come to class early each session (i.e., direct instruction or online courses), ensuring that I never keep my classmates waiting; I prepare to do well even when viewing a podcast, video, or television show, with total focus on whatever I must accomplish. I devote my normal, enthusiastic self to doing my best although I work full-time and also have home/family responsibilities.

Summary

I am an inquisitive student, who tends to ask **why not,** instead of **why** a great deal of the time. I read my assigned textbooks in their entirety prior to the course start date, outline the books (using my own color-coding technique), and read the supplementary books and materials. Additionally, I prepare color-coded file folders all alphabetized in advance for each module or section, and arrange other files with labels such as Internet Articles, Class Discussion Questions, Postings, Notes, Syllabus, Textbook Chapter Outlines, Field Experience (if any), Vocabulary, and Final Project.

Specifically, when I write a paper of any length, **I do the following when editing**:

- Write a rough draft; leave spaces, asterisks or question marks in sentences that might provide me with ideas on which to follow through.

- Edit the paper, filling in vocabulary terms to use; ask myself questions in writing.

- Check for mechanics such as grammar, punctuation, run-on sentences, tense, voice. Notice if there is parallel construction in sentences; correct them if not.

- Review for logical paragraph sequences, paragraph verb-tense consistency, signal terms such as 'moreover' or 'nevertheless' or 'however' i.e., transitions between paragraphs.

- Edit the paper again, looking for the main idea, supporting sections, and documentation for these ideas: who, did what, when, how, why, consequences, relevancy.

- Put the paper aside for a day or two, and then reread it for creativity, originality, and insightfulness, ensuring that I fulfilled the assignment according to the instructor's directions. I always check the instructor's rubric.

- Check and recheck all references used for correct spelling of author's name, date, following APA guidelines.

- Review the paper to see if the entire work follows APA format.

Usually, I also compile a list of specialized vocabulary terms used in the chapters I have read. I establish a personal schedule which allows me time to write, edit, rewrite, then step away from the project for a few days, then edit the paper again, before submitting it many days before the deadline.

Finally, over the weeks of each course, I schedule my Saturdays and Sundays at my office (home or elsewhere), doing research, writing and rewriting; during weekday evenings, I read my texts and supplementary materials. Thus, by at least one week prior to a course start-date, I have completed all papers for the course, read all materials and texts, and if it is an online course, I have done everything except for postings in response to my classmates' comments. Before the course ends, I have already started to prepare for the next course in the same manner.

What I learned:

I really learned a great deal about each course, from a variety of sources: weekly assignments, fellow students, postings, course handouts, discussion board, in-person or online professor lectures, and supplementary and textbook readings and papers. It is best to challenge yourself, and understand that you not only owe good learning to your professor and yourself, but to your fellow students as well.

I realize that some students have families and childcare issues and I am not minimizing life's challenges and distractions. Others have full-time and even part-time jobs, while maintaining a house or apartment, inside and out. However, once you identify your own personal challenges and roadblocks, you can then address each one. Identify the issue, list choices available in terms of cost, location, resources available, and so forth. Then choose if you can live with the option you select. If not, renegotiate with yourself or family.

Learning never happens in a vacuum! Be prepared! And I remember every undergraduate course where I received a grade of C. Yes, all seven of them. Yes, I received a few Bs too, but the more courses I took, the better I got. So, this advice I offer you here is from developing a system of study that actually works! What system do **you** have?

CH 50 Challenges Faced While Completing Doctoral Coursework

My Pearl of Wisdom: It Ain't Over 'Till It's Over

The significant problems we face cannot be solved

at the same level of thinking

we were at when we created them.

Albert Einstein

TAKING THE DOCTORAL level course, Qualitative Methods and Analysis mid-way through my program of study which I began in 2005, proved to be unexpectedly challenging, for several reasons.

Challenges

First, my loving (late) spouse (Daniel Atoigue) had a series of heart attacks, almost 14 years ago. It was early May, when I quickly drove Dan to the emergency room (ER) of one of the finest Honolulu hospitals which specializes in heart problems. Straub Hospital has an outstanding reputation nationally and throughout Pacific and Asia countries.

Cardiologists in the ER quickly moved my spouse to the critical care unit; they later performed an Angiogram or 'Cardiac Cath,' which is a highly sophisticated diagnostic test involving injecting dye through the arteries and veins of the heart, to determine if blood flow is restricted by blockage. This initial surgery is important but can be medically dangerous for high-risk patients. However, it was the test results that proved to be most devastating.

Dan had one major artery 100% occluded, and two other major arteries 85% or more blocked. **He needed emergency coronary triple bypass surgery**, but because of previous blood thinner use, he had to wait nearly a week, for the actual surgery. The cardio-thoracic surgeon was part of a team of 10 (including a profusion specialist who deals with the heart-lung machine, cardiologist, anesthesiologist, vein-surgeon, specially-trained cardiac nurses, and a special cadre of highly trained surgical technicians) who altogether perform bypass surgery weekly. They spent over six hours operating on my husband, repairing damaged arteries, striping good arteries from the leg (groin to knee), arm (elbow to wrist) and chest (near the major incision) and reattaching them in or near the heart.

Following surgery, doctors placed my spouse in the intensive care unit (ICU) where he subsequently needed at least five pints of blood and some extremely good nursing care. While all this was going on, I would race home to write doctoral course assignments, telephone friends and relatives with medical updates, or go to work for a few hours.

More Challenges

Secondly, my youngest adult son had **shoulder surgery** also in May so he had his own medical procedure just one day after his father's heart surgery. Once my son had recovered from the shoulder surgery, then he **had eye surgery the following week**. I felt totally overwhelmed, first driving back and forth to Straub Hospital after my husband was admitted, then later, driving both my son and spouse to various medical appointments, picking up prescription medications, driving them to hospital or clinic for special tests, etc. This was in addition to being the caretaker 24 hours a day for my bed-ridden spouse, who aside from bathroom trips, remained in bed recuperating.

Third, unfortunately, Dan's heart problem proved too severe, and it forced him (meaning me) to prepare and complete over 20 different forms including attending two weeks of pre- retirement counseling sessions, to retire from his state of Hawai'i job. Once he had recovered from his hospital stay, we met with a retirement expert, financial planner, social security administration technician, union representative, payroll officer, and our tax accountant, all between July-August.

Finally, my Argosy University professor **did not release the course syllabus** earlier than three days prior to the course start date. (Yes – I was still enrolling and completing my doctoral courses every seven and a half weeks!) This particular professor waited to send out the course syllabus for our online course until just a few days prior to the start date. (I discovered later that he had been quite ill and was just returning to work.) I prefer to organize all my class work **ahead of time**: color-code file folders, print and read the online lectures, read the book once if not twice, and outline the chapters. But you can only control yourself; you cannot control others! Life can be many times, unpredictable.

To say my life was hectic is a gross understatement. In hindsight, I should have taken more than two weeks of leave from a very demanding federal job. Ah – if only – I could've, should've, would've – isn't hindsight grand!

Learning Experiences

The most significant learning experience during this time was that it forced me to deal with the terrible fear that **my spouse of several decades might die**, first in the ER, then after the cardiologist moved him to the critical cardiac care bed while waiting for invasive tests to be completed, then surviving the open-heart triple bypass surgery itself.

Once my Dan was home, he was basically helpless — no lifting more than 10 pounds, no raising arms away from sides of body, no stooping, bending, driving, only brief but careful showering, standing up/sitting down; his stitches were over a foot in length on his leg and arm (for vein grafts) and on his chest, of course. So, I had to do almost everything for him.

What an experience! My husband survived his heart attacks and surgery, and my son, his double surgeries. I continued to work as the Army Reserve Education Services

Officer at Fort Shafter, completed demanding course work, and later, obtained my doctorate in education in mid-2010. Jonell Calloway, Education Director in St Louis, MO approved and funded my Ed.D. under the budget's training category for which I will be eternally grateful. I retired in late December 2012.

CH 51 My Personal Reflections:

Persistence, Enthusiasm, Choices

My Pearl of Wisdom: Tell Me Oh So Sweetly

Not all superheroes wear capes, some having teaching degrees.

Unknown Author

MY THREE STRONGEST abilities are **persistence in the face of great hardship or disorder, enthusiasm for what I believe in, and identifying, then selecting options/choices when sometimes others are unable to do so.**

Persistence

To me persistence is an inclination to continue, persist, or exist in spite of challenges or obstacles (Merriam-Webster, n.d.). Over the course of a lifetime, my persistence in following through on projects or tasks seems to have only increased. **Perhaps it is meeting resistance that has forced me onwards.** After high school, I ran into a roadblock to obtain funds for college. However, I worked diligently, earning a four-year State of Hawai'i scholarship, as well as a one-year journalism scholarship. I married briefly at age 18, divorced, but then remarried at age 19, to an English professor.

Children

After graduating from the University of Hawaii at Mānoa, I began a Masters in Audiology, but stopped to start a family. By the time I divorced my second husband due to his alcoholism, I had two young boys under the age of three to support.

After an eye-opening, horrendous experience with the Honolulu Food Stamp Program for three months, I found a job in 1969 **teaching 12 months a year full-time (eight hours a day)** for two years, at the Hawai'i Job Corps Center in Koko Head, near

Hanauma Bay, all the while taking evening courses as a half-time student working towards my teacher certification. (I was the first Job Corps female teacher who lasted more than a few months, and was their first teacher to become almost fully certified through the state of Hawai'i.)

To place both of my young boys in the *Wai Kahala* Nursery School, an exceedingly good school for children under age five, I applied for a scholarship for one of them and received it based on my 'terrific application letter' I later learned (from the nursery school director herself).

Tuition was $75 a month per child, a princely sum for someone trying to live on $350 a month income prior to finding a teaching position. (I ate the crusts from tuna sandwiches I made for my children's lunches, consumed all leftovers, and drank copious amounts of water at every meal. Yes, I could have asked my dear mother for some money but I was too proud. I was sometimes a bit hungry but my boys were always well fed. (I chewed a lot of gum when not working or in class.) In every phase of my life, there was great adversity but also profound joy; persistence truly paid off.

Teaching in Guam

I accepted a contract teacher position in Guam, to teach special education students, following my work at Job Corps, and concurrently to pursue a master's in reading education there. The job came with free housing for the duration of the two-year contract! I uprooted myself and my children. With barely $150 in cash (the total of my life's savings), we spent three weeks island-hopping from Hawai'i through Micronesia to Guam on Continental Air Lines (at no extra cost), staying with local families who were friends or relatives of Job Corp students.

Within two weeks of arrival in Guam, I had borrowed a pick-up truck from a 'friend of a friend' (with Hawai'i connections), enrolled in University of Guam graduate school, found an apartment, placed my two young sons in kindergarten and nursery school (respectively), and started a new job—teaching deaf and hard of hearing. I knew absolutely **no** sign language and had to quickly learn it within a few short weeks. I borrowed several books from the university library on finger spelling and sign language, asked my principal and fellow teachers a great many questions and took copious notes; my stubborn personality (of persistence and tenacity) proved to be a tremendous strength.

Enthusiasm

Enthusiasm has always been part of my personality. If one feels strongly about a subject, person, or idea, how can one not be excited, motivated, and spirited? If one makes a commitment to excellence, how can one accomplish this excellence without avid interest and attention? If one is basically a positive person, how can this natural enthusiasm one feels, be quelled? If one believes in a new concept, for example, how can one explain this concept to others, without some sort of positive emotional release or expression?

My Mother

My mother was enthusiastic about life and I owe this trait to her; she was a wonderful mother and mentor. Trude Michelson Akau, born in Boston, MA, earned her master's in education when I was four years old, the youngest of three sisters and two brothers. The community elected my mother (one of only five women out of a total of 63 delegates) to be a member of the State of Hawai'i Constitutional Convention in 1950 and she was instrumental with four others, in writing the state constitution. When the U.S. Congress voted Hawai'i into its fold in 1959, lawmakers used the 1950 Hawai'i State Constitution as a key element.

Trude began teaching part-time at age 40, full-time at age 60 and finally retired at age 74. In between, she wrote a book, *Kalihi Kids Can Communicate*, a compilation of her fifth- grade students' best poetry and stories, which I had the fortune to edit. My mother was tireless and wrote literally hundreds of letters to the Honolulu Advertiser for over 40 years, about numerous, diverse controversial subjects; the newspaper always published them and readers almost invariably responded to them. She had an extraordinarily high energy level, and that part of her personality must have flowed into my veins, by way of DNA.

Options, Choices in Life

The ability to understand problems, identify options or choices, and decide on one to put into action is a strength that I have always nourished. Initially, searching for options was a matter of survival.

Not enough money for undergraduate school? Look for grants and scholarships. Later, no money for food with two babies? Review the Food Stamp Program. No money for gasoline to drive to work? Rent out a portion of your *Hawai'i Kai* house because it had extra bedrooms. No money for nursery school for the two little boys? Get a scholarship for at least one of them. No time for graduate school in the summers because work at Job Corps was all-year-round? Leave Job Corps and accept a teaching contract where the government of Guam paid the rent. Don't know sign language? Learn it quickly, and ask the other teacher of that grade level to team-teach with me. Need a father for the children? Make a checklist of variables to consider when going out with eligible men. Need a better job to obtain a mortgage? Leave a teaching job with Department of Education in Hawai'i and work for the U.S. Army!

Be Logical, See the Choices

Life is full of choices. **It is what one chooses which is all-important**. People are a sum of all the choices they make is life. One must expect adversity. But at that moment of pain, indecision, chaos – it is what one decides to do, which path to take, when to follow a particular direction – that matters. Then, take the action you choose – do not procrastinate!

Knowing what options are available, what each option entails, what resources are needed, and the length of time involved are extremely important. For example, one may select Choice A – but doing so means that choice will take two years to complete and $10 thousand. Choice B is available too – but that means moving to another state at additional, perhaps prohibitive costs and will take four years. Choice C might be the best, if one can agree on spending $20 thousand over a three-year period to pay off significant bills and missing the youngest son's high school graduation, to accept a position in Germany. But in Germany, one might be promoted within a year rather than wait for five. And promotion equates to greater financial stability. And so, it goes, options, decisions, and consequences.

Professional Purpose

My professional purpose in life is to assist those who want to pursue their educational or vocational endeavors, first, as a teacher for delinquent young men for two years, then a special education teacher, regular and resource teacher K-12, and an adult school instructor. I wrote a federal grant and became a special summer school principal. I was also a federal program grant writer for Guam Teacher Center and Guam Teacher Corps (as well as innovative Title IV program grants), a Title I resource teacher, and an instructor for undergraduate and graduate students at the University of Guam for over eight years.

I wrote a well-received hard-back juvenile novel (a chapter book set in Guam) and edited a language arts resource book (set in Kalihi, HI). On Oahu, I taught at Punahou Summer School, Waipahu Intermediate School, Adult Evening School (DOE) and at Leeward Community College. Life has been quite challenging.

U.S. Army, DOD

In 1983, I began working full-time for the Department of the Army at Fort Shafter, and Schofield Barracks, HI, and subsequently accepted positions at active-duty Army Education Centers in Germany, Egypt, Hawai'i, Panama, Honduras, Saudi Arabia, Kuwait, Japan, Korea, Puerto Rico, and then returned to Fort Shafter, Hawai'i. In between these 25+ years overseas, I visited, trained, or worked at over 39 countries, temporarily or full-time.

Beginning in mid-2001, I continued to spread the education word to military personnel and their families located across the Pacific and Asia: Fairbanks and Anchorage, Alaska; Maui, the Big Island of Hawai'i, and Oahu; the Commonwealth of the Northern Marianas Islands, (to include Saipan, Rota, and Tinian); the U.S. Territories of Guam and American Samoa; Japan and Korea, too. I traveled to one of these various locations from Honolulu every six-eight weeks. I was terrifically busy for years! But oh – the work was so gratifying.

My Personal Contributions

I raised three children of whom I am very proud. Each is a contributing member of society – working, paying taxes, voting, and being a loving member of his or her family and community. I have four grandchildren, too. My loving husband (50 years) whom I adored recently passed away February 2021. Daniel was the great family nurturer! He worked as an excellent Adult Corrections Officer III at *Waiawa,* a minimum-security facility. And he was a great family cook, skilled handy man and family chauffer; he loved his Singer sewing machine as much as his Ryobi weed wacker.

Before moving to Hawaii, the U.S. Environmental Protection Agency certified Dan as a trained waste water treatment plant operator/supervisor for one of Guam's 12-million-gallon sewage plants after the Guam government sent Dan and five others to technical college in Neosho, Missouri. The irony i.e., moving from sewage plant to prison was not lost on either of us!

I live in Mililani, Central Oahu, and substitute teach in this same area (usually at Mililani Middle School and Mililani High School). Life can be good when one sees the rainbow and accepts the storm preceding it. Now, I love writing, so I can share my experiences with others.

My Professional Contributions

How should I be remembered professionally? It would be wonderful if I made a difference in people's lives for the better. It is a tremendously rewarding experience to have a student I helped e-mail or communicate to me that I counseled her or him and helped to solve an educational problem, thus making life better.

In the education office at 9th Regional Readiness Command, one staff member had only four courses left to complete her bachelor's degree but when she began working there, she did not yet have an associate's degree. Another staff member completed both his associate and bachelor's degrees while working in the education office, and had six courses remaining for the master's degree. A third staff member requested a foreign transcript evaluation, entered Honolulu Community College, took some coursework, and was just shy of a two-year degree.

Soldiers invited me to attend their graduation ceremonies – too many to count, and I felt deeply honored to be included in these soldiers' milestones. This is true transformational leadership.

Soldiers and civilians need assistance; they need to know their options in terms of funding, types of degree programs, distance education programs vs. direct instruction delivery methods, testing for college credit, obtaining credit for military schooling and experience on the job. Persistence, enthusiasm, and choices continue to make me the person I am today.

Notes

In late December 2012, I retired, because I had too many personal things I wanted to do and disliked the mindless, numbing DOD paperwork which was consuming too much time: daily, weekly reports no one really read, time sheets I had to complete using an Army computer even if I was on leave, meetings just for appearance where my input was not needed. I also wanted to spend more time with my family, write a book or two, and travel less. Yes – less! I knew I would miss helping the hundreds of military members and their families but felt secure in what I had accomplished.

It is now late 2021, and **the COVID-19 pandemic is sweeping over Mother Earth**. Our planet is facing a biological nightmare, which the world has not seen since the 1918-1919 Spanish Influenza Pandemic killed 20-50 million, worldwide. Some 500 million were infected but survived!

Presently, there are over 260 million confirmed cases of COVID-19 **infections** worldwide (about 10% of the world's population) and approximately 5.2 million **deaths.** There are some 48 million COVID infections in America and 775,000 American deaths. Yes, there are vaccines available (as some 7.63 billion doses have been administered worldwide), and yes, that will certainly help. But new strains of the virus are showing up in England, South Africa, America, India, and parts unknown. So, choices we make become even more important.

Eventually, I believe that society will require nearly 100% of us to be fully vaccinated – to include booster shots, just like the annual influenza shot. But that might not happen immediately.

Think of the Polio or Small Pox vaccination programs. The federal government did not need to ask us to vaccinate. We simply ate the sugar cubes laced with American virologist and medical researcher Dr. Jonas Salk's vaccine and rolled up our sleeves and took the mandated Small Pox vaccine (thank you Dr. Edward Jenner) knowing they were for the good of ourselves and society. (Polio was eradicated in America by the early 1950s and Small Pox was eradicated in America by the late 1970s.)

The vaccination programs stopped these and many other diseases in America, such as mumps, measles, chicken pox, tetanus, rubella, whooping coup, diphtheria – except for an occasional outbreak every few years affecting mostly unvaccinated individuals. (Many other diseases are controlled by vaccinations such as rabies, shingles, pneumonia, hepatitis A & B, and human papillomavirus (HPV) which prevents many cancers in young people.)

Our country needs to decide if personal freedom is more important than that of societal needs. Personally, I feel that if parents do not want to get vaccinated to include their children that is their right. But society (government at all levels and private company CEOs) then needs to tell parents to home-school them, because public schools will soon require all students to be fully vaccinated (or use distance learning) even 5 – 11 year-olds. If adults do not want to be vaccinated, I say fine. But then do not frequent supermarkets, movie theaters, gyms, drugstores, gas stations, malls or **any private or public facility open to the public**. Dentist offices, physicians, medical clinics, airlines, and restaurants may require all clients to be vaccinated. No vaccine? No service! Use only mail service, or order items online.

Note: I realize that public medical facilities such as the ERs must accept all patients. However, ill ER patients who are **not** vaccinated should not be seen ahead of those who are indeed vaccinated. And hospitals should **not** be accepting patients for elective surgeries, and dentists should not be accepting patients for routine dental care and cleaning, if they are **not** vaccinated. Airlines and restaurants should **not** be accepting those who are not vaccinated. Period.

Even fully vaccinated individuals can get sick with an infection, called a 'break-through' case despite using a mask, practicing social distancing, using hand sanitizers, and avoiding large gatherings. So, vaccinating as many members of society becomes even more important.

If prisoners who spread the virus to correctional workers, their own family members, and others think it is their right to opt out of vaccine, **then society must determine if personal freedom 'wins' or if society's needs come first.** Prisoners must **not** determine what is best for society and the public good. Law enforcement personnel such as correctional and police officers, water safety personnel, medical workers, educators and all school personnel, bus drivers, store clerks, and **all those dealing with the public** must be the first to be fully 100% vaccinated and receive booster shots!

Finally, perhaps health plan companies may decide to increase health care premiums for those who refuse to take the vaccine. And hospitals may decide to first care for those who are vaccinated, before others. Why should those of us who follow federal guidelines and vaccinate suffer because of those who refuse to do so?

Choices, choices, choices. But make no mistake. Unless society learns from this COVID-19 pandemic, mistakes will be repeated. When the next Ebola, Severe Acute Respiratory Syndrome Coronavirus 2 (SARS-CoV-2), Swine Flu, Avian Flu, Viral Hemorrhagic Fever, Middle East Respiratory Syndrome (MERS-COV) or another deadly disease strikes civilization again, just remember – history is bound to repeat itself unless we learn from our past actions and mistakes.

Persistence, enthusiasm, and selecting choices among many – all are my three strongest abilities. Each person must identify their own personal strengths, and embrace them. In this chapter, I mention in detail the pandemic ranging across the globe because of its tremendous effect on all of us citizens of Mother Earth. Readers –What are your best abilities? Can you identify them? Are you using them? Why not? What is stopping you? If not now, when? Yes – I am talking to you!

REFERENCES

Absher, J. (2020, September 29). *Military tuition assistance.* Military.com. https://www.military.com/education/money-for-school/tuition-assistance-ta-program-overview.html

Absher, J. (2021, June 29). *Reserve tuition assistance.* Military.com. https://www.military.com/education/money-for-school/reserve-tuition-assistance.html/

Agirdag, O. (2014). The long-term effects of bilingualism on children of immigration: Student bilingualism and future earnings. *International Journal of Bilingual Education and Bilingualism, 17,* 449-464.

Alber, R. (2017, January 17). *Gender equity in the classroom.* Edutopia. https://www.edutopia.org/blog/gender-equity-classroom-rebecca-alber

Aldridge, J., Calhoun, C., & Aman, R. (2000). *15 Misconceptions about multicultural education.* Weebly. https://tcreadingresa.weebly.com/uploads/2/3/5/8/23585408/_15_misconceptions_about_multicultural_education.pdf

Ali, A. R. (2005, February). *Reserve component education panel briefing.* Paper/PowerPoint presented at the meeting of the Council of College and Military Educators, New Orleans, LA.

Allen, R. (2004, May 3). *Brown v. Board of Education: How far have we come?* ASCD. https://www.ascd.org/el/articles/brown-v.-board-of-education-how-far-have-we-come

Allport, G. W. (2000). Theories of prejudice. In J. Noel (Ed.), *Notable selections in multicultural education* (pp. 93-101). Guilford, CT: McGraw-Hill.

American Association of University Professors [AAUP]. (2003, December 3). *Academic Bill of Rights.* https://www.aaup.org/report/academic-bill-rights

American Association of University Women [AAUW]. (n.d.). *Fellowships and grants.* https://www.aauw.org/resources/programs/fellowships-grants/overview/

American Civil Liberties Union [ACLU]. (2021). *Religion and public schools.* https://www.aclu.org/issues/religious-liberty/religion-and-public-schools

American Educational Research Association [AERA]. (2021). *Research ethics.* https://www.aera.net/About-AERA/AERA-Rules-Policies/Professional-Ethics

American Federation of Teachers [AFT]. (2007). *Academic freedom in the 21st century.* https://www.aft.org/sites/default/files/academicfreedomstatement0907.pdf

Anderson, L. W., & Krathwohl, D. R. (2001). *A taxonomy for learning, teaching, and assessing: A revision of Bloom's taxonomy of educational objectives.* NY: Addison Wesley Longman. https://www.uky.edu/~rsand1/china2018/texts/Anderson-Krathwohl - A taxonomy for learning teaching and assessing.pdf

Anti-Defamation League [ADL]. (2020). *Coordinator handbook & resource guide 2020-2021.* https://www.adl.org/media/11295/download

Anti-Defamation League [ADL]. (2020). *Lessons.* https://www.adl.org/education-and-resources/resources-for-educators-parents-families/lessons

Anti-Defamation League [ADL]. (2021). *Assessing children's literature.* https://www.adl.org/education/resources/tools-and-strategies/assessing-childrens-literature

Anti-Defamation League [ADL]. (2021). *Books matter.* https://www.adl.org/education-and-resources/resources-for-educators-parents-families/childrens-literature

Anti-Defamation League [ADL]. (2021). *Education glossary terms.* https://www.adl.org/education/resources/glossary-terms/education-glossary-terms

Anti-Defamation League [ADL]. (2021). *Religion in the public schools.* https://www.adl.org/education/resources/tools-and-strategies/religion-in-public-schools

Antley, T. (2020, July 16). *What is professional development and why is it important?* WebCE. https://www.webce.com/news/2020/07/16/professional-development

Anyon, J. (2014). *Radical possibilities: Public policy, urban education, and a new social movement,* (2nd ed.). Oxfordshire, UK: Routledge. https://www.routledge.com/Radical-Possibilities-Public-Policy-Urban-Education-and-A-New-Social/Anyon/p/book/9780415635585

Arizona State University Online [ASU]. (2021). *Online Master of Arts: Educating multilingual learners.* https://asuonline.asu.edu/online-degree-programs/graduate/master-arts-multilingual-education/

Athuraliya. A. (2020, January 7). *The easy guide to Kotter's 8 step change model.* Creately. https://creately.com/blog/?s=The+Easy+Guide+to+Kotter%27s+8+Step+change+Model&category_name=

Au, W., & Yonamine, M. (2021, March 23). *Dear educators, it is time to fight for Asian America.* Rethinking Schools. https://rethinkingschools.org/2021/03/23/dear-educators-it-is-time-to-fight-for-asian-america

Augenblick, Palaich, & Associates. (2020, January 20). *Hawaii teacher compensation study and recommendations.* Hawaii Public Schools. https://www.hawaiipublicschools.org/DOE Forms/OTM/Hawaii Teacher Compensation Study and Recommendations, Final Report 1.20.2020.pdf

Baker, B. D. (2018). *Educational inequality and school finance: Why money matters for America's students.* Cambridge, MA: Harvard Education Press.

Banks, J. (2021). *The eight characteristics of multicultural schools.* University of Northern Iowa. From J. Banks (1999), *The eight characteristics of multicultural schools* (2nd ed.). Boston: Allyn & Bacon. https://intime.uni.edu/eight-characteristics-multicultural-schools

Bear, J., & Bear, M. (2001). *College degrees by mail & Internet* (rev. ed.). Berkeley, CA: Ten Speed Press.

Benedict, A. E., Brownell, M. T., Griffin, C. C., Wang, J., & Myers, J. A. (2020). Leveraging professional development to prepare general and special education teachers to teach within response to intervention frameworks. In *accessibility and diversity in education: Breakthroughs in research and practice* (Vol. 1, pp. 143-162). Hershey, PA: IGI Global. http://www.igi-global.com/chapter/leveraging-professional-develoment-to-prepare-general-and-special-education-teachers-to-teach-withinin-response-to-intervention-frameworks/240977?camid=4v1a

The best fake diploma maker. (2020). DiplomaMakers. https://diplomamakers.com/

The Best Schools. (2021, April 23). *Online college versus diploma mills: Know the difference.* https://thebestschools.org/magazine/online-college-vs-diploma-mills/

Bigelow, C. S. (2018, July 11). *10 important examples of gender inequality happening today.* The Borgen Project. https://borgenproject.org/examples-of-gender-inequality/

Bilingual education in the classroom. (2021). Education Corner. https://www.educationcorner.com/k12-bilingual-education.html

Bolman, L. G., & Deal, T. E. (2003). *Reframing organizations: Artistry, choice, and leadership* (3rd ed.). San Francisco: Jossey-Bass.

BOL News. (2021). *About BOL news.* https://www.bolnews.com/about-us/

Bowles, S. (2000). Unequal education and the reproduction of the social division of labor. In J. Noel (Ed.), *Notable selections in multicultural education* (pp. 47-53). Guilford, CT: McGraw-Hill.

Boylan, P. (2021, June 3). *Police Commission nominee denies racism exists in Hawai'i.* Honolulu Star-Advertiser Newspaper. https://www.staradvertiser.com/2021/06/03/hawaii-news/police-commission-nominee-denies-racism-exists-in-hawaii/

Burns, M. (2015, July 22). *4 barriers to teachers' professional development in fragile contexts.* Global Partnership. https://www.globalpartnership.org/blog/4-barriers-teachers-professional-development-fragile-contexts

Buy a degree online. (2020). DiplomaMakers. https://diplomamakers.com/

Buy a degree online: Global scam exposed. (2021). GetEducated. https://www.geteducated.com/fake-diplomas/295-diploma-mills-buy-a-degree-epidemic/

Callahan, L. L. (2014). *Exploring characteristics of religious affiliated colleges labeled "diploma mills": A multi-case study of U.S. Court decisions* (Publication No. 3578707). [Doctoral dissertation, Northcentral University]. https://www.proquest.com/docview/1501732829

Cancian, M. F. (2019, November). *U.S. military forces in FY 2020: The struggle to align forces with strategy.* Center for Strategic International Studies [CSIS].

https://www.csis.org/analysis/us-military-forces-fy-2020-struggle-align-forces-strategy-1

Cancian, M. F. (2020, October). *US military forces in FY2021: Army.* Center for Strategic International Studies [CSIS]. https://www.csis.org/analysis/us-military-forces-fy-2021-army

Cardoza, K. (2014, December 12). *Demand for dual-language programs in D.C. public schools skyrockets.* WAMU. https://wamu.org/story/14/12/12/demand_for_dual_language_programs_in_dc_publi c_schools_skyrockets/

Cherry, K. (2020, March 5). *Transformational leadership: A closer look at the effects of transformational leadership.* Verywellmind. https://www.verywellmind.com/what-is-transformational-leadership-2795313

Children's Defense Fund. (2021). *The state of America's children: Child poverty.* https://www.childrensdefense.org/state-of-americas-children/soac-2021-child-poverty/

Chung, N. (2021, May 27). *I'm tired of trying to educate White people about Anti-Asian racism.* Time. https://time.com/6051948/educating-white-people-anti-asian-racism

Cimpian, J. (2018, April 23). *How our education system undermines gender equity.* Brookings. https://www.brookings.edu/author/joseph-cimpian/

Clifton, H., Chapman, M., & Cox, S. (2018, January 16). *Staggering trade in fake degrees revealed.* BBC. https://www.bbc.com/news/uk-42579634

College degree scams. (2021, May). Federal Trade Commission [FTC]. https://www.consumer.ftc.gov/articles/0206-college-degree-scams

College degrees for sale, legally. (2021). InstantDegrees. https://instantdegrees.com

Colorado State University [CSU]. (n.d.). *Undergraduate specializations.* CSU Global. https://csuglobal.edu/undergraduate/specializations

Commands: Geographic and functional. (n.d.). U.S. Army Reserve. https://www.usar.army.mil/Commands/

Conner, M. (n.d.). *Introduction to adult learning.* Marcia Conner.
https://marciaconner.com/resources/adult-learning/

Council for Higher Education Accreditation [CHEA]. (n.d.). *Important questions about degree mills.* https://www.chea.org/important-questions-about-degree-mills

Council for Higher Education Accreditation [CHEA]. (2021).
https://www.chea.org/international-directory/accreditation-service-international-colleges

Cramer, R. J. (2004, Sept 23). *Diploma mills are easily created and some have issued bogus degrees to federal employees at government expense.* Government Accountability Office [GAO]. https://www.gao.gov/assets/a111262.html

Creating a multicultural environment. (2020). Childcare Education Institute [CCEI].
https://www.cceionline.com/course/creating-a-multicultural-environment/

Cumming-McCann, A. (2003, February). *Multicultural education: Connecting theory to practice.* National Center for the Study of Adult Learning and Literacy [NCALL].
http://www.ncsall.net/index.html@id=208.html

Data: Race and ethnicity in U.S. schools today. (2014, May 13). Education Week.
https://www.edweek.org/ew/section/multimedia/data-package-us-schools-racial-ethnic-landscape.html

Day, F. A. (1999). *Multicultural voices in contemporary literature: A resource for teachers* (2nd ed.). Portsmouth, NH: Heinemann.

Defense Activity for Non-Traditional Education Support [DANTES]. (2006). *External degree catalog.* Pensacola, FL: U.S. Government Printing.
http://www.dantes.doded.mil

Defense Activity for Non-Traditional Education Support [DANTES]. (2006). *Mission and activities.* Pensacola, FL: U.S. Government Printing.

Delpech, S. D. (2021, February 3). *GoArmyEd is switching to ArmyIgnitED.* U.S. Army Reserve. https://www.usar.army.mil/News/Article/2492440/goarmyed-is-switching-to-armyignited/

Department of the Army. (2006). *Army Regulation 621-5.* ArmyIgnitED.
https://www.armyignited.com/app/

Department of the Army. (2019). *Army reserve benefits.* GoArmy. https://goarmy.com/reserve/benefits/education.html

Department of the Army. (2020). *Education resource.* ArmyIgnitED. https://www.armyignited.com/app/

Diaz, C. F. (Ed.). (2001). *Multicultural education for the 21st century.* New York: Addison-Wesley.

Diploma mills: how to recognize and avoid them. (2021, April 27). CollegeChoice. https://www.collegechoice.net/diploma-mills/

Diversity learning with impact. (2020). DiversityEdu. https://diversityedu.com/

Diversity lesson plan. (2016, March 2). Study.com. https://study.com/academy/lesson/diversity-lesson-plan.html

Doctoral Journey. (2018, March 29). *The essential characteristics of adult learners.* GCU. https://www.gcu.edu/blog/doctoral-journey/essential-characteristics-adult-learners

Dolch sight word list. (2021). https://sightwords.com/sight-words/dolch

East-West Center. (2021, July 21). In *Wikipedia.* https://en.wikipedia.org/wiki/East–West_Center

Essoyan, S. (2003, May 17). *Lab school at UH faces uncertain future.* Starbulletin. http://archives.starbulletin.com/2003/05/17/news/story6.html

Evaluating children's books for bias. (2020). University of Northern Iowa. https://intime.uni.edu/evaluating-childrens-books-bias

Ezell, A., & Bear, J. (2012). *Degree mills: The billion-dollar industry that has sold over a million fake diplomas.* Amherst, NY: Prometheus Books.

Facts and figures: Economic empowerment. (2018, July). UN Women. https://www.unwomen.org/en/what-we-do/economic-empowerment/facts-and-figures

Facts and figures: Women's leadership and political participation. (2021, January 15). UN Women. https://www.unwomen.org/en/what-we-do/leadership-and-political-participation/facts-and-figures

Fake diploma prices and information. (n.d.). Havocscope. https://havocscope.com/fake-diploma/

Fink, L. D. (2013). *Creating significant learning experiences: An integrated approach to designing college courses* (2nd ed.). San Francisco: Jossey-Bass.

Fink, L. D. (2013). A taxonomy of significant learning. In *Creating significant learning experiences: An integrated approach to designing college courses* (2nd ed., pp. 31-66). San Francisco: Jossey-Bass.

5 key challenges facing U.S. higher education. (2018, October 4). Digital Marketing Institute. https://digitalmarketinginstitute.com/blog/5-key-challenges-facing-us-higher-education

Gal, S., Kiersz, A., Mark, M., Su, R., & Ward, M. (2020, July 8). *26 simple charts to show friends and family who aren't convinced racism is still a problem in America.* Business Insider. https://www.businessinsider.com/us-systemic-racism-in-charts-graphs-data-2020-6

García, E., & Weiss, E. (2019, March 26). *The teacher shortage is real, large and growing, and worse than we thought.* Economic Policy Institute [EPI]. https://www.epi.org/publication/the-teacher-shortage-is-real-large-and-growing-and-worse-than-we-thought-the-first-report-in-the-perfect-storm-in-the-teacher-labor-market-series/

Gibson, K. (2017, May 9). *Your MD may have a phony degree.* CBS News. https://www.cbsnews.com/news/your-md-may-have-a-phony-degree

Goldenberg, C., & Wagner, K. (2015, Fall). *Bilingual education: Reviving an American tradition.* AFT. https://www.aft.org/ae/fall2015/goldenberg_wagner

Grant, M. (2019, August 22). *Easy to get fake degrees creating real problems.* FOX 46. https://www.fox46.com/news/easy-to-get-fake-degrees-creating-real-problems/

Guskey, T., & Huberman, M. (Eds.). (1995). *Professional development in education: New paradigms & practices.* New York: Teachers College Press.

Hall, E. T. (2000). The silent language. In J. Noel (Ed.), *Notable selections in multicultural education* (pp. 81-83). Guilford, CT: McGraw-Hill.

Hawai'i KHON 2. (2012, January 14). *Groundbreaking ceremony held for off-leash dog park* [news video]. KHON 2. https://www.khon2.com/local-news/groundbreaking-ceremony-held-for-off-leash-dog-park/

Hawai'i News Now. (2007, August 30). *City renames park after Patsy Mink.* https://www.hawaiinewsnow.com/story/7008899/city-renames-park-after-patsy-mink/

Hawai'i State Department of Education. (2019). *Employment report school year 2018-19.* Hawai'i Public Schools. https://www.hawaiipublicschools.org/Reports/Employment Report 18-19.pdf

Hawai'i State Department of Education. (2020). *Multilingualism.* Hawai'i Public Schools. https://www.hawaiipublicschools.org/TeachingAndLearning/StudentLearning/Multilingualism/Pages/default.aspx

Hawai'i State Department of Education. (2020, February). *Teacher salary modernization project.* Hawai'i Public Schools. http://www.hawaiipublicschools.org/DOE%20Forms/OTM/Teacher%20Salary%20Modernization%20Project.pdf

Heick, T. (n.d.). *The 6 stages of a teaching career.* TeachThought. https://www.teachthought.com/pedagogy/6-stages-teaching-career/

Heick, T. (n.d.). *What is the taxonomy of significant learning?* TeachThought. https://www.teachthought.com/learning/what-is-the-taxonomy-of-significant-learning/?fbclid=IwAR2FqctVFll38rGT6mXooBoTIiblSnjYUTZqVZMa5vNnRK_5iSN7AowFBts

Hersey, P., Blanchard, K. H., & Johnson, D. E. (2001). *Management of organizational behavior: Leading human resources* (8th ed.). Upper Saddle River, NJ: Prentice-Hall.

History of bilingual education. (n.d.). Rethinking Schools. https://rethinkingschools.org/articles/history-of-bilingual-education/

Hostetler, K. D., Sawyer, R. M., & Prichard, K. W. (Eds.). (2004). *The art and politics of college teaching: A practical guide for the beginning professor* (2nd ed.). New York: Peter Lang.

How to detect a diploma mill (part 2). (2018, May 30). USAcollegex. https://www.usacollegex.com/not-to-be-fooled-by-a-diploma-mill-part-2/

How to encourage gender equity and equality in the classroom. (2020, July 16). Waterford. https://www.waterford.org/education/gender-equality-in-the-classroom

Inouye, D. K. (n. d.). *U.S. Senate: Daniel K. Inouye: A featured biography.* https://www.senate.gov/senators/FeaturedBios/Featured_Bio_Inouye.htm

International Woman's Day. (2014, March 8). Women and girls education: Facts and figures. UNESCO. http://www.unesco.org/new/en/unesco/events/prizes-and-celebrations/celebrations/international-days/international-womens-day-2014/women-ed-facts-and-figure/

Investing in sexual and reproductive health in low- and middle-income countries. (2020, July). Fact sheet. Guttmacher Institute. https://www.guttmacher.org/fact-sheet/investing-sexual-and-reproductive-health-low-and-middle-income-countries

Jenkins, R. (2016, November 29). *Community-College FAQ: How long before I get tenure?* The Chronicle of Higher Education. https://www.chronicle.com/article/community-college-faq-how-long-before-i-get-tenure

Jhunjhunwala, P. (2019, February 6). *International Day of zero tolerance for female genital mutilation/cutting* [press release]. U.S. Agency for International Development. https://www.usaid.gov/news-information/press-releases/feb-06-2021-statement-international-day-zero-tolerance-female-genital-mutilation-cutting

Jimenez, C. (2021, March 4). *Inside U.S. border patrol immigration checkpoints.* KYMA News. https://kyma.com/news/immigration/2021/03/04/special-report-inside-u-s-border-patrol-immigration-checkpoints/

Kelly, A. (2020, July 22). *Army Reserve to be commanded by woman for the first time.* The Hill. https://thehill.com/changing-america/respect/equality/508502-army-reserve-to-be-commanded-by-woman-for-the-first-time

Kimmelman, P. L. (2006). *Implementing NCLB: Creating a knowledge framework to support school improvement.* Thousand Oaks, CA: Corwin Press.

Klein-Collins, R. (2018, December 23). *In 'Never too Late,' finally, a guide for adults going to college* [Interview by E. Nadworny]. NPR. https://www.npr.org/2018/12/23/678799694/in/never-too-late-finally-a-guide-for-adults-going-to-college

Knowles, M. S., Holton, E. F., III, & Swanson, R. A. (2005). *The adult learner* (6th ed.). San Diego, CA: Elsevier.

Koppelman, K. L. (2017). *Understanding human differences: Multicultural education for a diverse America* (5th ed.). Upper Saddle River, NJ: Pearson.

Kotter, J. P., & Cohen, D. S. (2002). *The heart of change: Real-life stories of how people change their organizations.* Boston: Harvard Business School Press.

Krashen, S. (1997). *Why bilingual education?* ERIC Digest. https://www.ericdigests.org/1997-3/bilingual.html

Ladson-Billings, G. (2000). But that's just good teaching! In J. Noel (Ed.), *Notable selections in multicultural education* (pp. 206-215). Guilford, CT: McGraw-Hill.

Lankster, N. M. (2020, January 17). *The importance of multicultural education in American schools.* drnlankster. https://www.drnlankster.com/single-post/2020/01/17/The-Importance-of-Multicultural-Education-in-American-Schools

Lieb, S. (1991). *Principles of adult learning.* Petsalliance. https://petsalliance.org/sites/petsalliance.org/files/Lieb 1991 Adult Learning Principles.pdf

Lipsky, M. (2005, April 19). *Under the radar.* The American Prospect. https://prospect.org/special-report/radar/

List of accreditation agencies used by fake colleges. (2019). GetEducated. https://www.geteducated.com/college-degree-mills/204-fake-agencies-for-college-accreditation/

List of degree mills and distance learning accreditation reports. (2021). GetEducated. https://www.geteducated.com/diploma-mill-police/degree-mills-list/

List of unaccredited institutions of higher education. (2021, August 11). In *Wikipedia*. https://en.wikipedia.org/wiki/List_of_unaccredited_institutions_of_higher_education

Littlefield, J. (2020, January 28). *What you need to know about diploma mills.* ThoughtCo. https://www.thoughtco.com/what-you-need-to-know-diploma-mills-1097946

Lynch, M. (2015, December 31). *6 ways to implement a real multicultural education in the classroom.* The Edvocate. https://www.theedadvocate.org/6-ways-to-implement-a-real-multicultural-education-in-the-classroom-2/

Manning, R. (2018, December 13). *Oregon educators prioritize bilingual education.* Wallowa County Chieftain. https://www.wallowa.com/news/oregon-educators-prioritize-bilingual-education/article_4cf3d6ff-ec8e-5aba-9a47-f37de2629d90.html

Matsumoto-Grah, K. (2002, Fall.). *Diversity in the classroom: A checklist.* http://152.6.15.92/Documents/ncate/Standard 4/8-11-2014/Diversity in the Classroom.pdf

McGarvey, A. (2004, January 20). *The best investment we can make.* The American Prospect. https://prospect.org/special-report/best-investment-can-make/

McNamee, G. L. (n.d.). Mazie Hirono: United States senator. In *Encyclopedia Britannica.* https://www.britannica.com/biography/Mazie-Hirono

Meckler, L., & Rabinowitz, K. (2019, September 12). *Six findings in The Post's analysis of diversity in school districts.* The Washington Post. https://www.washingtonpost.com/educa tion/2019/09/12/six-findings-posts-analysis-diversity-school-districts

Merriam-Webster. (n.d.). *Merriam-Webster dictionary.* https://www.merriam-webster.com/

Mertens, R. (2012, September-October). *Patsy Mink, JD'51, was a tenacious and determined politician.* University of Chicago Magazine. https://mag.uchicago.edu/law-policy-society/political-pioneer

Moody, J. (2021, April 27). *A guide to the changing number of U.S. universities.* U.S. News. https://www.usnews.com/education/best-colleges/articles/how-many-universities-are-in-the-us-and-why-that-number-is-changing

Moore, D., Hoskyn, M., & Mayo, J. (2018). Thinking language awareness at a science centre: iPads, science, and early literacy development with multilingual kindergarten children in Canada. *International Journal of Bias, Identify and Diversities in Education (IJBIDFE)*, *3*(1), 40-63. http://doi.org/10.4018/IJBIDE.2018010104

Mulcahy, E. (2017, December 18). *What can schools do to reduce pupils' prejudice?* The Centre for Education & Youth [CFEY]. https://cfey.org/2017/can-schools-reduce-pupils-prejudice/

Multicultural and diversity guide for students. (2021, May 28). Accredited Schools Online. https://www.accreditedschoolsonline.org/resources/student-diversity-multicultural/

Multiculturalism lesson plans. (2020). Study.com. https://study.com/academy/topic/multiculturalism-lesson-plans.html

Myers, I. B. (1998). *Introduction to type* (6th ed.) [Brochure]. Palo Alto, CA.

National Association for Multicultural Education [NAME]. (2021). *Advancing and advocating for social justice & equity.* https://nameorg.org/headline_news.php

National Association for Multicultural Education [NAME]. (2021). *Definitions of multicultural education.* https://www.nameorg.org/definitions_of_multicultural_e.php

National Association for Multicultural Education [NAME]. (2021). *NAME supports educators with resources.* https://www.nameorg.org/docs/NAMECovid-19Tools-5-5-2020-FINAL_to_post.pdf

National Association for Multicultural Education [NAME]. (2021). *Position statements.* https://www.nameorg.org/name_position_statements.php

National Association of Special Education Teachers [NASET]. (2021). https://www.naset.org/

National Center for Education Statistics [NCES]. (2019, February). *Characteristics of public school teachers by race/ethnicity.* https://nces.ed.gov/programs/raceindicators/spotlight_a.asp

National Center for Education Statistics [NCES]. (2010). *Status and trends in the education of racial and ethnic minorities.* https://nces.ed.gov/pubs2010/2010015/index.asp

National Center for Education Statistics [NCES]. (2020). *The condition of education 2020 at a glance.* https://nces.ed.gov/pubs2020/2020144_AtAGlance.pdf

National Center for Education Statistics [NCES]. (2021, May). *Characteristics of postsecondary students.* https://nces.ed.gov/programs/coe/indicator/csb

1960 United States census. (1961). In *Wikipedia.* https://en.wikipedia.org/wiki/1960_United_States_census

Nkabinde, Z. P. (2017). Multiculturalism in special education: Perspectives of minority children in urban schools. In J. Keengwe (Ed.), *Handbook of research on promoting cross-cultural competence and social justice in teacher education* (pp. 382-397). Hershey, PA: IGI Global. http://doi:10.4018/978-1-5225-0897-7

Noel, J. (Ed.). (2000). *Notable selections in multicultural education.* Guilford, CT: McGraw-Hill.

Nolen, J. L., & Duignan, B. (2021, June 3). No Child Left Behind. In *Encyclopedia Britannica.* https://www.britannica.com/topic/No-Child-Left-Behind-Act

Office of Civil Rights [OCR]. (2008, December 31). *Hawaii State Department of Education Civil Rights Violation No. 10051060.* https://stopsexualassaultinschools.org/wp-content/uploads/2015/06/OCR-FOIA-cases-Hawaii.pdf

Ordway, D. (2021, January 25). *Multicultural education: How schools teach it and where educators say it falls short.* Journalist's Resource. https://journalistsresource.org/education/multicultural-education-schools/

Our View. (2020, September 3). *COVID-19 deepens gender inequality and work is needed to address it* [Editorial opinion]. Joplin Globe. https://www.joplinglobe.com/ opinion/editorials/our-view-covid-19-deepens-gender-inequality-and-work-is-needed-to-address-it/article_5df149bc-38b3-5ea7-b13f-0ced906816e0.html

Patsy Mink. (2021, August 21). In *Wikipedia.* https://en.wikipedia.org/wiki/Patsy_Mink

Patton, M. Q. (2002). *Qualitative research & evaluation methods* (3rd ed.). Thousand Oaks, CA: Sage.

Peterson, D. (2019, October 7). *5 Principles for the teacher of adults*. ThoughtCo. https://www.thoughtco.com/principles-for-the-teacher-of-adults-31638

Prejudice, discrimination & stereotypes: definitions & examples. (2014, October 22). Study.com. https://study.com/academy/lesson/prejudice-discrimination-stereotypes-definitions-examples.html

Qualities of effective change agents. (2019, May 28). Michigan State University. https://www.michiganstateuniversityonline.com/resources/leadership/qualities-of-effective-change-agents/

Rabinowitz, K., Emamdjomeh, A., & Meckler, L. (2019, September 12). *How the nation's growing racial diversity is changing our schools*. Washington Post. https://www.washingtonpost.com/graphics/2019/local/school-diversity-data/

Race and ethnicity in Hawai'i. (2018, September 4). Statistical Atlas. https://statisticalatlas.com/state/Hawaii/Race-and-Ethnicity

Ridgeway, M. & Pewewardy, C. (2005). Linguistic imperialism in the United States: The historical eradication of the American Indian languages and the English-only movement. In F. Schultz (Ed.), *Annual editions: Multicultural education, 2005/2006* (12th ed., pp. 214-220). Dubuque, IA: McGraw-Hill/Dushkin.

Roy, K. (2017, September 14). *Why we need gender equity now*. Forbes. https://www.forbes.com/sites/ellevate/2017/09/14/why-we-need-gender-equity-now/?sh=277fb8c577a2

Rosa Parks biography. (2021, March 26). Biography.com. https://www.biography.com/activist/rosa-parks

Rosa Parks history. (2021, January 21). History. https://www.history.com/topics/black-history/rosa-parks

Rumbaut, R. G. (2014). English plus: Exploring the socioeconomic benefits of bilingualism in Southern California. In R. M. Callahan & P. C. Gándara (Eds.), *The bilingual advantage: Language, literacy and the US labor market* (pp. 182-209). Bristol, UK: Multilingual Matters.

Rutakumwa, R., Mugisha, J. O., Bernays, S., Kabunga, E., Tumwekwase, G., Mbonye, M., & Seeley, J. (2019, November 7). Conducting in-depth interviews with and without voice recorders: A comparative analysis. *Qualitative Research, 20*(5), 565-585. https://doi.org/10.1177/1468794119884806

Sanders, C. (2019, September 9). *65 years after Brown v. Board of Education, more suits over education equity.* Center on Budget And Policy Priorities [CBPP]. https://www.cbpp.org/blog/65-years-after-brown-v-board-of-education-more-suits-over-education-equity

Santora, L. A. (2013). *Assessing children's book collections using an anti-bias lens.* Anti-Defamation League [ADL]. https://www.adl.org/sites/default/files/documents/assets/pdf/education-outreach/Assessing-Children-s-Book-Collections.pdf

Schools may perpetuate gender inequality without realising it. (2019, November 14). Study International. https://www.studyinternational.com/news/gender-inequality-school

Schultz, F. (Ed.). (2005). *Annual editions: Multicultural education, 2005/2006* (12th ed.). Dubuque, IA: McGraw-Hill/Dushkin.

Sciupac, E. P., & Schwadel, P. (2019, October 3). *For a lot of American teens, religion is a regular part of the public school day.* Pew Research Center. https://www.pewforum.org/2019/10/03/for-a-lot-of-american-teens-religion-is-a-regular-part-of-the-public-school-day/

Seifert, K., & Sutton, R. (2009). Student diversity. In *Educational psychology* (pp.66-84). http://home.cc.umanitoba.ca/~seifert/EdPsy2009.pdf

Seigfried, S. (2019, April 12). *Gender inequality in education.* P4H Global. https://p4hglobal.org/p4h-blog/2019/4/12/gender-inequality-in-education

Silbey, M. (2014, September 2). *World-wise Northwest parents drive demand for bilingual preschools.* Seattle Globalist. https://seattleglobalist.com/2014/09/02/bilingual-preschool-seattle-french-spanish-language/28747

Sixty years after Brown v. Board of Education, its promise of integrated, equitable schools is still elusive. (2014, May 15). Opinion. https://www.cleveland.com/opinion/2014/05/sixty_years_after_brown_v_boar.html

Sleeter, C. E., & Puente, R. (2001). Connecting multicultural and special education. In C.F. Diaz (Ed.), *Multicultural education for the 21st century* (Chapter 8). New York: Addison-Wesley.

Snyder, T. D., & Dillow, S. A. (2012). *Digest of Education Statistics, NCES 2014-015.* ERIC. https://eric.ed.gov/?q=ED544576&id=ED544576

Sociology. (2010). Chapter 10.3: Prejudice. In *Understanding and changing the social world.* https://open.lib.umn.edu/sociology/chapter/10-3-prejudice/

Soken-Huberty, E. (2020). *10 Causes of gender inequality.* Human Rights Careers. https://www.humanrightscareers.com/issues/causes-gender-inequality/

Spring, J. (2000). The great civil rights movement and the new culture wars. In J. Noel (Ed.), *Notable selections in multicultural education* (pp. 11-19). Guilford, CT: McGraw-Hill.

Strategies to promote gender equality. (2018, October 15). Elesapiens. https://www.elesapiens.com/blog/strategies-to-promote-gender-equality-in-the-classroom/

Stringer, K. (2018, March 27). *Women's history month: These female trailblazers changed American education for you and your kids. Do you know their names?* The 74. https://www.the74million.org/series/educationsfemaletrailblazers/

Takaki, R. T. (2000). A different mirror: A history of multicultural America. In J. Noel (Ed.), *Notable selections in multicultural education* (pp. 3-10). Guilford, CT: McGraw-Hill.

Teachers reduce gender bias. (2018, August 15). Teachers: 20 ways to reduce gender bias at school. Thinkorblue. https://thinkorblue.com/teachers-reduce-gender-bias-at-school/

10 tips to avoid diploma mills. (2020). Medical Assistant Career Guide. https://www.medicalassistantcareerguide.com/10-tips-to-avoid-diploma-mills/

10 ways to spot a diploma mill. (2020). GetEducated. https://www.geteducated.com/college-degree-mills/161-college-degree-or-diploma-mill/

Tobar, H. (2016, November 15). *The Spanish lesson I never got at school.* NY Times. https://www.nytimes.com/2016/11/15/opinion/the-spanish-lesson-i-never-got-at-school.html

Tokenism. (2021). Psychology Research and Reference. https://psychology.iresearchnet.com/counseling-psychology/multicultural-counseling/tokenism/

Trueba, H. T. (2000). The dynamics of cultural transmission. In J. Noel (Ed.), *Notable selections in multicultural education* (pp. 84-91). Guilford, CT: McGraw-Hill.

Umansky, I. M., & Reardon, S. F. (2014). Reclassification patterns among Latino English learner students in bilingual, dual immersion, and English immersion classrooms. *American Educational Research Journal, 20*(10), 1-34. https://files.eric.ed.gov/fulltext/ED566368.pdf

University of Chicago. (n.d.). *Daughter of Patsy Mink '51 remembers her mother on anniversary of Title IX Legislation.* Law School. https://www.law.uchicago.edu/news/daughter-patsy-mink-51-remembers-her-mother-anniversary-title-ix-legislation

University of Hawai'i at Mānoa. (2021). *Experience the education of a lifetime at UH Mānoa!* Mānoa. https://manoa.hawaii.edu/

University of Hawai'i at Mānoa. (2021). *2021-2022 catalog.* Mānoa. https://manoa.hawaii.edu/catalog/

University of Hawai'i at Mānoa Athletics. (2021). *Traditions.* Hawai'i Athletics. https://hawaiiathletics.com/sports/2012/6/18/GEN_0618120234.aspx

University of Hawai'i Leeward Community College. (2021). *2020-2021 catalog.* Leeward. https://www.leeward.hawaii.edu/catalog

University of Hawai'i Leeward Community College. (2021). *Faculty and staff.* Leeward. https://catalog.leeward.hawaii.edu/faculty-and-staff

U.S. Agency for International Development [USAID]. (2021, September 7). *Gender equality and women's empowerment.* https://www.usaid.gov/what-we-do/gender-equality-and-womens-empowerment

U.S. Army Reserve [USAR]. (2021). *Educational benefits.* https://www.usar.army.mil/Resources/Educational-Benefits/

U.S. Department of Education. (n.d.). *Database of accredited postsecondary institutions and programs.* Office of Postsecondary Education. http://ope.ed.gov/accreditation

U.S. Department of Education. (2004, February 10). *Executive summary of the No Child Left Behind Act of 2001.* Ed.gov. https://www2.ed.gov/nclb/overview/intro/execsumm.html

U.S. Department of Education. (2007, December). *Accreditation and quality assurance: Diploma mills and fraud.* U.S. Network for Educational Information [USNEI]. https://www2.ed.gov/about/offices/list/ous/international/usnei/us/fraud.doc

U.S. Department of Education. (2008, February 26). *Recognition of foreign qualifications.* U.S. Network for Educational Information [USNEI]. https://www2.ed.gov/about/offices/list/ous/international/usnei/us/edlite-visitus-forrecog.html

U.S. Department of Education. (2009, December 23). *Diploma mills and accreditation--diploma mills.* Ed.gov. https://www2.ed.gov/students/prep/college/diplomamills/diploma-mills.html

U.S. Department of Education. (2012). *National evaluation of Title III implementation: Report on state and local implementation.* AIR. https://www.air.org/sites/default/files/downloads/report/AIR_Title_III_Implementation_0.pdf

U.S. Department of Education. (2015). *Every Student Succeeds Act [ESSA].* Ed.gov. https://www.ed.gov/essa?src=rn

U.S. Department of Education (2019). *Accreditation Handbook.* Office of Postsecondary Education. https://www.ed.gov/sites/default/files/accreditation/accreditation-handbook.pdf

U.S. Department of Education. (2020). *Accreditation: Postsecondary education institutions.* Ed.gov. https://www.ed.gov/accreditation?src=m

U.S. Department of Homeland Security. (2021, March 10). *CBP announces February 2021 operational update.* Customs and Border Protection [CBP].

https://www.cbp.gov/newsroom/national-media-release/cbp-announces-february-2021-operational-update

U.S. Department of Labor. (2017). *Career training programs.* Job Corps. https://www.jobcorps.gov/train

U.S. Department of Labor. (2017). *Careers begin here.* Maui Satellite Job Corps Center. https://maui.jobcorps.gov/

U.S. Department of Labor. (2017). *Parents guide.* Job Corps. https://www.jobcorps.gov/parents

U.S. Department of State. (2016). *U.S. strategy to prevent and respond to gender-based violence globally.* https://www.state.gov/wp-content/uploads/2019/03/258703.pdf

Villiers, A. J. (2021, May 7). James Cook. In *Encyclopedia Britannica.* https://www.britannica.com/biography/James-Cook

Vo, E. (2019, November 15). *What are the key components of a strategic plan?* Small Biz Ahead. https://sba.thehartford.com/business-management/key-components-of-strategic-plan/

Walsh, D. (2015, May 18). *Fake diplomas, real cash: Pakistani company Axact reaps millions.* NY Times. https://www.nytimes.com/2015/05/18/world/asia/fake-diplomas-real-cash-pakistani-company-axact-reaps-millions-columbiana-barkley.html?auth=link-dismiss-google1tap

Walsh, J. (2020, March 12). *7 tips for adult learners returning to school.* Peterson's. https://www.petersons.com/blog/7-tips-for-adult-learners-returning-to-school

Ward, C. S. (2003). Expanding appreciation for "others" among European-American pre-teacher populations. In F. Schultz (Ed.), *Annual editions: Multicultural education, 2005/2006* (12th ed., pp. 76-78). Dubuque, IA: McGraw-Hill/Dushkin.

Wawrzynski, M. R. (2004, January/February). Creating significant learning experiences. *Journal of College Student Development, 45*(1), 105-106. https://doi.org/10.1353/csd.2004.0016

Wellein, M. D. (1976). *The endless summer: An adventure story of Guam.* New York: Vantage Press.

Wellein, M. D. (2010). *Factors associated with Army reservists using educational programs and services at 9th Mission Support Command* (UMI No. 3429228) [Doctoral dissertation, Argosy University, Hawaii]. ProQuest Dissertations and Theses Global.

Wellein, M. D. (2021). *Education essays from my perspective: 50 years as a professional educator offering pearls of wisdom for your journey Book 1*. U.S.: MD Wellein, Inc.

Whiting, K. (2019, March 8). *7 surprising and outrageous stats about gender inequality.* World Economic Forum. https://www.weforum.org/agenda/2019/03/surprising-stats-about-gender-inequality/

Willoughby, B. (2004). Brown v. Board: An American legacy. *Teaching Tolerance, 25,* para.7. https://www.learningforjustice.org/magazine/spring-2004/brown-v-board-an-american-legacy

Woolhouse, M. (2020). *Geena Davis: Leading the fight for gender parity in Hollywood.* Boston University Alumni Magazine. https://www.bu.edu/articles/2020/geena-davis/

Yamane, J. K. (2014, January). *Sunrise analysis: Regulation of unaccredited degree granting institutions: A report to the Governor and the Legislature of the State of Hawaii, Report No. 14-03*. Docplayer. http://docplayer.net/3120258-Sunrise-analysis-regulation-of-unaccredited-degree-granting-institutions.html

Yeros, J. (2021). *Sharing many cultures in the elementary classroom.* Globe Trottin' Kids. https://www.globetrottinkids.com/sharing-many-cultures-elementary-classroom/

Appendix A

REMEMBERING THOSE WHO HAVE MADE A DIFFERENCE IN UNITED STATES MILITARY VOLUNTARY EDUCATION

Biographical Entry of 225 Top U.S. Military Educators, all service branches,

including

Marsha Diane Akau Wellein

By Dr. Clinton L. Anderson, Editor

DoD, Servicemembers Opportunity Colleges, Washington, D.C.

I am thankful for all of those who said NO to me.
It's because of them I'm doing it myself.
Albert Einstein

Marsha Diane Akau Wellein, in more than twenty years of service to the Army community, worked to open the classroom doors to education opportunity for thousands of military servicemembers and their families by ensuring they had full access to the financial benefits available to them. From the 1980s to the 21st century, Wellein continued to use her creativity to introduce new programs for accessing financial benefits and publicize them throughout the local Army community to ensure that Soldiers knew how to use those benefits to achieve their education goals. At Army installations in Hawaii, Germany, Egypt, Panama, Honduras, Saudi Arabia, Kuwait, to Japan, Korea, Puerto Rico, and back again to Hawaii, Wellein spread the news that financial assistance was available to those who wished to learn.

One of Wellein's major contributions was the development of a telephone and fax process for tuition assistance programs at Camp Zama, Japan in the late 1990s, making it easier for Soldiers with busy work schedules to take advantage of the education opportunities available to them. She later took this concept to other installations, showing how technology could be used to expand Soldiers' access to education in even the most remote areas.

Wellein also initiated Veterans Affairs Work Study Programs at several installations, thus allowing eligible veterans to access the education benefits available to them through this VA program. This was of particular importance to the Army Reserve Soldiers Wellein served as the Army Reserve Regional Director of Education for Pacific and Asia for the 9th Regional Readiness Command of the U.S. Army Reserve in the early 2000s, many of whom were eligible for such benefits.

But Wellein was not content with simply developing new programs to access financial assistance; she also worked tirelessly to advertise those programs throughout the community, often using innovative marketing techniques to reach her target audience. Education and Career Fairs, radio talk shows, unit and command briefings, newspaper articles, posters and brochures--Wellein used all of these to inform the Soldiers, civilians, and family members of the programs available to help fund their education. Her hard work broke through financial barriers to education for many in the Army community.

Wellein's success in opening doors to military education opportunities to servicemembers and their families throughout the globe was recognized through numerous awards throughout her career, including the 2003 Outstanding Education Services Officer Award of the U.S. Army Reserve.

Note:

Prepared for **2006 Department of Defense Worldwide Education Symposium**

17-20 July 2006, at Orlando World Center Marriott Resort & Convention Center, FL.

Compact Disk Productions Co-Sponsored by:

American Association of State Colleges & Universities and

The American Association of Community Colleges

Disclaimer:

The contents of these working papers have not been coordinated with the United States Department of Defense or the Military Services and, therefore, should not be construed as having any official endorsement from any federal agency.

Appendix B

THE COMMAND SERGEANT MAJOR
MARCIAL M. TUMACDER STORY

Military Educator Newsletter of the AAACE Commission on Military Education and Training, Edited and Distributed by the Servicemembers Opportunity Colleges, Wash. DC Volume 19, No. 1, April 2011, Supplements, Be All You Can Be

By Dr. Marsha D. Wellein,
Army Reserve Regional Director of Education, Pacific & Asia,
9th Mission Support Command, HI

We want the education by which character is formed,

strength of mind is increased,

the intellect is expanded and by which one can stand on one' own feet.

Swami Vivekananda

Command Sergeant Major (CSM) Marcial M. Tumacder, U.S. Army Reserve, 9th Mission Support Command, Hawaii, had a dream, and did not let go of it! "I am not sure where to start but it was always one of my dreams to continue my education. With the support of family, friends, and mentors, I succeeded." The journey, however, was not without some bumps, or perhaps boulders in the road.

CSM Tumacder, born and raised in Bacarra, Philippines Islands (PI), only spoke the country's Ilocano dialect until the tender age of six, when his first-grade teacher began instruction in Tagalog (the official language of the PI) and English. It was a rude awakening, but a challenge (think of his first, huge boulder in his path) in which young Tumacder excelled.

Now fast forward to 1987, when young Tumacder joined the Army Reserve in Honolulu and completed his associate degree in Hotel Management from Kapiolani Community College, University of Hawaii (another boulder moved out of his way). He used Army tuition assistance and completed his bachelor degree in Human Resources from Regents College, now Excelsior College in 2000. Many people would stop at this point. But not CSM Tumacder!

With a wife and two children under the age of ten, Tumacder earned a promotion to the Safety and Occupational Health Specialist (a federal position) in early 2008. "It had been almost ten years since I received my BS degree and as a safety professional, I felt strongly that I needed some formal education for my job," Tumacder continued. "When I accepted this job, I did not have any formal safety schooling, so I started looking around to continue my education. One of my mentors, Major Straus Scantlin, recommended Columbia Southern University. In December 2008, I enrolled in their **O**ccupational **H**ealth and **S**afety (OHS) graduate program and completed all the course requirements this past December for a Masters in Science degree in OHS." (Another enormous boulder surpassed....)

Despite holding down a full-time job with the federal government (traveling nine times in 2010 all over the Pacific, Alaska, Hawaiian Islands, Guam, Saipan, and American Samoa) and a part-time job holding the highest enlisted rank in the Army Reserve, Tumacder enrolled in the two-year residency Sergeants Major Academy in August 2010. "It took a lot of sacrifice, determination, and self-discipline to go over, around, under, these life-size boulders in reaching my dreams with the unwavering support from my family and my boss. I attribute the Army Reserve Tuition Assistance Program and Chapter 33 Post 9-11 GI Bill for making a true financial difference," remarked CSM Tumacder.

But anyone who knows this CSM understands that despite having to master three languages, three cultures (Filipino, American, and Military), and dealing with the enormous stress of family responsibilities, CSM exceeded even his own expectations. He had monthly Battle Assemblies (drills), annual 2-3 weeks of full-time training usually in a foreign country, thousands of miles of travel with the Army Reserve – 9th Mission Support Command (MSC) as the CSM, and a stint from 2004-2005 in Iraq as an activated US Army Reserve Soldier. CSM Tumacder is not one to rest on his laurels.

"I am still mystified how I did it but guess when you set a goal or believe in a dream and you keep on marching forward, you will get there with the help of many helpful people to include the Army Reserve Education staff," he explained. CSM Tumacder is presently considering continuing his education by completing the requirements of a graduate certificate in Human Resources Management.

CSM Tumacder is quite modest. He outperformed more than nine other CSMs to win the 2009 Army Reserve-wide Level One US Army Reserve Excellence in Safety Award and won runner up for this award in 2010.

This article was written when CSM Tumacder was the CSM of 330 1st Mobilization Support Battalion at Fort Richardson, Alaska. Presently, he is the Safety & Occupational Health Manager, M.S., U.S. Army Dental Health Command – Pacific, 512 Palm Circle DR., Bldg. T118, Ft Shafter, HI 96858 E-mail Marc96701@gmail.com URL https://safety.army.mil/

Appendix C

UNITED STATES SENATE
WASHINGTON, D.C.

DANIEL K. INOUYE
HAWAII

November 19, 2012

Dr. Marsha D. Wellein
Theater Support Group – Education Services Office
9th Mission Support Command, Army Reserve, Pacific
Honolulu, Hawaii 96819-2135

Dear Dr. Wellein:

It is my pleasure to extend my sincere congratulations to you on your retirement after 43 years of dedicated work, which includes your service with the federal government and State of Hawaii.

I am pleased to join your family, friends and colleagues in celebrating your long and illustrious career. I commend you on your diligent efforts over the years. You can be proud of your personal accomplishments.

May you enjoy your retirement years. It is my hope that you take this time to plan to do the things in life you have always dreamed of doing. I wish you continued success in all your future endeavors.

Aloha,

DANIEL K. INOUYE
United States Senator

Appendix D

THE COMMAND SERGEANT MAJOR

SCOTT MARTIN STORY

My Pearl of Wisdom: Talk the Talk Then, Walk the Walk

Try a thing you haven't done three times.

Once, to get over the fear of doing it.

Twice, to learn how to do it.

And a third time, to figure out whether you like it or not.

Virgil Thomson

The Military Educator Newsletter, Be All You Can Be, August 2007, p. 7 by Marsha D. Wellein, Education Director, Army Reserve, Pacific & Asia, 2007

CSM Scott Martin used the eArmyU, Dept. of Defense education program, to achieve the bachelor's degree he never had time to complete as he moved around the world in the Army, married, and started a family.

He took college classes at the University of Phoenix while stationed in Arizona, but that ended when he moved to Milwaukee, and then Hawaii.

Marsha Wellein, Director of Army Reserve Education for Pacific & Asia at the 9th Regional Readiness Command, Fort Shafter suggested Martin try the eArmyU, an online program for degree completion offered to military personnel by several colleges and universities around the world.

Martin began working for an applied management degree through Franklin University.

"I've been knocking out the classes ever since" said Martin who is currently stationed at the Pentagon, G1- Section. Martin had to drop out of his Franklin courses when he volunteered for six months in Afghanistan. But he re-enrolled once he got there, despite being based 35 miles north of Kabul, where electricity was minimal and Internet connections sketchy.

He did much of his class work in the middle of the night. But Martin says the 18-hour days were worth it. He graduated from Franklin University on May 15, 2006.

When Martin returned to Hawaii from Afghanistan, although busy with his wife and four young children, he completed his degree and now is short two course for his masters.

"I've done a lot of things. I've jumped out of airplanes, gotten a pilot's license. I've got years of experience in the military. But I've always wanted to finish my studies at a college level. I wouldn't have gotten the degree any other way."

Note: Franklin University in Ohio created a statue – full size – in Martin's likeness and unveiled it on campus on July 20, 2017, in recognition of his many accomplishments!

Appendix E

DANIEL K. AKAKA
HAWAII

WASHINGTON OFFICE:
141 HART SENATE OFFICE BUILDING
WASHINGTON, DC 20510
TELEPHONE: (202) 224-6361

HONOLULU OFFICE:
3106 PRINCE JONAH KUHIO
KALANIANAOLE FEDERAL BUILDING
P.O. Box 50144
HONOLULU, HI 96850
TELEPHONE: (808) 522-8970

United States Senate

WASHINGTON, DC 20510-1103

COMMITTEES:
ARMED SERVICES
BANKING, HOUSING AND
URBAN AFFAIRS
HOMELAND SECURITY AND
GOVERNMENTAL AFFAIRS
INDIAN AFFAIRS
VETERANS' AFFAIRS

November 19, 2012

Dr. Marsha Diane Akau Wellein
Regional Director of Education, Pacific and Asia
U.S. Army Reserve, 9th Mission Support Command
Theater Support Group, Pacific
1557 Pass Street
Honolulu, Hawaii 96819-2135

Dear Dr. Wellein:

Congratulations and best wishes on your retirement after 43 years as a professional educator, the last 30 of which was with the Department of the Army within the Department of Defense. Mahalo for your outstanding service.

You should be very proud of your work as Regional Director of Education, Pacific and Asia, 9th Mission Support Command, U.S. Army Reserve. As an education specialist in Hawaii, you have traveled worldwide to make contributions in countries such as Germany, Sinai-Egypt, Panama, Honduras, Kuwait, Saudi Arabia, Japan, Korea, Puerto Rico, the Commonwealth of the Mariana Islands-Saipan, Guam, and American Samoa to fulfill your ultimate mission. You have earned the respect of all who have been fortunate enough to have worked with you over the years and who benefitted from your expertise. With your retirement, you leave behind a host of friends and admirers. This celebration warmly reflects the respect and affection you have won over the years and the solid friendships you formed.

The awards and honors you received are clear evidence of your leadership and character. Your dedication to our community is further shown by your writing *The Endless Summer–An Adventure Story of Guam* and editing *Kalihi Kids Can Communicate (1976)*.

Mahalo, congratulations, and best wishes. I extend my warmest aloha to you and your ohana as you pursue other opportunities and challenges. May you be blessed with much happiness and good health in your retirement.

Aloha pumehana,

Daniel K. Akaka

DANIEL K. AKAKA
U.S. Senator

Appendix F

TEACHING STAGES AND CYCLES:

INNOVATION AND CHANGE

My Pearl of Wisdom: Count Your Blessings

Efforts and courage are not enough without purpose and direction.
Honorable **John Francis Kennedy**

IN EDUCATION, "Every successful person has been learning and working at their skills for a long time – taking advantage of professional development opportunities over the entirety of their career" (Antley, 2020, p. 2). Let us hope that this is true.

Professional Development (P.D.) research suggests five stages teachers go through when implementing innovative ideas. **These five basic stages include survival and discovery, exploration and bridging, adaptation (using new technology, for example, in the classroom), conceptual change, and invention** (Guskey & Huberman, 1995).

Other noted educators (Heick, 6 Stages, 2020) believe that these sequential stages include teachers new to the subject. Other teachers do not immediately use information discussed in P.D. as they might initially fear change. Some teachers like the new procedures or practices learned in P.D. but do not use that information due to possible disapproval by administrators or fellow teachers. Finally, there are teachers who actually work out a schedule as to when to begin using the new technique or activity, and then implement changes (Wellein, 2021).

Terry Heick (6 Stages, 2020) also writes about six stages of a teaching career, including pride (new teachers), survival (getting lots of practice), experimentation and disillusionment (even more confusion about the job and self-doubts), rebellion (teaching begins to be fun again) and finally ongoing mastery. I discuss these stages briefly below:

Teaching Life Stages or Cycles

I want to relate these teacher-cycles or stages, with teachers after undergoing P.D. and then trying these techniques out in their classrooms. Terry Heick (6 Stages, 2020) discusses what he calls, '**life cycles**' in teaching which include the following:

First – a jump at the far end of the pool without proper swimming instruction– This is usually the first year of teaching, the newbie is full of vinegar and spit, and it is lots of fun – at least **until the first minute of the first hour of the first class**. It is like implementing a new process in the classroom after a P.D. activity, an introduction to survival and discovery, Heick, (6 Stages, 2020) explains. You discover the importance of flexible lesson plans and then realize you can use some of the same lesson plans for the same subject, same grade level, the following school year!

Survival and Discovery – The change from theory to reality is a head spinner; work is exhausting because it is so stressful, and there is a lot of time spent 'second-guessing,' and asking 'what if' questions. As the teacher, you finished the P.D. activity, thought you knew what to do, and now find that you know nothing! You planned, revised, and then planned again, but gosh, the students are not behaving the way they should behave – at least not how they are supposed to, based on those P.D. exercises!

Exploration, Experimentation, and Bridging – Good teachers try out ideas, hoping they will work; great teachers are flexible and waste little time in sifting the wheat from the chafe, learning quickly what works and why, and expanding on the positive feedback from students. The use of P.D. and learning from a network of peers to garner new ideas and mentoring tips continue to expand, states Heick (6 Stages, 2020). As a teacher, you are delighted you tried out the new P.D. activity, but you are 'waiting for 'the other shoe to drop.'

Adaptation and Disillusionment – Super teachers ask themselves if they are making a difference in their students' lives; if they cannot reach all, has the 'system failed'? The growing, negative voices in the back of their minds, the realization that huge amounts of money are wasted on items perhaps **not** needed, (and needing money for items really essential), new educational policies which do **not** appear to be in the students' best interests all combine to cause great confusion. "Is this what I really wanted to do with my life?" asks teachers at this teaching stage. P.D. activities might not work for you now (Heick, 6 Stages, 2020). But be patient, persistent, and you might persevere.

Conceptual Change, Invention, and Rebellion – Great teachers think long and hard and most critically. Terry Heick states that teachers in this stage "don't do what they're told…[they] push back…subvert…go around…[they] don't sabotage or cause unrest, but [they] agitate. . .[ask] questions" (Heick, 2020 p. 4). Teaching becomes fun again, because teachers can "make a mess without getting…fired" (p. 4). Teachers explore better approaches to reach all learners. P.D. really has paid off. All is not lost!

Ongoing Mastery – After some 10,000 hours of teaching to become an expert, teachers can relax a bit. **Teaching is not just something one does but it becomes one's life.** That is right, you are really a teacher and cannot think of having a different job, ever. **"Teaching changes because the world changes, so what you're becoming an expert of isn't teaching, but change"** (Heick, 6 Stages, 2020, p. 4). You cannot only benefit from P.D. courses, but perhaps become part of a team offering such courses. Who would have thought this was possible!

Once classroom teachers pass through some of the basic stages listed above, **they will be able to implement** what they learned in P.D. sessions quite easily. And they may adapt these new P.D. learning procedures, and skills based on their students' needs and abilities.

Personal Experiences

I have experienced the stages mentioned by Guskey and Huberman (1995) as have most senior teachers. However, teachers can become "stuck" at any of these stages and be unable to move on to the next one. **For example,** I attended a series of P.D. sessions on Guam some years ago, but the funds were diverted by the school superintendent for one of her pet projects and thus, the planned sessions stopped. Teachers could only use a fraction of these P.D. techniques.

In another instance, we reading specialists introduced a new reading series (Pre-K-6th grade) to use in all Guam public-schools district wide. Training went well. At the end of the year, the education department placed new orders for textbooks, workbooks, and end-of-level tests needed for the following year. However, a supervisor in the district office told her supply clerk to 'cut 10% off the textbook order' to meet budgetary needs. This dutiful clerk cut the bottom section of the order list (which represented a 10% savings) but which unfortunately sliced off the teachers' manuals and most of the end-of-level exams (and answer keys) from the book order. This disastrous error was not discovered until late that summer.

Many Guam teachers became quickly disillusioned with the P.D. training they had received on using the new textbook series, somehow blaming the book ordering error with that training by sheer association. (The brain does funny things, right? How unfortunate!) However, a few astute school principals fixed this 10% cut-problem, by going directly to the superintendent, and the new reading series was implemented, with teacher lesson plans and end-of-level exams with answer keys, albeit two months late, at all schools!

Many educators discuss barriers to good P.D. training such as Mary Burns (2015) in her article, *4 Barriers to Teacher's PD in Fragile Contexts*. She cites difficult working conditions, systematic challenges, conflicts in general, and poorly designed P.D. activities, as examples; so does Trevor Antley (2020). But we educators should not give up, simply because P.D. can be difficult. Read about how P.D. activities can enrich your career and energize you as well (Wellein, 2021).

If you are a teacher, at what stage or cycle are you right now?

INDEX

NAME INDEX

SUBJECT INDEX

Made in the USA
Las Vegas, NV
08 January 2022